Slavery
Throughout History
Almanac

Slavery
Throughout History
Almanac

Theodore L. Sylvester
Edited by Sonia Benson

AN IMPRINT OF THE GALE GROUP

DETROIT · SAN FRANCISCO · LONDON
BOSTON · WOODBRIDGE, CT

Theodore L. Sylvester

Staff

Sonia Benson, *U•X•L Senior Editor*
Carol DeKane Nagel, *U•X•L Managing Editor*
Thomas L. Romig, *U•X•L Publisher*

Erin Bealmear, *Permissions Assistant (Pictures)*

Rita Wimberley, *Senior Buyer*
Evi Seoud, *Assistant Production Manager*
Dorothy Maki, *Manufacturing Manager*

Martha Schiebold, *Cover Art Director*
Pamela A. E. Galbreath, *Page Art Director*
Cynthia Baldwin, *Product Design Manager*

Graphix Group, *Typesetting*

Library of Congress Cataloging-in-Publication Data
Sylvester, Theodore L.
    Slavery throughout History. Almanac / Theodore L. Sylvester ;
Sonia Benson, editor.
        p.cm.
    Includes bibliographical references and indexes.
Summary: A comprehensive examination of the institution of
    slavery throughout the world, from ancient Mesopotamia to
    the present day.
ISBN 0-7876-3176-0 (hardcover)
1. Slavery—History Juvenile literature. 2. Slavery Cross-cultural
    studies Juvenile literature. 3. Slave trade—History Juvenile lit-
    erature. [1. Slavery—History.] I. Benson, Sonia. II. Title.
HT861.S94 1999
306.3'62'09—dc21

99-34277
CIP

Printed in the United States of America

10 9 8 7 6 5 4 3 2

This book is dedicated
to the greatest teacher in the world,
Mrs. Joyce L. Sylvester

A slave market in Atlanta, Georgia, in the nineteenth century. *Courtesy of the Library of Congress.*

Contents

Egyptian laborers. *Archive Photos, Inc.*

Africans being forced into slavery. *The Granger Collection, New York.*

A slave coffle. *Archive Photos, Inc.*

A slave auction. *Corbis-Bettmann.*

Richard Allen, founder of the AME Church. *Archive Photos, Inc.*

An abolitionist medallion. *AP/Wide World Photos, Inc.*

A camp cook in the Civil War. *Archive Photos, Inc.*

Thai girls rescued from slavery, 1980. *AP/Wide World Photos, Inc.*

Reader's Guide

Slavery is broadly described by the United Nations (UN) as the condition of a person over whom any or all of the powers connected to the right of ownership are exercised. We know that slavery has existed as an institution in human civilizations all over the world for thousands of years and that it continues to this day. But there is much we don't know. For the most part enslaved people throughout the world have lived and died without an opportunity to tell their own tales. Although slaves who found freedom were able to record their experiences, the records kept by slave holders are more often the only documentation left to us of many slaves' lives. How many millions of people in the world have lived their lives from birth to death in slavery and are now hidden from history is difficult to estimate and painful to imagine.

Through the records that do exist, though, it is possible to fill out our understanding of the people who lived in slavery, not only as victims of a terrible system, but in terms of their individuality, their ways of coping and surviving, their own stories, and their struggles to be free. The Slavery Throughout History Reference Library provides a unique forum for a student or general interest reader to approach this difficult subject. The *Almanac* presents the overall history of slavery throughout the Western world and beyond, with facts, figures, and plenty of contextual information on the economics, politics, law, culture, religion, and social trends that developed around the institution. The *Biographies* volume presents slavery from the perspective of individual lives: the stories of people of diverse beliefs, personalities, and circumstances who were slaves themselves or who had a profound impact on the institution. Finally, the *Primary Sources* volume features the first-hand accounts of slaves, lawmakers, abolitionists, and slaveowners, offering the immediate voices of the times on the events, issues, and ideas that arose in the history of slavery.

Related reference sources:

Slavery Throughout History: Almanac provides an overview of the institution of slavery from the time it developed among the earliest permanent settlers in Mesopotamia (perhaps as early as 3500 B.C.E.) to the present day. Civilizations covered in the volume include ancient Egypt, Israel, Greece, and Rome; western Europe and Africa in the Middle Ages; Latin America and the United States from colonial times through emancipation; and modern-day slavery worldwide.

Five of the twelve subject chapters in this volume are dedicated to slavery in the United States. Along with information about the commercial history of the vastly profitable slave trade, the draining of Africa, and the labor-intensive cotton industry, the reader will find stories of slave uprisings, black troops fighting in the American Revolution and the Civil War, the brutal punishments, the restrictive slave codes, the auction blocks, and the heroic abolitionist efforts. The final chapter presents examples of slavery still claiming millions of lives around the world at the end of the twentieth century.

One hundred fifteen black-and-white photographs, illustrations, and maps appear throughout the *Almanac*. A "Fact Focus" sidebar highlights key facts in each chapter. Other sidebars present information on a variety of interesting events, customs, and people. Cross references aid the reader in finding related material. *Slavery Throughout History: Almanac* begins with a Words to Know section defining key terms and a timeline of important events in the history of slavery. The volume concludes with a bibliography and a thorough subject index.

Slavery Throughout History: Biography presents biographies of thirty men and women who made an impact on the institution of slavery or were profoundly impacted by it. Featured are slaves and resistance fighters such as Moses, Spartacus, Toussaint L'Ouverture, Sojourner Truth, Harriet Tubman, Frederick Douglass, Nat Turner, John Brown, and Alexander Solzhenitsyn.

Slavery Throughout History: Primary Sources features twenty full or excerpted documents pertaining to the institution of slavery, from the Code of Hammurabi to the American slave narratives to the United Nations 1956 declaration of intent to end slavery worldwide. Included are poems, narratives, autobiographical essays, legal documents, speeches, newspaper articles, and other first-hand accounts of slavery. Ample introductory and sidebar information aid the reader in understanding the historical and biographical context of the primary source; black-and-white photographs and illustrations, glossaries, a timeline, a thorough subject index, and cross references provide easy and engaging access.

Special thanks

Grateful acknowledgment is extended to Laurie J. Wechter and Maxine A. Biwer for their editorial assistance with this book. Special thanks also to Sonia Benson, a perceptive, patient editor.

Comments and suggestions

We welcome your comments about *Slavery Throughout History: Almanac* as well as your suggestions for other topics in history to be covered in this series. Please write: Editors, *Slavery Throughout History: Almanac,* U•X•L, 27500 Drake Rd., Farmington Hills, Michigan 48331-3535; call toll-free: 1-800-877-4253; fax to: 248-699-8055; or send e-mail via http://www.galegroup.com.

Words to Know

A

Abbot: The head or ruler of a monastery for men.

Abolition: The act of getting rid of slavery. An abolitionist is someone who fights against the institution of slavery.

Agricultural slaves: People owned as property by owners of farms and forced to labor in the fields.

Amnesty: An official act of pardon for a large group of people.

Antebellum: Before the war; particularly before the Civil War (1861–65).

Apprentice: Someone who learns an art or trade by serving for a set period of time under someone who is skilled at the trade.

Auction: A sale of property in which the buyers bid on the price, and the property goes to the highest bidder.

B

Baptism: A Christian ceremony marking an individual's acceptance into the Christian community.

Benevolent societies: Organizations formed to promote the welfare of certain groups of people determined by the society's members. In antebellum America, benevolent societies were very important social, cultural, and economic organizations for free blacks.

Black codes: Bodies of law that emerged in the states of the U.S. South that restrictively governed almost every aspect of slaves' lives.

Black Death: A deadly contagious disease often called "the plague" that started around 1350 and killed about one-third of Europe's population and even more in Asia.

Bondage: The state of being bound by law in servitude to a controlling person or entity.

Branding: Marking something, or someone, usually by burning them with a hot iron with a particular mark that shows ownership.

C

Cacao: Seeds used to make chocolate and cocoa.

Chain gangs: Groups of workers chained together at the ankles while performing forced hard labor.

Chattel slavery: A permanent form of slavery in which the slave holder "owns" a human being—the slave—in the same way that property (chattel) is owned: permanently and without restrictions. Historically, chattel slaves had no legal rights and were considered property that their owners had the right to possess, enjoy, and dispose of in whatever way they saw fit. Slaves could be bought, sold, given away, inherited, or hired out to others. Slave masters had the right, by law and custom, to punish and, in some times and places, to kill their slaves for disobedience. Slaves were forced to work where and when their masters determined. They could not own property or freely marry whom they chose, and their children were born as slaves.

City-state: An independent political unit consisting of a city and its surrounding lands.

Coffle: A group of people chained together.

Colonialism: Control by one nation or state over a dependent territory and its people and resources.

Colony: A territory in which settlers from another country come to live while maintaining their ties to their home country, often setting up a government that may rule over the original inhabitants of the territory as well as the settlers.

Commerce: The making and selling of goods for local and foreign markets.

Commodity: Something that is to be bought and sold for a profit.

Compromise: To arrive at a settlement or agreement on something by virtue of both parties giving up some part of their demands.

Compromise of 1850: A decision by the U.S. Congress to admit California as a free state and that left the status of territories to be determined when they applied for statehood. It also outlawed the slave trade in the District of Columbia and strengthened the fugitive slave laws.

Confederate States of America: Often called the Confederacy, the government established in 1861 when seven states of the South—South Carolina, Georgia, Louisiana, Mississippi, Florida, Alabama, and Texas—seceded from the Union.

Concentration camps: Prison camps where inmates are detained, often, historically, under severe conditions and for political or ethnic reasons.

Concubine: A sex slave.

Conspiracy: The act of two or more parties secretly joining together to plan an illegal action.

Cotton gin: A machine invented by Eli Whitney in 1793 that separated cotton fibers from the seed. With just two people working it, Whitney's cotton gin cleaned as much cotton as 100 workers could by hand, thus freeing up laborers for the cultivation of the crop.

Crucifixion: Being nailed or bound to a cross until death; any horrible and painful punishment.

Crusades: A series of military expeditions from the eleventh century to the thirteenth century launched by the Christian powers to conquer the Holy Land from the Muslims.

Curfew: A rule or regulation that forbids certain people from being out in public after a certain time of day.

D

Dark Ages: A period of the Middle Ages in western Europe from 500 to 750 when there was no central government, lords ruled over small territories, and education and the arts were minimal. The term is also used to mean the entire span of the Middle Ages (500–1500).

Debt slavery: A form of forced servitude usually taking place when a person has borrowed money against a pledge, or a promise, of work. If the loan goes unpaid, the borrower or members of his family are enslaved for a period of time to the lender to clear the debt.

Democracy: Government ruled by the people or their representatives.

Democratic party: A party founded by Thomas Jefferson in the early days of the United States favoring personal liberty and the limitation of the federal government. In 1854 the political party names changed to reflect the proslavery forces of the South versus the antislavery forces of the North. The Democrats were the proslavery forces of the South; the Republicans were the antislavery party of the North.

Domestic slaves: Slaves who worked in the homes of the slaveowners, usually cooking, cleaning, serving, or performing child care.

E

Emancipate: To free from bondage.

Emancipation Proclamation: The 1863 order by President Abraham Lincoln during the Civil War that freed all slaves in the rebel states that had seceded and were battling against the Union.

Empire: A large political unit that usually has several territories, nations, or peoples under one governing authority.

Essenes: A Jewish brotherhood in ancient Palestine that was opposed to violence, war, and slavery.

Exodus: Departure.

Exploitation: An unfair or improper use of another person for one's own advantage.

F

Feudalism: The system of political organization in the Middle Ages in Europe based on the relationship of lord and vassal. The king or ruler basically owned all the land in his realm, but he could not govern it all. Thus he partitioned it out to nobles for a pledge of loyalty and military service. The nobles then divided their lands among lords for their pledge of service. Peasants, serfs, and slaves lived and worked on the lords' estates.

Forced migration: The movement of a large group of people by force.

Free state: A state in which slavery is not permitted.

Freedman's Bureau: Also called the Bureau of Refugees, Freedmen, and Abandoned Lands, an organization formed in 1865 by Congress to provide food, land, clothing, medicine, and education to the newly freed peoples of the South.

Freedpeople: Former slaves.

Fugitive: Someone who is running away or escaping from something.

Fugitive slave laws: Federal acts of 1793 and 1850 that required the return of escaped slaves between states. Thus, a citizen of a free state was required to return an escaped slave to his or her owner in a slave state.

G

Gladiator: Trained fighters in ancient Rome who fought each other—and sometimes wild beasts—to the death in huge arenas in front of crowds of spectators.

H

Heathen: A disrespectful word for non-Christian people.

Holocaust: Mass slaughter.

Human rights: Rights that belong to every person by virtue of their being a human being; the idea that everyone should be provided with the civil, political, economic, cultural, and social opportunity for personal human dignity.

Husbandry: The taming and raising of domestic animals as a branch of farming.

I

Imperial slaves: Slaves owned by the emperor.

Indentured servants: Servants who work under a contract, bound to their masters for terms usually between two and fourteen years. In American history the terms of service were generally part of the deal that paid for an indentured servant's passage from England to the New World. Upon completion of their contract, indentured servants were promised their freedom and perhaps some food, clothing, tools, or land.

Indigo: A plant used for making dyes.

Industrial Revolution: A period of great economic changes in Europe due to new technology, starting in England in the mid-1700s.

Industrial slaves: Slaves who labored in factories, mines, quarries, and other fields of production.

Infidel: A disrespectful word for a non-Christians.

Insurrection: Rebellion.

Irrigation farming: An agricultural system using ditches and canals built to bring water to dry fields from a river or lake in order to grow crops.

J

Jim Crow laws: Laws passed in the South after the Reconstruction period (1865–77) that separated black people from white people in many public places.

K

Kansas-Nebraska Act: An 1854 act that organized Kansas and Nebraska as territories and left the question of slavery to be determined by the settlers when they applied for statehood. This act, in effect, erased the prohibition of slavery north of the Mason-Dixon line as established in the Missouri Compromise.

Kidnaping: The holding of captured people for ransom (money or goods paid for the return of the captured person).

Knight: A trained soldier who fought on horseback in the service of a lord or superior, especially in the Middle Ages.

L

Labor camp: A prison camp in which forced labor is performed.

Latin America: A vast region comprised of the countries of South and Middle America where Romance languages (languages derived from Latin) are spoken. Geographically, it includes almost all of the Americas south of the United States: Mexico, Central America, South America, and many of the islands of the West Indies.

M

Magna Carta: A British document created in 1215 by King John guaranteeing certain rights, but perhaps mainly guaranteeing feudal relations.

Manor: In Medieval England, the castle and surrounding land belonging to a lord, who ruled locally.

Manumission: Formal release from bondage.

Mason-Dixon line: The boundary between the states of Pennsylvania and Maryland. Before the Civil War the Mason-Dixon line became the boundary between the free states of the North and the slave states of the South.

Massacre: The act of killing a group of people who are not prepared to adequately defend themselves; the word connotes a cruel or atrocious act.

Medieval: Relating to the Middle Ages (500–1500), particularly in Europe.

Mestizos: People of mixed Indian and European ancestry.

Middle Ages: A period of European history that dates from about 500 to 1500, beginning after the fall of the Roman empire in 476 and characterized by a unified Christian culture, economy, politics, and military and a feudal hierarchy of power.

Middle Passage: The voyage from Africa to the Americas; the middle stretch of the slave-trading triangle that connected Europe to Africa, Africa to the Americas, and the Americas back to Europe.

Militant: Ready to fight, or aggressively active.

Militia: A unit of armed forces that is trained and ready to do battle or patrol in an emergency.

Missionary: A person with a religious mission, usually a minister of the Christian church who tries to convert non-Christians to the faith.

Missouri Compromise: A series of measures passed in 1820 and 1821 admitting to the Union Missouri as a slave state and Maine as a free state and prohibiting slavery in all other territory north of Missouri's southern boundary.

Monasteries: Churches and residences for monks and nuns.

Monk: A man who belongs to a religious order and lives in a monastery, where he serves the church and devotes himself to his religion.

Mulatto: A word—used mainly in past times—meaning a person of mixed white and black ancestry.

Muslims: Members of the Islam religion.

Mutilation: The act of cutting something or someone in a way that is permanently disfiguring or removes an essential part of the body.

N

Narratives: Something that is told like a story. Slave narratives in the years before the Civil War were written personal stories about what life was like as a slave. They were either written by former slaves or told out loud by them and then written down by someone else. Either way, they were presented in the manner of a spoken story.

Near East: A region of southwest Asia that includes the Arab nations.

Nobles: Wealthy families of landholders in Europe, usually holding the titles of dukes, counts, and lords.

P

Passive resistance: Not cooperating with authority by purposefully not doing what is expected of one, but without using violent or aggressive means.

Patriarch: A tribal chief, or a man who is the father and founder of a people.

Peasants: A class of people throughout the history of Europe and elsewhere who were poor and lived by farming the land, either as small landowners or laborers.

Peculium: Money, such as wages, tips, or gifts, that slaves in ancient Rome earned by doing extra jobs; they were allowed to keep it after giving their master part of the income.

Piracy: The seizure by force of people and property on land or water.

Pharaoh The supreme ruler, as a king, of ancient Egypt.

Pillory: A wooden frame in which there were holes to lock up the head and hands used to punish and humiliate people.

Plantation: A vast farming estate that is worked by a large staff living on the premises.

Plebs: Short for plebeians; Rome's majority middle class.

Pope: The bishop of Rome and head of the Roman Catholic church.

Prostitution: The practice of engaging in sexual activities for payment.

Public slaves: Slaves owned by cities or towns who did administrative, construction, public-safety, or maintenance work or worked in temples.

Q

Quakers: A religious body formally known as the Religious Society of Friends that originated in seventeenth-century England. Its founders believed that people could find the spiritual truth that was provided by the Holy Spirit within themselves, having no need of church services or its hierarchy. The Quakers believed in the equality of all human beings and were staunch abolitionists in the eighteenth and nineteenth century.

Quarry: A dug out pit from which stone, slate, or limestone is taken.

R

Ratification: The formal approval or confirmation of a document or act, such as an amendment to the Constitution.

Reconstruction acts: Acts passed in 1867 by Congress that divided the former Confederacy into five military districts under the command of army generals. They stripped the right to vote from whites who had supported the Confederate government. Elections were ordered for state constitutional conventions, and black men were given the right to vote. Withdrawal of the federal forces in 1877 marked the end of the Reconstruction period.

Reenslavement: Being forced back into slavery once one has achieved freedom from bondage.

Republic: A form of government run by elected representatives and based on a constitution.

Republican party: A party formed in 1854 by the antislavery forces of the North. The first Republican president was Abraham Lincoln, elected in 1860.

Rural: Relating to the country, country people, and agriculture; the opposite of urban or city life.

S

Secede: To withdraw

Segregation: The separation of people along racial lines. For example, in many churches before and after the Civil War, black people were forced to sit in separate sections than white people; in public transportation in some places there were separate sections for blacks and whites; in education, there were sometimes separate schools.

Serfdom: From the Latin word for "servant," a form of servitude that differed from chattel slavery in that the enslaved were not considered "movable" property. Serfs were bound to the land they lived on, generation after generation, serving the owners of the land, known as lords. If the lord left the land, the serf served its next owner.

Servile: Submissive, or slavelike; being always at the bidding of a controlling person.

Sexual slavery: The control and ownership of one human being by another for the purpose of engaging in sexual activities with that person, often forcibly, or selling the person's sexual services to others.

Sharecropping: A system of farming in which one person farms land owned by another in exchange for a share of the crop.

Slave codes: The body of laws held by the states governing the slaves themselves and the ownership of them. Many slave code laws severely restricted slaves because of the slaveowner's strong fear of slave uprisings.

Slave raids: Military expeditions for the purpose of capturing slaves.

Slave trading forts: Sometimes called "slave factories," trading posts operated by Europeans mainly on the west coast of Africa with dungeons capable of holding thousands of captured Africans until they could be placed on the next ship to the Americas.

Slaver: A person who is involved in the slave trade for profit.

Supreme Court: The highest court of the United States, and the highest authority on all cases that arise under the Constitution, laws, and treaties of the federal government.

T

Territory: An area, or a vast stretch of land in eighteenth and nineteenth century America that had settlers and local communities but had not yet organized as a state of the Union.

Terrorism: Attacks on unarmed civilians.

Textile: Cloth, usually a woven or knit fabric.

Therapeutae: A Jewish community in ancient Alexandria, Egypt, that opposed war and slavery.

Tribute: A payment made by one group or state to another, either in acknowledgment of having been conquered or for protection.

U

Underground Railroad: A secret network of people, black and white, who guided runaway slaves to freedom and sheltered them along their way in the eighteenth and nineteenth century United States.

United Nations (UN): An international organization established after World War II (1939–45) that includes most of the world's countries. The UN's mission is to maintain world peace and security, to achieve cooperation among countries in solving problems, and to promote international humanitarianism.

V

Vassals: Lower nobles in medieval Europe who pledged loyalty and services to the local ruler, the lord.

Vigilante group: A group that organizes independently of official authority, setting its task to suppress or punish other people, for real or perceived offenses, without going through the due processes of law.

Timeline

c. 3500 B.C.E. Mesopotamians settle into permanent communities with successful agricultural techniques. Constantly at war with neighbors, the Mesopotamians begin to capture and enslave prisoners, forcing them into labor instead of killing them.

1780 B.C.E. King Hammurabi becomes the sixth ruler of Babylon, a city in northern Mesopotamia. With Babylon as his capital, Hammurabi unites all of the competing kingdoms of Mesopotamia under one government. He establishes the Code of Hammurabi, a list of about 300 laws that regulate all aspects of Babylonian life, including slavery.

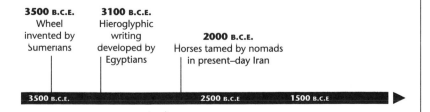

3500 B.C.E.
Wheel invented by Sumerians

3100 B.C.E.
Hieroglyphic writing developed by Egyptians

2000 B.C.E.
Horses tamed by nomads in present–day Iran

3500 B.C.E.   2500 B.C.E   1500 B.C.E

Females slaves in Athens.
Archive Photos, Inc.

The death of Spartacus.
Corbis-Bettmann.

1570 B.C.E. The Egyptians drive the ruling Hyksos from Egypt and enslave all foreigners who remain, including thousands of Hebrews, who are forced to work in the fields making bricks for the construction of new cities and temples.

597 B.C.E. Nebuchadrezzar II captures the city of Jerusalem and sends most of the city's population, about 3,000 Hebrews, into slavery in Babylonia. The Hebrews, who are eventually freed in 539 B.C.E., call this period "The Great Captivity."

594 B.C.E. Debt slavery for Greek citizens is outlawed in Athens, creating a demand for foreign slaves to do the work of the freed Greek debt slaves. At the same time, the introduction of coinage makes the slave trade easier, and slavery increases significantly.

431 B.C.E. The city-state of Athens in Greece has so many slaves it becomes the world's first example of a slave society. Of the 155,000 residents of the city of Athens, 70,000 are slaves, 60,000 are citizens, and 25,000 are resident foreigners.

431–404 B.C.E. The Peloponnesian War, a civil war between the Greek city-states Athens and Sparta, produces tens of thousands of slaves.

264–27 B.C.E. Rome, during the second half of the Republic, fights many overseas wars that produce hundreds of thousands of slaves for central Italy. Giant agricultural estates develop—the world's first plantations—relying on slave labor.

73 B.C.E. Roman gladiator/slave Spartacus leads a breakout of about seventy gladiators from their training school. The rebels build a vast army of runaway slaves and hold off the Roman army effectively for two years.

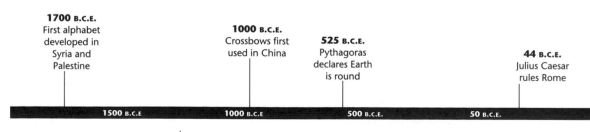

1700 B.C.E.
First alphabet developed in Syria and Palestine

1000 B.C.E.
Crossbows first used in China

525 B.C.E.
Pythagoras declares Earth is round

44 B.C.E.
Julius Caesar rules Rome

1500 B.C.E   1000 B.C.E   500 B.C.E.   50 B.C.E.

41–54 C.E. The Roman Emperor Claudius makes it a crime to murder a slave or to turn a sick slave out to die. More laws follow that uphold the institution of slavery but take a more humane stand in the treatment of slaves.

476 The fall of the Roman Empire changes slavery in Europe dramatically. A new class of people develops, called serfs—peasants who are not allowed to leave the land where they work. If the land changes hands, the serfs stay, "bound" to the soil. Serfdom is hereditary: the children of serfs become serfs at birth. Beneath serfs on the social scale there is still a small population of slaves.

1000 As many as 80 percent of Europe's peasants are living on feudal estates. One-half of those peasants are free, able to live and work where they choose; the other half are serfs, legally bound to the land they work. The number of slaves is now very low, as descendants of slaves, through the years, have risen to the level of serfs.

1300 Europe emerges from the feudal era. The laws and customs of the villages are being replaced by the common law of entire kingdoms.

1441 Fourteen African slaves arrive in Lisbon, Portugal, beginning the network for shipping slaves from Africa to the New World. The Africans had been captured in a raid on one of the many voyages Portuguese explorers had made along Africa's Atlantic coast.

1455 The pope of the Catholic church approves slave raids and gives Portugal blanket permission to enslave all non-Christian people.

1481 The Portuguese establish a trading post at Elmina, Gold Coast.

Farm workers in France, fifteenth century. *The Granger Collection, New York.*

Africans captured by slavers. *The Granger Collection, New York.*

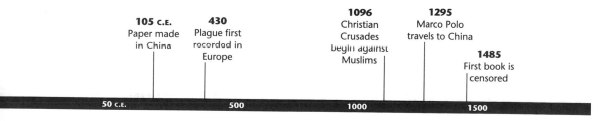

105 C.E. Paper made in China

430 Plague first recorded in Europe

1096 Christian Crusades begin against Muslims

1295 Marco Polo travels to China

1485 First book is censored

50 C.E.   500   1000   1500

Inside the slave ship *Gloria*.
The Granger Collection, New York.

1493 The pope grants Spain sole shipping rights to the New World, and throughout the 1500s, Spain dominates the Atlantic slave trade. Portugal continues the African part of the trade.

1494 Christopher Columbus sends 500 Indians to Spain as slaves.

1500 The Portuguese are taking 3,000 slaves a year from Africa's Atlantic coast.

1518 The first cargo of slaves from the Guinea coast of West Africa arrives in the West Indies.

1524 The Spanish bring slaves to Guatemala; by the end of the century they have shipped at least 60,000 Africans to Mexico.

1526 The first slave revolt in what is now the United States takes place in the first known settlement on mainland North America. Disease wipes out many of the 600 people—500 Spanish colonists and 100 African slaves—who arrive in modern-day South Carolina. The slaves revolt and flee to live with the local Indians. The surviving settlers flee to Haiti, leaving the rebel slaves as the first permanent immigrants in North America.

1538 The Portuguese bring slaves from the coasts of Africa to their colonies in Brazil.

1565 The Spanish settle Saint Augustine, Florida, the earliest example of an established colony using slaves on the North American mainland.

1574 The queen of England abolishes serfdom in her nation.

1600 About 367,000 African slaves have crossed the Atlantic to the Americas.

1492
Christopher Columbus lands in the Americas

1517
Martin Luther posts his 95 theses, sparking the Protestant Reformation

1556
Tobacco seeds from the New World reach Spain

1587
Galileo states the law of falling bodies

1500   1525   1550   1600

1619 Jamestown, Virginia, is the first English colony to receive Africans.

1630 The Republic of Palmares is established by runaway slaves in the heavy inland forests of northeastern Brazil. At its peak it has a population of 20,000. The Republic of Palmares is destroyed by the Portuguese in 1697—after surviving almost 70 years.

1638 A Salem ship named *Desire* unloads New England's first cargo of African slaves at Boston Harbor. A profitable New England slave trade has begun. Ships leave New England loaded with cargo to trade, sailing first to the West Indies, where they trade most of their cargo for rum. The "rum boats" then sail to Africa, where they trade the liquor for slaves. The ships then sail back to the West Indies, where they trade the freshly captured African slaves to the sugar islands for "seasoned" slaves and other products of the islands. These slaves are taken to New England slave ports, where they are sold in local markets, mainly to southern planters.

1641 Massachusetts is the first colony to officially recognize the institution of slavery.

1663 Planters are offered 20 acres for every African male slave and 10 acres for every African female slave they bring into the Carolinas.

1672 The Royal African Company is chartered by the British king and soon becomes the number-one slave trader in the world by securing, under an agreement with Spain, the exclusive rights to ship West African slaves to the Spanish colonies in the Americas. England becomes the dominant slave-trading force to the Americas.

1686 Carolina's colonial legislature begins creating laws that ensure the domination of black slaves by their

The introduction of slavery to Virginia. *Archive Photos, Inc.*

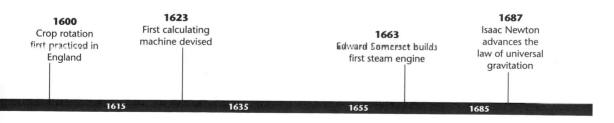

1600 Crop rotation first practiced in England

1623 First calculating machine devised

1663 Edward Somerset builds first steam engine

1687 Isaac Newton advances the law of universal gravitation

1615   1635   1655   1685

A slave in stocks. *The Library of Congress.*

white masters. In time, the slave code of the Carolinas becomes a model for the Black Codes that harshly regulate slaves throughout much of mainland North America.

1688　Pennsylvania's influential population of Quakers voice their religious opposition to slavery.

1739　A man named Jemmy leads a slave revolt in South Carolina, killing two warehouse guards and seizing weapons and ammunition. One hundred slaves join him as he marches south to Spanish-held Florida, where they hope to be free. Along the way they kill about 20 whites before entering into an intense battle with the local militia, in which about 50 slaves are killed.

1770　Runaway slave Crispus Attucks is the first man to die for the cause of the American Revolution in the Boston Massacre.

1775　As the American Revolution begins, the British governor of Virginia, Lord Dunmore, declares that all slaves who join the British side will be set free. After Dunmore's Proclamation, slaves run away by the tens of thousands. Hundreds of slaves join Dunmore, who forms all-black fighting units in what he calls his "Ethiopian Regiment."

1776　General George Washington, after learning that Lord Dunmore is enlisting blacks into the British troops, allows blacks to enter the war on the American side. Thousands of black soldiers fight against the British. Many states promise freedom after a set period to slaves who fight the war.

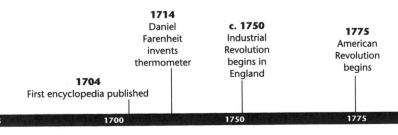

1714
Daniel Farenheit invents thermometer

c. 1750
Industrial Revolution begins in England

1775
American Revolution begins

1704
First encyclopedia published

1685　　1700　　　　1750　　　　1775

1780s The Underground Railroad begins to take shape when Quakers in a number of towns in Pennsylvania and New Jersey assist slaves in their escape.

1787 At the Constitutional Convention, the new nation's founding fathers decide that the slave trade can continue for at least 20 more years, three-fifths of the slave population can be counted toward determining the number of each state's Congressional representatives, and all states are required to return fugitive slaves to their owners.

1787 Haiti, as the world's greatest producer of sugar and its by-products rum and molasses, brings in 40,000 slaves in this year alone to work on sugar plantations and in sugar mills. The island has more than 600 sugar plantations and more slaves in proportion to its size than any other place in the New World.

1787 Various British abolitionist organizations come together to form the Society for Effecting the Abolition of the Slave Trade.

1791 A rebellion in Haiti led by a slave named Toussaint L'Ouverture results in the abolition of slavery on the island in 1794 and ultimately to Haiti's independence from France in 1803.

1793 Eli Whitney invents the cotton gin. With just two people working it, Whitney's cotton gin cleans as much cotton as 100 workers could by hand, thus freeing up laborers for the cultivation of the crop. The rise of cotton as the number-one crop of the nation has a tremendous impact on the institution of slavery.

1793 The federal government passes the fugitive slave laws, which require that slaves who escape to a different

The slave revolt in Haiti. *The Granger Collection, New York.*

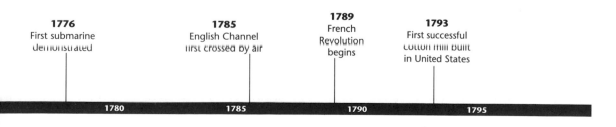

1776
First submarine demonstrated

1785
English Channel first crossed by air

1789
French Revolution begins

1793
First successful cotton mill built in United States

1780   1785   1790   1795

Mother Bethel AME Church.
Archive Photos, Inc.

state be returned to their owner by the authorities of the state to which they fled.

1794 Richard Allen founds the first independent church for blacks in America, the Bethel African Methodist Episcopal (AME) Church.

1800 Gabriel Prosser prepares slaves for revolt in the city of Richmond, Virginia, hoping to ignite a widespread rebellion among all slaves. About 1,000 slaves arm themselves, ready to attack the city, but a severe storm stops them. Troops hunt them down, and at least 35 rebels, including Prosser, are hanged.

1807 The U.S. federal government officially abolishes the African slave trade. The law is poorly enforced and consequently ignored by the people who profit most from the trade—the New England shipowners, the Middle Atlantic merchants, and the southern planters.

1808 After great pressure from the abolitionists and repeated legislative attempts in the House of Commons led by William Wilberforce, the British Parliament outlaws the slave trade. Unlike the Americans, the British pass laws that contain harsh penalties for violators and rewards for those who catch them.

1815 The four Philadelphia branches of the Masons, a fraternal organization, pool their resources and build the country's first black Masonic Hall.

1816 Sixteen black Methodist congregations, from New York, New Jersey, Delaware, and Maryland, come together for a convention at Richard Allen's Bethel AME church in Philadelphia—until then, the only black Methodist church in America. Together they withdraw from the white-dominated mother church and

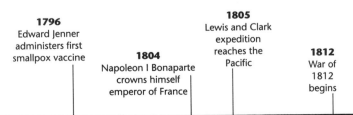

1796
Edward Jenner administers first smallpox vaccine

1804
Napoleon I Bonaparte crowns himself emperor of France

1805
Lewis and Clark expedition reaches the Pacific

1812
War of 1812 begins

1795   1800   1810   1815

form the nation's first independent black church, the African Methodist Episcopal (AME) Church. Allen is ordained a church elder and the AME Church's first bishop.

1816   The American Colonization Society (ACS) forms with a plan to ship blacks to land in Africa that will later be known as Liberia.

1819   Towns in Ohio and North Carolina join New Jersey and Pennsylvania in acting as way stations and shelters for fugitive slaves on the Underground Railroad. Historians estimate that in the 50 years before the Civil War, at least 3,200 "conductors" help about 75,000 slaves escape to freedom.

1820–21 In a series of acts known as the Missouri Compromise, Congress admits Missouri as a slave state and Maine as a free state. It prohibits slavery in all other territory north of Missouri's southern boundary (the 36th parallel).

1822   Denmark Vesey, a freed slave and carpenter, prepares slaves around Charleston, South Carolina, for a major uprising after whites close down the African Methodist church he has helped establish. The planned attack, said by one of the witnesses to involve as many as 9,000 slaves, never takes place because information about it reaches the authorities and the leaders are hanged.

1827   Samuel Cornish and John Russworm start the country's first black newspaper, *Freedom's Journal*.

1829   David Walker, a free black in Boston, publishes *Walker's Appeal ... to the Colored Citizens of the World But in Particular and Very Expressly to Those of the United States*

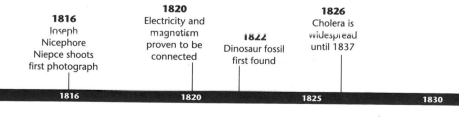

1816 Joseph Nicephore Niepce shoots first photograph

1820 Electricity and magnetism proven to be connected

1822 Dinosaur fossil first found

1826 Cholera is widespread until 1837

1816   1820   1825   1830

of America, which calls for blacks to violently rise up and defeat the forces of slavery.

1830 Richard Allen organizes the first Free People of Color Congress in Philadelphia. At that gathering, black delegates from six states begin what will come to be known as the National Negro Convention Movement. Every year until the Civil War, blacks convene in different cities "to devise ways and means of bettering our condition."

1831 William Lloyd Garrison begins publishing the abolitionist newspaper *The Liberator.*

1831 Nat Turner, a slave and preacher, leads a slave revolt in Southampton, Virginia. The rebels go from plantation to plantation killing whites. Within 24 hours, about 70 slaves have joined the revolt, and 57 whites—men, women, and children—are slaughtered. White troops force the group to scatter, and retaliation against all blacks in the area is severe.

1833 Abolitionist William Lloyd Garrison helps establish the American Antislavery Society (AAS). Only 3 black people are among the 62 signers of the society's Declaration of Sentiments.

1835 The right for blacks, slave or free, to assemble in groups for any purposes without a white person present is denied throughout the Deep South.

1836 Sixty thousand slaves are brought to Cuba in this year alone, but not all of them will stay on the island to work the sugar plantations. Cuba has become the largest slave market in the New World, supplying African slaves to colonies far and wide.

The capture of Nat Turner.
The Library of Congress.

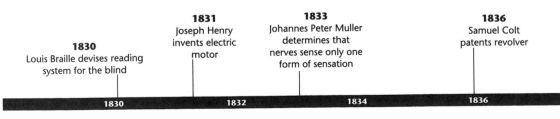

1830
Louis Braille devises reading system for the blind

1831
Joseph Henry invents electric motor

1833
Johannes Peter Muller determines that nerves sense only one form of sensation

1836
Samuel Colt patents revolver

1830   1832   1834   1836

1839　Anti-Slavery International (ASI), a London-based organization, is founded. It will continue to fight slavery into the twenty-first century.

1840　There are more than 100 antislavery societies in the free states of the North, with at least 200,000 black and white members. Abolitionists, however, are not well received in most places.

1845　The autobiography of Frederick Douglass, *Narrative of the Life of Frederick Douglass*, becomes an international best-seller.

1847　Frederick Douglass begins publishing his abolitionist and reform-minded newspaper, the *North Star.*

1850　In the Compromise of 1850, Congress admits California as a free state, leaves the status of territories to be decided later, outlaws the slave trade in the District of Columbia, and puts real teeth into the fugitive slave laws of 1793.

1852　*Uncle Tom's Cabin,* an antislavery novel by Harriet Beecher Stowe, sells 300,000 copies in its first year and convinces many readers that slavery must end.

1853　William Wells Brown publishes his novel *Clotel; or, The President's Daughter: A Narrative of Slave Life in the United States,* the first published novel written by a black person in the United States.

1854　The Kansas-Nebraska Act of 1854 organizes Kansas and Nebraska as territories and leaves the question of slavery to be decided by the settlers when they apply for statehood. The act, in effect, erases the thirty-four-year-old prohibition of slavery above the Mason-Dixon line as established in the Missouri Compromise.

Frederick Douglass. *AP/Wide World Photos, Inc.*

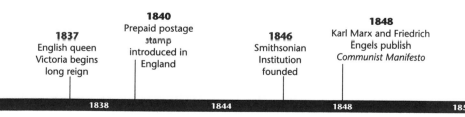

1837
English queen Victoria begins long reign

1840
Prepaid postage stamp introduced in England

1846
Smithsonian Institution founded

1848
Karl Marx and Friedrich Engels publish *Communist Manifesto*

| 1838 | 1844 | 1848 | 1854 |

Dred and Harriet Scott.
Archive Photos, Inc.

Cotton workers. *Archive Photos, Inc.*

1854 After the passage of the Kansas-Nebraska Act (sponsored by the northern Democrats as a "compromise"), the northern Whigs unite with antislavery Democrats and Free Soilers (an antislavery political party formed in 1848) and found the antislavery Republican Party. The southern Whigs join the southern Democrats as a united party firmly on the proslavery side.

1857 Responding to Dred Scott's lawsuit, in which he contended that he and his wife should be free from slavery because they lived with their owner in territories where slavery was not allowed, the Supreme Court rules that blacks, free or slave, are not citizens of the United States; that slavery is a property right established by the U.S. Constitution and therefore owners still retain title to their slaves, even when visiting or living on free soil; that territories are common lands of the United States where the property rights of all citizens—including slaveholders—apply. The court, in effect, declares the Missouri Compromise unconstitutional and opens all territories to slavery.

1859 John Brown, a white abolitionist, carries out a raid on Harpers Ferry, Virginia, hoping to capture the federal arsenal and arm slaves for a massive uprising to end slavery. The revolt is crushed, and Brown and his followers are hanged.

1860 There are about 4 million slaves in the United States at this time, 90 percent of them living in the rural South. The United States is producing more than 5 million bales of cotton annually. Mississippi, Alabama, Louisiana, and Georgia produce 70 percent of the cotton and are at the top of the list in the number of large slaveholders.

1850 Levi Strauss sews first pair of jeans

1851 Linus Yale patents lock

1854 Florence Nightingale founds modern nursing practices

1857 Toilet paper introduced

1854   1856   1858   1860

1860–61 When Republican Abraham Lincoln is elected president on an antislavery platform in November 1860, seven southern slaveholding states withdraw from the Union and form their own government. Those states—South Carolina, Mississippi, Florida, Alabama, Georgia, Louisiana, and Texas—form the Confederate States of America.

1861 The Civil War officially begins on April 12, when Confederate soldiers open fire on Fort Sumter, a Union-held fort located in the harbor of Charleston, South Carolina. Union forces surrender after a thirty-one-hour battle. The defeat costs the Union four more slave states, as Virginia, North Carolina, Tennessee, and Arkansas join the Confederacy.

1861 The Confiscation Act passed by the U.S. Congress states that any property used in aiding or abetting insurrection against the United States can be captured and kept as a prize of war. When the "property" consists of slaves, the law declares them to be forever free. Thousands of slaves seek refuge and freedom on the lands occupied and controlled by the Union armies.

1862 On June 19, the United States abolishes slavery in the territories. On July 19, an act proclaims that all slaves who make it into Union territory from Confederate states are to be set free. On September 22, President Abraham Lincoln issues a preliminary draft of the Emancipation Proclamation, freeing all slaves. At the same time, he allows the enlistment of blacks into the Union's armed forces. These acts mark a huge change of policy: the war's goal is no longer just to save the Union, but to crush slavery.

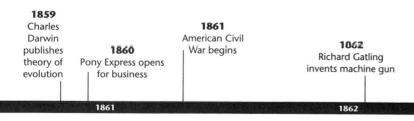

1859 Charles Darwin publishes theory of evolution

1860 Pony Express opens for business

1861 American Civil War begins

1862 Richard Gatling invents machine gun

1861

1862

Abraham Lincoln reading the Emancipation Proclamation. *The Library of Congress.*

The 107th U.S. Colored Infantry. *Archive Photos, Inc.*

1863 President Abraham Lincoln issues the final Emancipation Proclamation, declaring approximately 4 million enslaved people in the United States free.

1865 The Civil War ends on April 9, when the Confederate army, led by General Robert E. Lee, surrenders at Appomattox Courthouse, Virginia.

1865 By the end of the Civil War more than 185,000 blacks have served in the Union army. About 93,000 came from the rebel states, 40,000 from the border slave states, and about 52,000 from the free states. More than 38,000 black soldiers died in the war.

1865 The Thirteenth Amendment to the U.S. Constitution, which abolishes slavery in America, is ratified (officially approved by popular vote) by the states on December 18, 1865.

1865–66 Black Codes become the law of the land in the post-war South, gravely violating the rights of blacks.

1865 Congress establishes the Bureau of Refugees, Freedmen, and Abandoned Lands, or the Freedman's Bureau, to provide aid, such as food, education, medicine, and to help in resettling recently freed blacks in the South.

1866 The Republican-controlled U.S. Congress passes a Civil Rights bill that repeals the Black Codes of the South. The bill grants citizenship to blacks and equal rights with whites in every state and territory.

1867 The Reconstruction era begins when Congress passes a series of acts that divide the former Confederacy into five military districts under the command of army generals; strip the right to vote from most whites who had supported the Confederate govern-

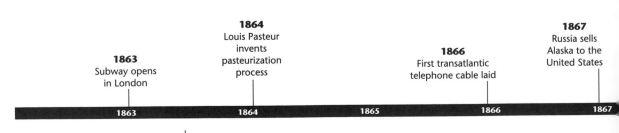

1863
Subway opens
in London

1864
Louis Pasteur
invents
pasteurization
process

1866
First transatlantic
telephone cable laid

1867
Russia sells
Alaska to the
United States

1863   1864   1865   1866   1867

ment; order elections for state constitutional conventions; and give black men the right to vote, in some states by military order. Black voters soon make up a majority in the states of Alabama, Florida, Louisiana, Mississippi, and South Carolina. Blacks are elected to state legislatures and, in much smaller numbers, to the U.S. House and Senate.

1868 The Fourteenth Amendment, which grants citizenship to blacks, is made law.

1870 The Fifteenth Amendment, guaranteeing the protection of U.S. citizens against federal or state racial discrimination, is ratified by the states.

1871 Brazil passes a gradual emancipation law.

1877 The withdrawal of all federal troops from the South in 1877 marks the end of the Reconstruction period; southern Democrats regain political dominance and restrict the rights of blacks.

1880 Cuba passes a gradual emancipation law, and the shipping of Africans across the Atlantic ends.

1885–1908 European powers grant King Leopold of Belgium the right to rule over the Congo Basin. He directs his troops in the Congo to round up whole communities of Africans. Millions of Congo people face inhuman conditions of hard labor—harvesting ivory and wild rubber and building facilities needed for trade—and atrocious brutality and violence at the hands of Leopold's forces. As Leopold's private African kingdom falls apart in the early twentieth century, his troops resort to wholesale slaughter of the Congo people as punishment.

1927–53 The Union of Soviet Socialist Republics (USSR), ruled by the dictator Joseph Stalin, enslaves millions of So-

Relief at the Freedmen's Bureau. *Archive Photos, Inc.*

Brutality and enslavement in the Congo under Belgian King Leopold. *Anti-Slavery International.*

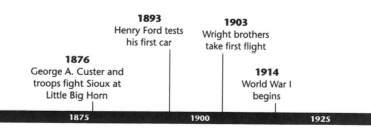

1893
Henry Ford tests
his first car

1903
Wright brothers
take first flight

1876
George A. Custer and
troops fight Sioux at
Little Big Horn

1914
World War I
begins

1868   1875   1900   1925

Jewish women laboring in a Nazi camp. *USHMM Photo Archives.*

viet citizens in labor camps in Siberia, Central Asia, and above the Arctic Circle.

1942–45 In Nazi Germany under Adolf Hitler, millions of Jews are enslaved in concentration camps, where they are systematically murdered. At the same time, millions of foreigners are enslaved in labor camps.

1956 The United Nations (UN) defines slavery as the condition of someone over whom any or all of the powers connected to the right of ownership are exercised and dedicates itself to ending all forms of slavery, including chattel slavery, serfdom, debt bondage, child labor, child prostitution, child pornography, the use of children in armed conflict, servile forms of marriage, forced labor, and the "white slave" traffic, or sexual slavery.

1990s In war-torn Sudan, human-rights groups estimate that in the 1990s, 30,000 to 90,000 Sudanese have been enslaved by a government-sponsored Arab militia. The militia regularly raids civilian villages and cattle camps in the south and hauls away hundreds of black Africans at a time to be marched north and sold into slavery.

1990s Despite the ban on slavery in Mauritania, tens of thousands of blacks remain the property of their Arab masters.

1991–96 According to official figures from the Chinese, police in China catch and prosecute 143,000 slave dealers and rescue 88,000 women and children who had been sold into slavery, marriage, or prostitution. Human-rights groups claim the real number of enslaved women and children was much higher.

1992 It is estimated that hundreds of thousands of political prisoners are forced to work in slave-like conditions in

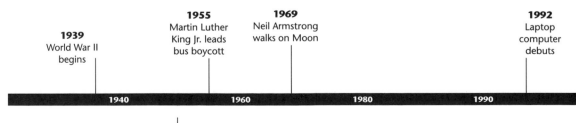

1939
World War II begins

1955
Martin Luther King Jr. leads bus boycott

1969
Neil Armstrong walks on Moon

1992
Laptop computer debuts

1940   1960   1980   1990

China's vast network of labor reform camps, some of which are nothing more than secured factories staffed with inmates. For years the official policy of China has been to use prison labor to produce cheap products for export.

1993 The Pakistan Human Rights Commission estimates the number of bonded child workers in Pakistan is 20 million. (A child labor survey conducted in 1996 by the Pakistani government, however, declares that there are a maximum of 4 million bonded child workers in the country.)

1996 The United Nations reports that children are being sold for prostitution, pornography, and adoption at increasing rates worldwide. In Asia alone, more than 1 million children are exploited sexually and live in conditions virtually identical to slavery.

1996 New York-based Human Rights Watch estimates that there are between 10 million and 15 million bonded child workers in India.

1996 The Pastoral Land Commission, a Catholic Church organization, reports 26,047 cases of slavery in Brazil, mainly involving Indians who work in charcoal production.

1998 The International Labor Organization (ILO) estimates the number of children exploited in labor markets around the world is between 200 million and 250 million, with nearly 95 percent living in poor countries.

1999 Anti-Slavery International (ASI) estimates that there are more than 200 million slaves in the world. Most of the slaves, according to ASI, live in Asia, Africa, and Latin America.

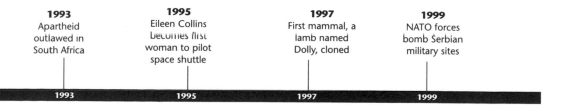

1993
Apartheid outlawed in South Africa

1995
Eileen Collins becomes first woman to pilot space shuttle

1997
First mammal, a lamb named Dolly, cloned

1999
NATO forces bomb Serbian military sites

1993   1995   1997   1999

Slavery
Throughout History
Almanac

Slavery Through the Ages (An Introduction)

Many times, many peoples

When we think of slavery, most Americans picture the American South in the 1800s, before the Civil War. Our mental image probably includes hundreds of black slaves on a plantation, picking cotton in the hot sun under the watchful eyes of their white masters. This vision is slavery in its simplest form: one person owning another and forcing the slave to work on the owner's behalf. This form of slavery is known as chattel slavery. Chattel means property, capital, or livestock, and it has been applied to slaves through the ages.

What may surprise many of us is that this form of slavery is as ancient as civilization itself, and it was alive and thriving in various places in the world at the end of the twentieth century. Chattel slavery is one of five traditional forms of slavery that the United Nations (UN; an international organization including most of the world's countries), in 1956, dedicated itself to ending. The other four forms are serfdom, debt bondage, the exploitation of children, and servile (slave-like) forms of marriage. As the twentieth century ended, the word "slavery" came to mean an even wider variety of

1

human-rights violations, including forced labor and various forms of sexual slavery. Counting all the people in traditional forms of enslavement, as well as people in more modern forms of slavery such as child pornography, the UN estimated that there were still millions of people enslaved in 1999.

While our mental picture of American slavery is fairly accurate, it is only one snapshot in the history of human slavery. The U.S. model of slavery was just one of many slave systems the world has known. The social, economic, and political forces that shaped the ancient societies of Mesopotamia, Egypt, Israel, Greece, and Rome; Western Europe in the Middle Ages; and the New World Latin American colonies all produced different systems of slavery. And still more ways of enslaving people were invented and practiced in the twentieth century, as the world became more industrialized, overcrowded, polluted, and dependent on technology.

The ancient world (5000 B.C.E.–500 C.E.)

The first slaves

The institution of slavery has existed throughout recorded history. Exactly when people began to enslave other people is impossible to say, but historians believe it happened around 10,000 years ago. For perhaps 1 million years before that time, humans lived constantly on the move, always searching for food. When they fought with one another, they killed rather than enslaved their defeated enemies. As people slowly began to replace hunting and gathering with husbandry (the taming of wild beasts for food and labor) and farming, they began to produce enough food to stay in one place.

By 5000 B.C.E., the desert and mountain people of the Near East (a region of southwest Asia that includes the Arab countries) were successfully farming the deserts of Mesopotamia, having constructed a vast system of canals and waterways to irrigate fields with water from the desert's only water sources—its rivers. Historians believe that at that time people began keeping their prisoners of war alive, feeding them minimum amounts, and making them slave laborers. Having gained some control over nature through farm-

ing and taming wild beasts, people turned to taming their own kind. Like cattle, sheep, or dogs, chattel slaves were trained to do the hardest and dirtiest work for the advancement of their masters.

When people started living together in villages and cities in Mesopotamia, around 3500 B.C.E., another form of bondage developed called debt slavery. Typically, a person would borrow money against a pledge, or a promise, of work. If the loan went unpaid, enslavement for a period of time was the only way to clear the debt. This form of enslavement was widespread in ancient societies right up to the Roman Empire (27 B.C.E.–476 C.E.). Debt slavery was supposed to be temporary, but it often resulted in lifelong servitude for debtors and even their families. Extreme poverty also drove many people into selling their children and their families into slavery.

Iberians (people from the Spanish peninsula) being sold as slaves by the Romans. *Engraving from a painting by R. Cogghe. The Bettmann Archive. Reproduced by permission.*

Person or property?

In the most general terms, chattel slaves throughout the ancient world had no legal rights. Slaves were considered property that their owners had the right to possess, enjoy, and dispose of in whatever way they saw fit. Slaves could be bought, sold, given away, inherited, or hired out to others. Slave masters had the right, by law and custom, to punish and, in some times and places, to kill their slaves for disobedience. Slaves were forced to work where and when their masters determined. They could not own property, they were not allowed to marry, and their children were born as slaves.

In ancient Mesopotamia, Egypt, Israel, Greece, and Rome, prisoners of war were the single greatest source of slaves. Children born to slave parents were the second greatest source. As slavery became more essential to the economies of the ancient world, the buying and selling of slaves became an important part of commerce. The Romans often sold their prisoners of war right on the battlefield to slave traders for transport and sale in the markets of central Italy. When wars could not keep up with the demand for slaves, piracy (the seizure by force of people and property on land or water) and kidnaping (the holding of captured people for ransom) thrived as profitable businesses.

Built on slave labor

The number of slaves in ancient Mesopotamia, Egypt, and Israel was small compared with the slave societies of Greece and Rome. Ownership was generally limited to the ruling classes—the kings, the pharaohs (rulers of ancient Egypt), the high priests, and the wealthy. There were no kings in the "democracies" (governments ruled by the people) of Greece and Rome, but there were plenty of slaves. Both the Greeks and the Romans built huge empires in Europe and the Mediterranean region, and in the process they enslaved millions of people from North Africa, Europe, and southwest Asia.

It was the Romans, though, who built the largest empire and held the most slaves of the ancient world. Every Roman who could afford to owned a slave or two—and that included peasants (poor people who lived off the land) and laborers. The wealthy owned hundreds of slaves, and Rome's rulers kept thousands. Between 200 B.C.E. and 200 C.E., between 30 and 40 percent of Rome's population were slaves.

Western Europe in the Middle Ages (500–1500)

The rise of serfdom

The dominant form of slavery in western Europe in the Middle Ages was serfdom. Serfdom was different from chattel slavery in that the enslaved were not considered "movable" property. That is, serfs (from the Latin word for servant) were bound to the land they lived on, generation after generation. Serfs served the owners of the land, known as lords. (Lords in turn served counts, counts served dukes, and everyone served the king.) If the land changed ownership, for whatever reason, the serfs worked for the new owners.

The Black Death, also known as the plague, killed nearly one-third of the population of Europe. This illustration of a dying plague victim with servants burning perfume in the sickroom comes from the *Fasiculus Medicinae*, Venice, 1500. *Archive Photos, Inc. Reproduced by permission.*

Chattel slavery did not entirely disappear with the end of Roman rule in western Europe and the Mediterranean. The Germanic tribes that moved into the territories of the old Roman Empire—such as the Franks, Angles, Saxons, Bavarians, Lombards, and Burgundians—set up a much different society from the Greeks or Romans before them. The process took hundreds of years, but the sharp distinctions between free people and slaves that were present in Greece and Rome slowly disappeared.

Feudal equality

By the year 1000, chattel slaves made up only 10 percent of Europe's population. The vast majority of people—around 80 percent—were peasants. Half of the peasants were considered "free"; the other half were serfs. The slaves, serfs, and free peasants lived and worked side by side under very similar conditions. All were in one way or another dependent on the noble class of landowners for their safety and their livelihoods.

Free peasants had more personal freedom than serfs and slaves. They were allowed to move off the land, marry, and control their possessions. Free peasants and serfs received plots of land from their lord in exchange for part of their crops and a pledge of work. Serfs, however, could not leave the land without severe punishment (whipping or branding). Serfs could not marry without their lord's permission, and all their possessions technically belonged to their lord. The small number of chattel slaves had no rights at all. They were the lord's property and could be sold independent of the land and punished at his will. They were allowed to marry, but only with their master's permission.

Hard times for all

Most of the free peasants, serfs, and slaves lived in little one-room huts with their entire families. Their lives were full of suffering and hardship, and the differences among them in terms of personal freedom must have at times seemed minor. In times of war, it was their huts, not the lords' castles, that burned. When disease and hunger gripped the land, their children, their old, and their weak died first. Life was so difficult that about two-thirds of all children in the Middle Ages died before the age of ten.

The Holy Crusades (a series of wars waged by Christians against Muslims from 1096 to 1204) and the Black Death (a deadly contagious disease, often called "the plague") both contributed to the end of serfdom in western Europe. Many serfs legally left their lands for the first time to serve in the Christian armies of Europe as they tried to take over parts of the Near East that were under Muslim control. The Black Death, starting around 1350, killed about one-third of Europe's population. The result was an extreme shortage of labor, which led to serfs gaining their freedom and ultimately receiving wages for their work. By the fifteenth century, serfdom in western Europe was virtually extinct.

The New World (1500–1900)

The rape of Africa

Christopher Columbus's "discovery" of the New World in 1492 led to the rebirth of large-scale chattel slavery and the largest forced migration in human history. Between 1441 and 1880, about 11 million Africans were transported to the European colonies of the Americas. The vast majority of slaves came from West Africa, although some East Africans also made the voyage across the Atlantic Ocean. Roughly 95 percent of all slaves taken from Africa, or about 10.5 million slaves, went to the Spanish, French, Dutch, Danish, and Portuguese colonies of Latin America (the West Indies, Mexico, and Central and South Americas). The other 500,000 slaves were taken to mainland North America—what is now the United States.

By 1600, about 367,000 Africans had been shipped to the New World. Although slavery had existed in Africa since ancient times, most slaves were prisoners captured in small wars between local tribes. When the Europeans began trading guns for slaves from West Africa's coastal tribes, tribal wars in

Africans chained and yoked in the slave trade. Slaves were often captured in the interior of West Africa and marched hundreds of miles to coastal forts from which they were shipped to the Americas. *The Granger Collection, New York. Reproduced by permission.*

Africa's interior increased in size and number. Slaves were captured hundreds of miles from the coastal European slave-trading forts. Many were bought and sold several times on their march to the slave ships. The voyage across the Atlantic Ocean, known as the Middle Passage, was a two-month nightmare for the captured Africans, and many of them died at sea from the inhumane conditions aboard the slave ships.

Slavery for profit

Throughout the slave period in the Americas, the shipping of slaves from Africa across the Atlantic Ocean to the colonies was a very big business. The Spanish, British, and Americans at one time or another dominated the trans-Atlantic trade. Much of the commercial success of England and the United States in the eighteenth and nineteenth centuries, in fact, was based on profits made from trading in human cargo.

The New World colonists put their slaves to work on their vast plantations, growing crops such as sugarcane, tobacco, coffee, and cotton for export to Europe. The Spanish colonists at first tried to enslave the native Indian populations of the West Indies. There and elsewhere, the natives refused to be enslaved and were slaughtered in great numbers. The New World colonists, especially the British, also tried using white indentured servants from Europe as workers, but they were not available in the numbers needed for large-scale farming.

The vast majority of slaves in the Americas worked in agriculture and lived in rural areas. Slaves were also used in large numbers for industrial purposes. Some of the worst conditions and highest death rates were in mines, quarries, factories, and workshops. Slaves also worked as domestic servants for plantation owners and small farmers. In general, domestic servants—or house slaves—had better food and living quarters than agricultural and industrial slaves. Slaves who lived in cities enjoyed more personal freedoms than rural slaves. City slaves often were allowed to hire out their own labor and live in their own quarters provided that they paid their masters part of their wages.

Unequal before God

Slaves were treated quite badly throughout the New World. In the West Indies, where most of the slaves were taken before being shipped on to the mainland colonies, about 30 percent died in their first three to four years due to overwork, poor diet, diseases, and severe and frequent beatings. In Brazil, where almost one-half of all slaves ended up, five out of six slaves worked on sugar, coffee, cotton, and cacao (seeds used to make chocolate and cocoa) plantations. The strategy of the slave masters in Brazil was to get as much out of their investment as quickly as possible. If twenty-five out of one hundred plantation slaves lived longer than three years, planters felt that they had gotten their money's worth.

Despite the brutality and high death rates of slaves in Brazil and the West Indies, slaves in Latin America were generally treated better than in British North America. This was due largely to the Catholic church's influence on Spain, France, and Portugal, the main colonizers of Latin America. The Catholic church demanded that the colonists baptize their slaves into the Christian religion. As Catholics, slaves attended Mass with their masters and participated in all the Church's holy rituals and sacraments, including marriage.

The British colonists—and, after the revolution, the American planters—never granted their slaves one iota of a chance of being equal, even in the eyes of God. Marriages between slaves were never legal in the United States, and slaves began attending church with their masters only in the 1830s.

Possibilities of freedom

In general, punishments for slaves in the New World were excessive and frequent. Slaves were whipped, beaten, branded, burned, mutilated, and killed throughout the Americas. The slave systems of Latin America, however, also offered the possibility of freedom to their slaves, hoping to secure their cooperation and good services by promising liberty as a reward. The manumission (formal release from bondage) of slaves by Latin American slaveowners, like the ancient Greeks and especially the Romans, resulted in a large number of freedpeople (former slaves) in these societies. Ex-slaves in Latin America immediately enjoyed the same rights and privileges as the free whites.

The long-term result of this practice was that Africans who gained their freedom in Latin America were able to integrate into society. In the United States, however, manumission

The Death of Spartacus, a drawing of the renowned Roman gladiator (trained fighter) who led a huge slave uprising in 71–72 B.C.E. *Drawing by H. Vogel. Corbis-Bettmann. Reproduced by permission.*

for slaves was very rare. And if slaves found their way to freedom (usually by running away), they were often denied equal rights with free whites even in the "free" states of the North.

Resistance and rebellion

Throughout history, slaves have resisted their masters by running away and rebelling. The penalties for both have always been the most severe possible—if for no other reason than to discourage other slaves from following their example. Slave rebellions in the Americas, however, were more frequent, more violent, and more successful at changing conditions than at any other time in history. There were more than 250 rebellions in the United States alone. Although blacks lost more of their freedom after each failed revolt, the total effect of the bloodshed actually advanced the cause of abolition (the destruction of slavery) by forcing society to face the consequences of its unjust system.

The most successful slave revolt in history began in the French colony of Haiti in 1791. Inspired by the American Revolution (in which the colony won independence from Britain), Haiti's slaves rose up in arms against the French. After thirteen years and the death of 100,000 African slaves and 60,000 French soldiers and colonists, Haiti won its freedom and became the second independent republic in the Western Hemisphere. Haiti's slave revolution became a shining symbol to slaves throughout the Americas that freedom was possible, even if it came at a very heavy price.

The twentieth century (1900–1999)

Modern monsters

The abolition of slavery in all of the countries in the New World by 1888 and the freeing of millions of slaves in

North and South America was a great step forward for the human race, but it was hardly the end of slavery. Slavery flourished in the twentieth century. One human-rights group estimated that in 1999, there were more than 200 million slaves in the world. That's *fifty* times more than the 4 million slaves who were freed in the United States after the Civil War (1861–65).

During the 1900s, as the world changed more rapidly than ever before, people found even more ways to enslave their fellow humans. King Leopold of Belgium (1835–1909) perpetrated the century's first holocaust (mass slaughter) on the people of central Africa. More than 10 million Africans lost their lives as Leopold drained the Congo Basin of its rubber and ivory through the mass enslavement and forced labor of its inhabitants.

Millions of prisoners, including many political opponents of the state, were enslaved in labor camps in the Union of Soviet Socialist Republics (USSR) from 1917 to 1991, and in the People's Republic of China since 1949. In addition to killing 6 million Jews in concentration camps (prison camps where inmates were starved, executed, or worked to death) in Nazi-occupied Europe in World War II, German dictator Adolf Hitler had nearly 10 million non-German civilians and captured soldiers working as slaves in German arms factories, on farms, and as domestic servants in households.

Japan instituted another form of slavery from 1932 to the end of World War II in 1945. The Japanese systematically

A Chronology of Abolition

1794: A slave revolt begun in 1791 results in the abolition of slavery in Haiti.

1804: Denmark abolishes the slave trade.

1807: Great Britain abolishes the slave trade.

1808: The U.S. Congress outlaws the importation of slaves.

1813: Sweden abolishes the slave trade.

1818: France abolishes the slave trade.

1823: Chile abolishes slavery.

1829: Mexico abolishes slavery.

1833: Great Britain passes the Emancipation Act, freeing all slaves in the British Empire after a five-year period.

1848: France abolishes slavery in its colonies.

1850: Brazil abolishes the slave trade.

1863: Abraham Lincoln issues the Emancipation Proclamation abolishing slavery in the United States.

1888: Brazil emancipates all slaves.

1948: The United Nations issues the *Universal Declaration of Human Rights* on December 10. Article 1 of the document proclaims "All human beings are born free and equal in dignity and rights."

forced women from its occupied lands to go to its battle-grounds in China, the South Sea Islands, Korea, and other areas of conflict. There, the women were forced to serve the Japanese soldiers as sex slaves, often called "comfort women." About 200,000 women were drafted as comfort women, the majority of them Korean.

Slavery today

As the twentieth century came to an end, there were millions of slaves in dozens of countries around the world. In 1999, most of the slaves in the world lived in Africa and Asia, with a smaller number in Latin America. For example, there were at least 100,000 chattel slaves in the West African country of Mauritania and almost as many slaves in the East African country of Sudan. In south Asia—in the countries of India, Pakistan, Nepal, and Bangladesh—there were from 15 million to 20 million bonded child laborers working in conditions of virtual slavery, making carpets, sporting goods, and clothing. The chief markets for these slave-produced items were in the United States, Europe, and Japan—countries where slavery had been outlawed for years.

In 1999 the People's Republic of China continued to imprison thousands of political opponents in forced labor camps, where they made products for export to world markets—including the United States. And in Latin America, debt slavery was being practiced in the Amazon region of Brazil, where at least 26,000 Indians were trapped in a cycle of debt that forced them into slave labor on isolated charcoal-production farms.

The selling of children into slavery and wife-selling, both ancient Chinese practices, also continued throughout the century in Southeast Asia. Child prostitution, child pornography, and child labor, all relatively modern forms of slavery, were widespread and growing in countries around the world, according to the UN. In 1996 there were 300,000 child prostitutes walking the streets of the United States, some as young as nine years old.

Looking ahead

Of course, there are exceptions to every generalization about slavery made in this chapter. The treatment of slaves throughout history has always depended on the character of their master and the time, place, and circumstances of their relationship. Some slaves, we can be sure, were treated with human kindness somewhere along the way. But make no mistake: slavery involves the ownership of human beings by other human beings, and under any conditions, in any place or time, it is always wrong. To paraphrase an old saying, as long as there is one slave in the world, none of us is truly free. And with millions of slaves in the world at the end of the twentieth century, organizations such as the United Nations, Anti-Slavery International, the International Labor Organization, and many more were still working hard to rid the world of the monstrous institution and to raise the public's awareness and concern over the abuse and atrocities that are being practiced in our modern world.

Slavery in Ancient Mesopotamia, Egypt, and Israel

Mesopotamia (c. 3500–539 B.C.E.)

Mesopotamia (pronounced mes-oh-poe-TAY-me-uh) is the name of an ancient country in the southwest desert of Asia where people settled and lived on the land between two great rivers: the Tigris (pronounced TIE-griss) River and the Euphrates (pronounced you-FRATE-ees) River (in what is now a country called Iraq).

Land of invention and abundance

Mesopotamians were the first people to live in cities (c. 3500 B.C.E.), and one of the first cultures to use writing and to calculate in numbers. They invented the plow, the wheeled cart, and sailing ships. They discovered how to use metals and made tools, weapons, and art from copper, bronze, silver, and gold instead of the stone, bone, and wood used by their ancestors.

Mesopotamians were also one of the first peoples—perhaps as early as 5000 B.C.E.—to practice irrigation farming (a system of ditches and canals constructed to bring water to

Fact Focus

- Most of the slaves in Mesopotamia, Egypt, and Israel were prisoners of war.

- Some slavery was permanent and life-long. A form of temporary slavery was known as debt slavery.

- In Mesopotamia, kings and priests of the temples owned the most slaves. Under the Assyrians and Babylonians, however, some of the richer Mesopotamian households had as many as 100 slaves.

- The pharaohs owned all the slaves in Egypt and put many of them to work in their farms, factories, workshops, mines, quarries, bakeries, kitchens, wineries, and breweries.

- Slavery in Egypt reached its peak during the New Kingdom, when thousands of Hebrews and other foreign-born slaves were forced to work in the fields making bricks for the construction of new cities and temples.

- As a people, the Hebrews knew slavery from both sides: as the enslaved and as the enslavers.

- The earliest laws of the Bible's Old Testament prohibited the enslavement of Hebrews by other Hebrews, but in practice these laws were mostly ignored.

dry fields from a river or lake in order to grow crops). The successful use of irrigation farming to grow food in the desert was an amazing achievement. For the first time, people could settle down in one place, no longer forced to move constantly in search of food.

Slavery: A step forward?

With an abundance of food, Mesopotamians, who were always at war with one another over water and land, began enslaving rather than killing those defeated in battle. War captives were taken prisoner for life, kept alive with minimal rations of food, and put to work. In this context, some historians argue that slavery was a step forward in the development of civilization, reasoning that for prisoners of war, the loss of liberty and a life of hard labor were better than death.

Slaves in Mesopotamia may have been happy to be alive, but their lives must have been full of misery. In general, they did the hardest, most backbreaking work. Slaves dug the irrigation ditches, turned the potters' wheels, wove the cloth, and toiled in the fields, often working from dawn until dark.

Sumer (c. 3500–2000 B.C.E.)

The growth of slavery

About 5000 B.C.E., people began to settle in Sumer (pronounced SOO-mare), an area between the Tigris and Euphrates Rivers in southern

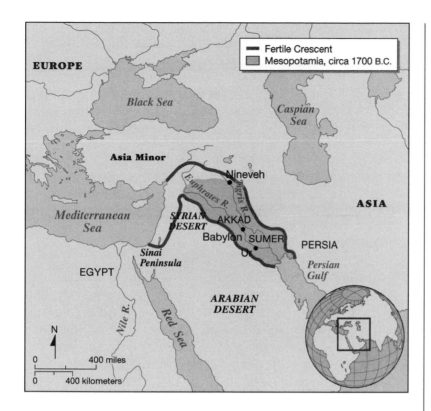

Mesopotamia, close to the Persian Gulf. The successful use of irrigation farming along the lower Tigris and Euphrates Rivers led to the growth of villages. By 3500 B.C.E., several of the larger villages in Sumer had come to resemble small cities, some with as many as 10,000 residents. By 2500 B.C.E., there were at least thirteen major city-states (a city and its surrounding lands) in Sumer. One city-state, Lagash, had 35,000 residents.

Sumerian city-states were politically independent, each ruled by its own king. Sumerian society was divided into two distinct classes: a very small upper class of nobles and priests, and a very large lower class of farmers, laborers, craftspeople, and tradespeople. Outside these classes were the slaves.

At first, when people lived in small farming villages, there was little use for a huge labor force. Families relied more on their children than on slaves to provide labor for private households and farms. The use of slave labor increased, however, as the city-states grew larger and more labor was needed to build additional houses, temples, and palaces and to work on larger farms and in expanded workshops and factories.

Slaves in Sumer were mostly those captured in the frequent wars between the city-states. The captives belonged to the king of the victorious city-state, who disposed of them as he saw fit. Some slaves served the personal needs of the king and his family. Some were sent to work on the king's farms or in the royal workshops. The king also gave many slaves to the temples of the gods, where the priests put them to work on the upkeep of the temple or on temple-owned farms.

Permanent vs. temporary slavery

Foreigners (people from another city-state) captured in war were subjected to lifelong slavery and were marked as such by branding, piercing, or special haircuts. Legally and socially they made up a specific class, with the least amount of rights and with very little hope for freedom for themselves or their children. Privately owned slaves, obtained on the open market or as gifts from the king, were sometimes adopted into the family or set free.

Another kind of less permanent slavery was also common in ancient Sumer: debt slavery. A creditor (moneylender) could enslave a free person for a period of time (three to six years) for failing to pay back a loan. Borrowers who were unable to pay off their debts were often forced to sell into slavery their sons or daughters, whom Sumerian society considered the father's property.

If found guilty of certain crimes, free persons could also be forced into temporary enslavement (rather than jail) as compensation to the victim. Permanent or temporary, slaves were considered to be property. They could be bought, sold, traded, given away, inherited, and rented out for use by others.

Babylonia (c. 2000–539 B.C.E.)

The First Dynasty of Babylon (c. 1800–1600 B.C.E.)

Around 2025 B.C.E., people known as the Amorites (pronounced AM-uh-rites) invaded Mesopotamia from northern Syria and formed the kingdom of Babylonia (pronounced

bab-ill-OWN-ee-uh). In 1780 B.C.E., King Hammurabi (pronounced ham-oo-RAH-bee), an Amorite, became the sixth ruler of Babylon, a city located on the Euphrates River in northern Mesopotamia. With Babylon as his capital city, Hammurabi united all of the competing kingdoms of Mesopotamia (including the Sumerian city-states) under one government.

The empire started by King Hammurabi grew to encompass an area more extensive than present-day Iraq. The First Dynasty of Babylon, as it came to be known, lasted for about two centuries (c. 1800–1600 B.C.E.) and is considered one of the world's first great empires.

The Code of Hammurabi and slavery

King Hammurabi's Babylonian empire was prosperous, made rich by his efforts to expand both agriculture and

Hammurabi, king of the Babylonian empire, presides at a trial. The Bettmann Archive. Reproduced by permission.

trade. His vast kingdom required a large labor force to build and maintain a huge network of irrigation canals; to carry out trade; to bake and glaze bricks; and to construct temples, houses, and other buildings. Slaves, again mostly prisoners of war, were an important but not dominant source of labor in the Babylonian economy. As more individuals in the empire became wealthy, the number of privately owned slaves increased as well (but it remained fairly low in this time period).

Like the Sumerians, the Babylonians accepted slavery and regulated it in their laws, many of which are contained in the Code of Hammurabi. The code, a list of about 300 laws, dealt with every aspect of Babylonian life. Much of Hammurabi's written code was derived from the customs and laws of the Sumerians, which were passed as an oral tradition from king to king, generation to generation.

Slaves as private property

Many of the laws governing slavery were for the protection and benefit of the slaveowner. Slaves were considered private property, and Hammurabi's code had very specific rules about buying, selling, and leasing slaves. As private property, slaves could be bought, sold, given away, exchanged, inherited, or rented out. Masters were allowed to brand, cut, or otherwise mark slaves, with harsh punishment for altering or removing such a mark. If someone caused a slave to lose an eye or break a bone, they would pay a fine of one-half the value of the slave to the owner, not to the injured slave. The code did not prevent the sexual exploitation of female slaves by their masters. Slaveowners often fathered children by female slaves and were allowed to use their female slaves as prostitutes.

Debt slavery

Free persons, such as farmers, craftspeople, merchants, and peddlers, sometimes needed loans to see them through lean times. A creditor could seize a borrower for failing to pay back a loan and turn him into a temporary slave until the debt was considered paid. The enslavement of the debtor's wife and children, in Babylonian society considered to be his property, was more often the result.

Runaway slaves

Hammurabi devoted six paragraphs of the code to the subject of runaway slaves. In Sumer, the punishment for aiding or harboring a runaway slave had been a fine. In Babylonia, under Hammurabi's rule, it was punishable by death.

Manumission

The Code of Hammurabi recognized four legal ways that a slave could be granted manumission (formal release from bondage) independent of his master's wish. First, wives and children in bondage as debt slaves were freed after three years. Second, children born to a free woman married to a slave were considered free. Third, a female slave concubine (pronounced CON-cue-bine; sex slave) and her children were freed after her master's death. Fourth, a Babylonian slave ransomed from a foreign land—that is, the required price was paid to his or her captors—was a free person upon return to the native city.

However, it was very rare for a permanent slave to gain his or her freedom. It was far more likely that a free person would become a temporary slave by failing to pay a debt or a permanent slave by being taken as a prisoner of war.

Assyrian domination (c. 1100–612 B.C.E.)

Slavery peaks in Mesopotamia

By 1100 B.C.E., the Assyrians (pronounced ah-SEER-ee-ans), a people living in northwest Mesopotamia, started to dominate Babylonia. The Assyrians established their capital in the northern city of Ashur (pronounced ah-SHUR) and then moved it to Nineveh (pronounced NIN-eh-vuh), on the banks

A stele (an inscribed stone pillar) of the Code of Hammurabi, with a figure carved into the top depicting Hammurabi dispensing law to a subject. The codes are listed below the carving. *The Bettmann Archive. Reproduced by permission.*

of the upper Tigris River. Although wars were a fact of life throughout Mesopotamian history, the Assyrians made war their trade, and they created their empire by brute force. The Assyrians, with their superior military power, had a simple formula for expanding their empire: invade, destroy, and enslave.

Since prisoners of war (and the children they gave birth to) were the main source of slaves throughout

Mesopotamian history, the number of slaves increased dramatically under the Assyrians. Records from one Assyrian ruler (c. 800 B.C.E.) list some of the riches taken from just one conquered city: "460 horses, 2,000 cattle, 5,000 sheep, the ruler's sisters, the daughters of his rich nobles with their dowries, and 15,000 of his subjects." (A dowry is the money or goods that a woman brings to her husband in marriage.)

Assyrian rulers put these huge slave-labor forces to work in state-controlled industry and agriculture. And, because war was so important and demanded such great resources, for a period of time the Assyrians even forced large numbers of slaves into their army.

The New Babylonian Empire (c. 612–539 B.C.E.)

Conquer and enslave: The trend continues

The tyrannical Assyrian empire fell to the Babylonians and their allies in 612 B.C.E., and its conquerors divided up its lands. In 605 B.C.E., King Nebuchadrezzar II (pronounced ne-buh-cuh-DREZ-er) became the first king of the New Babylonian Empire. He restored the capital city of Babylon (destroyed by the Assyrians, c. 689 B.C.E.) and turned it into the greatest city the world had known.

The Babylonians were not as brutal as the Assyrians, but they were every bit as ambitious in their quest to rebuild their empire (see "The First Dynasty of Babylon," above). They repeatedly sent their armies to conquer and collect tributes (gifts or payments for protection) from cities far and wide in the Near East. On one such campaign (597 B.C.E.), Nebuchadrezzar II captured the city of Jerusalem (pronounced jeh-ROO-sah-lem) and sent most of the city's population, about 3,000 Hebrews, into slavery in Babylonia (see "Captive in Babylon," later in this chapter). The Hebrew slaves were freed in 539 B.C.E., when Babylonia fell to the invading Persians (people from the east).

Assyrian and Babylonian slavery

The number of slaves increased steadily during both the Assyrian and Babylonian empires (c. 705–539 B.C.E.).

Oddly, so did the level of independence that masters granted
their slaves. Slaves in Babylonia during these two centuries
were given many of the rights of free persons. Slaves could
marry and own livestock, land, and other property (including
other slaves). Slaves could become apprentices and learn a
trade such as carpentry, shoemaking, baking, or weaving.
They could carry on a profession or business, engage in trading and banking, and appear in court as witnesses.

Throughout Mesopotamian history, wealthy families
owned slaves but not in great numbers, usually from one to five
(though in some cases as many as fifteen) slaves per household.
The number of privately owned slaves, however, increased
under the Assyrians and Babylonians. Some of the richer households had as many as one hundred slaves, and a middle-class
family might own as many as five slaves ("Middle class" is a rel-
ative term; most people were too poor to own any slaves.)

Egypt (c. 3110–332 B.C.E.)

Pharaohs, pyramids, and peasants

Ancient Egypt, a country in the northeast corner of
Africa, is known as the land of pharaohs (pronounced FAIR-
rows) and pyramids—the tombs of the pharaohs. "Pharaoh"

is what the Egyptians called their king; it means "great house" or "royal palace." The Egyptians considered their pharaohs to be both gods and kings. They ruled Egypt almost continuously for more than twenty-seven centuries and provided a political and spiritual unity to Egyptian society that was rare in ancient times.

Like the Mesopotamians (see "Land of invention and abundance," earlier in this chapter), the Egyptians settled close to water (the Nile River) and practiced irrigation farming. They built ships for trading, used writing, and knew how to use metals such as bronze, copper, silver, and gold. Unlike the Mesopotamians, almost all of the Egyptians lived in the countryside, not in cities.

One river, one kingdom

From 5000 B.C.E. to 3110 B.C.E., before the reign of the pharaohs, Egypt was divided into two kingdoms along the Nile River: Lower Egypt and Upper Egypt. Around 3110 B.C.E., a king of Upper Egypt named Menes (pronounced ME-nees) united the two kingdoms.

Pharaohs ruled over Egypt from 3110 B.C.E. to 332 B.C.E. Historians divide this period into three parts: the Old Kingdom (3110–2258 B.C.E.), the Middle Kingdom (2000–1786 B.C.E.), and the New Kingdom (1570–1085 B.C.E.).

From 1786 to 1570 B.C.E., and again after 1085 B.C.E., Egypt was ruled by foreigners: people from neighboring lands such as the Libyans (pronounced LIB-ee-ans; people to the west of Egypt), the Assyrians, and the Persians. The foreigners governed Egypt by assuming the position of pharaoh or by making the Egyptian pharaoh and his officials pledge their loyalty and pay tributes to them. In 343 B.C.E., the last native-born Egyptian pharaoh lost the throne. In 332 B.C.E., Egypt fell without a fight to the invading Greeks, led by Alexander the Great.

Slavery: A matter of degree

The pharaoh and his queen (usually his sister, since pharaohs were allowed to marry only within the family) were at the top of Egypt's social pyramid. The pharaoh owned everything in Egypt: the land, the mines, the quarries, the

Men erecting public buildings in Egypt. Most often peasants—not slaves—were forced into service by the pharaoh for public works. *Archive Photos, Inc. Reproduced by permission.*

factories, and the workshops. Below the pharaoh in status were the nobles (the pharaoh's relatives), the government officials (people who oversaw the pharaoh's business), and the priests. The nobles, officials, and priests were served by a class of scribes (educated men who could read and write). Below the scribes were workers such as soldiers, shepherds, tradespeople, craftspeople, and ship pilots. The bottom of the social pyramid, and by far the largest of all these groups, was a huge population of peasants.

Technically, peasants were not slaves (they were not owned, and they could not be sold), but they "belonged" to the land and its owner (either the pharaoh, the nobles, or the priests). The peasants worked the land as sharecroppers (they gave a portion of their crops to the landowner as rent). If the land was sold, the peasants stayed to serve the new owner.

Historians point to this large peasant class when they say that Egyptian civilization developed without the widespread use of slaves. In Egypt the peasants did most of the manual labor usually done by slaves. When they were not actively farming, peasants were regularly forced into service by the pharaoh. Ordered to various sites around the country, they went to work building pyramids, palaces, temples, roads, and canals. And, when the pharaoh needed soldiers for the army, he could draft them from the peasant class.

Slaves: "Bound for life"

Slaves in Egypt were mostly foreigners who were captured during wartime and in military raids on neighboring lands. The Egyptian word for these prisoners of war meant "bound for life." All slaves in Egypt belonged to the pharaoh. Like the kings of Mesopotamia (see "The growth of slavery," earlier in this chapter), the pharaohs of Egypt gave slaves to the temples of the gods, where the priests put them to work. The pharaohs also gave away slaves as rewards, usually to government officials or army generals.

Slaves given to individuals by the pharaohs were considered "property" that could be sold or given to someone else. The slaves kept by the pharaohs were put to work on the royal farms and in the pharaohs' factories, workshops, mines, quarries, bakeries, kitchens, wineries, and breweries.

Slavery in the Kingdoms

Military campaigns were rare in the Old and Middle Kingdoms. Since prisoners of war and their offspring were the main source of slaves in Egypt, the number of slaves remained low. Records from the Middle Kingdom provide the earliest evidence of privately held slaves. Whether in possession of the state (the pharaoh) or private individuals, escaped slaves in this era faced death if they were caught. In contrast, peasants who deserted a construction project or the army were sentenced to life in a labor camp.

Slavery in Egypt reached its peak during the New Kingdom (1570–1085 B.C.E.), when Egypt had just recovered from its first invasion and foreign rule in fifteen centuries. From 1786 B.C.E. to 1570 B.C.E., Egypt was ruled by the Hyksos (pronounced HIK-sose), a nomadic tribe from Syria. When the Egyptians drove out the Hyksos, they enslaved all foreigners

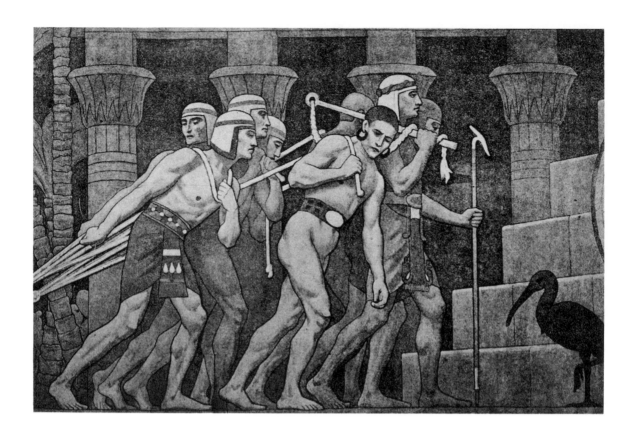

"Egypt," a frieze in the Grand Palace of Fine Arts.
Archive Photos, Inc. Reproduced by permission.

who remained. This included thousands of Hebrews (see "Captives in Egypt," later in this chapter). The Egyptians forced their Hebrew slaves, and thousands of other foreign-born slaves, to work in the fields making bricks for the construction of new cities and temples.

The New Kingdom was a time of empire-building for the Egyptian pharaohs. The pharaohs used their military power to enlarge Egypt's territory by conquering neighboring lands. These wars of expansion resulted in the capture of tens of thousands of slaves.

Ownership and status

Slaveownership by private individuals also increased in the New Kingdom. Slaves could be bought from foreign merchants in the local slave market. Slaves were not cheap, but their ownership was not restricted to the wealthy. Such people as herdsmen, stable masters, merchants, and entertainers owned slaves.

Private slaveowners usually had only one or two slaves, but some had as many as ten. Many of the slaves in private households were females obtained for domestic work such as child rearing, cleaning, and cooking. All slaves were considered property that could be sold, traded, rented out, inherited, or given away.

In the New Kingdom, slaves participated more in the economic and social life of Egypt than in the past. They were allowed to own property, inherit possessions, bear witness in court, marry freewomen, and learn how to write. Slaves could also be granted manumission from their owners or gain the status of a free person by marrying a free person (sometimes their own master) or by being adopted by a free family.

Israel (c. 1850–539 b.c.e.)

The enslaved and the enslavers

The history of slavery among the Hebrews (also known as Israelites, or Jews) in the ancient Near East is unique. As a people, the Hebrews knew slavery from both sides: the enslaved and the enslavers. Twice they were enslaved, by the Egyptians in 1570 b.c.e., and by the Babylonians in 597 b.c.e.

The Hebrews also owned slaves. Slavery for non-Hebrews was permanent, and slaves' children were born slaves. Most slaves were foreigners captured in battle; some were bought from slave traders on the open market. Hebrews also enslaved other Hebrews in a form of debt slavery. By Hebrew custom, a moneylender could seize a free person for failing to pay back a loan and turn the borrower into a temporary slave until the debt was considered paid. This form of slavery was supposed to be temporary—but it often wasn't. Various Hebrew laws tried to regulate the length of time a person was enslaved (see "Slave laws of the Old Testament," below).

Guests in Egypt

Though the Hebrews are associated with the state of Israel in the ancient country of Palestine (pronounced PAL-eh-stine; a country on the eastern shore of the Mediterranean

Sea), their ancestors were tribes that wandered far and wide in the deserts of the Near East, constantly searching for food and water. The ancient Hebrews of 2000 B.C.E. possessed no land or cities. They worked as shepherds, artisans, and merchants, and were led by a tribal chief, known as a patriarch (pronounced PAY-tree-ark).

Around 1850 B.C.E., the Hebrew patriarch Abraham led one of the tribes of Israel (there were twelve), to the city of Hebron (pronounced HEE-brun) in central Palestine, where they settled. In 1700 B.C.E. Joseph, a descendent of Abraham, led a tribe of Hebrews from Palestine into Egypt at the invitation of the pharaoh. The Hebrews settled and prospered in northern Egypt, on the lands just east of the Nile River.

Captives in Egypt

Generations later, the Egyptians enslaved the Hebrews. In 1570 B.C.E., Egypt drove out invaders (see "Slavery in the Kingdoms," earlier in this chapter) who had ruled their country for two centuries. The Egyptians then enslaved all remaining foreigners—including thousands of Hebrews, forcing them to work in the fields making bricks for the construction of new cities and temples.

The exodus (departure) of the Hebrews from their bondage in Egypt and their return to Palestine to establish the state of Israel is one of the most famous events in Jewish history, as told in Exodus, the second book of the Bible's Old Testament. Sometime between 1300 B.C.E. and 1200 B.C.E. (historians are unable to fix a more exact date), a Hebrew lawgiver named Moses led a group of slaves in an escape from Egypt. After wandering in the Sinai Desert for "forty years," according to the Bible, Moses and his people reached the borders of the Promised Land (Palestine), at which point Moses is said to have died.

One people, two kingdoms

Joshua, the next leader of the Hebrews, reunited and led the twelve tribes of Israel in the conquest of Canaan (pronounced KAY-nun; the name of Palestine at the time). This resulted in the establishment of the Jewish national homeland: Israel. Once settled (c. 1200 B.C.E.), the Israelites built cities and farmed.

The leadership of the patriarchs gave way to elected chiefs, or "judges" as they were called. Then, about 1000 B.C.E., Saul established the first Hebrew kingdom. David, the next king, conquered the city of Jerusalem (pronounced jeh-ROO-sah-lum) and made it the capital. In 940 B.C.E. the kingdom split into two parts: Israel in the north, with Samaria (pronounced sah-MAR-ee-uh) as its capital, and Judah (pronounced JOO-duh) in the south, with Jerusalem as its capital.

In 722 B.C.E., Samaria fell to the Assyrians (see "Assyrian domination," earlier in this chapter), marking the end of the kingdom of Northern Israel. Samaria's fall led to the deportation of ten of the twelve tribes of Israel (more than

The bondage of Hebrews in Egypt: Israelite slaves making bricks for the construction of Egyptian cities. *Archive Photos, Inc. Reproduced by permission.*

The people of Jerusalem are taken captive by the king of Babylon, Nebuchadrezzar, and his army, c. 597 B.C.E. The Hebrews called their years of slavery in Babylon "The Great Captivity." *Picture Collection, The Branch Libraries, The New York Public Library.*

27,000 people) into Assyria. The Assyrians spared Jerusalem when the king of Judah sent the Assyrians a tribute that included his own daughters, as well as other treasures.

Captive in Babylonia

In 597 B.C.E., Jerusalem and the nation of Judah fell to the Babylonian king Nebuchadrezzar II. Jerusalem's destruction resulted in the enslavement of some 3,000 Hebrews. Nebuchadrezzar sent the captured Hebrews to Babylonia to serve as slaves. The Hebrews toiled in Babylonia for almost fifty years; this period is known in Jewish history as "The Great Captivity."

The Israelites were not treated badly in Babylonia, but they longed to return to their homeland, and many of them did so when the Persians captured the city of Babylon in 539 B.C.E. and encouraged the Jews to return to Jerusalem to rebuild their temple and city.

Slave laws of the Old Testament

Religion was very important to the Hebrews and played a strong role in how they viewed and practiced slavery. The Hebrews believed their laws were dictated by their god, Yahweh (pronounced YAH-way), through the Hebrew leaders and prophets. Many of the Hebrew laws about slavery can be found in the Bible's Old Testament. Biblical slave laws were rarely concerned with non-Hebrew slaves. Prisoners of war and other foreign slaves had about the same legal status as cattle or other private property.

The earliest laws of the Old Testament prohibited the enslavement of Hebrews by other Hebrews, yet in practice these laws were mostly ignored. People unable to pay a debt became the slaves of wealthy landowners, merchants, and moneylenders. Sometimes people were faced with such extreme poverty that they had to sell their children or even themselves into slavery.

The First Abolitionists

Slavery was a fact of life in ancient times. Neither the kings of Mesopotamia, the pharaohs of Egypt, nor the kings and prophets of Israel condemned slavery or tried to abolish it. Organized opposition to the practice of slavery was virtually unheard of until the appearance in the first century B.C.E. of two Jewish sects (small communities of people who share common beliefs), the Essenes (pronounced eh-SEENS) and the Therapeutae (pronounced thair-ah-PUTE-eye).

The Essenes, who lived in secluded brotherhoods next to the Dead Sea near the river Jordan in eastern Palestine, and the Therapeutae, who lived in Alexandria, Egypt, did not own slaves. The Essenes and Therapeutae opposed violence and war, and they considered slavery unnatural.

The Essenes actively worked to end slavery by purchasing slaves from their masters and setting them free. The beliefs and practices of the Essenes were so similar to the teachings of Jesus and the apostles that some historians believe that one or more of the founders of Christianity may have been an Essene or influenced by their philosophy.

Softening the blow

Biblical slave laws recognized the existence of debt slavery in Hebrew society and tried to regulate some of its harsher practices. A master who killed his Hebrew slave was punished severely (not just fined), and slaves injured by their masters were granted freedom in compensation (this applied to non-Hebrew slaves as well).

As for runaway slaves, Old Testament laws encouraged their protection, not punishment. In fact, if the Hebrews had obeyed this law to the letter, slavery would have ended. In general, Hebrew leaders and lawmakers encouraged owners to treat their Hebrew slaves as family. Slaves, like their masters, were to take a day of rest on the Sabbath. (Saturday, the seventh day of the week in the Hebrew calendar, was named by the Ten Commandments as the Sabbath, a day of worship and rest.)

Manumission

Bondage for Hebrew debt slaves in Israel was not supposed to be permanent. Hebrew laws granting manumission to slaves tried to limit the time of the enslavement. Early Hebrew laws required masters to set their slaves free after seven years. Later laws required masters to set their slaves free after fifty years.

In early Hebrew law, female slaves did not have the same opportunity for manumission as male slaves. According to Exodus, the second book of the Bible's Old Testament, if a female was sold into slavery by her father, she was to remain in bondage for her lifetime: "she shall not go out like the male slaves do." Female slaves were often both manual laborers and concubines (used for sexual purposes) for their masters. Female slaves were eventually granted the same manumission rights as their male counterparts.

Slaves could also gain their freedom by purchase (somehow paying off the loan or debt, perhaps with help from free relatives). More common, however, was a commitment by slaves to serve their masters for life. After declaring their loyalty to their masters, slaves were marked by having an ear pierced with an awl (a pointed tool for making holes).

Slavery in Ancient Greece and Rome

Slavery in Greece (c. 1200–330 B.C.E.)

What little is known about slavery in early Greek history comes to us from Greek literature. The stories contained in the *Iliad* (pronounced ILL-ee-ad) and the *Odyssey* (pronounced ODD-iss-ee), written by the Greek poet Homer, depict a world of domestic life, farming, adventure at sea, and warfare and conquest abroad. Homer lived in the ninth century B.C.E. (900–800 B.C.E.) but wrote about the Greece of around 1200 B.C.E. Homer's stories are more about the ruling class of Greece than the peasants and slaves. Yet his epic poems contain many situations that involve slaves, from which historians are able to piece together what slavery may have been like in a period they call "Homeric" Greece (roughly 1200 B.C.E.–800 B.C.E.).

Homeric Greece (c. 1200–800 B.C.E.)

In Homeric Greece, power in society belonged to a small number of family patriarchs (pronounced PAY-tree-arks). The patriarchs were wealthy men who owned estates (houses in the country with large amounts of land), which

Greek poet Homer singing to the people, an illustration. Much of what we know today about slavery in ancient Greece comes to us through Homer's epic poems, the *Iliad* and the *Odyssey*. *Archive Photos, Inc. Reproduced by permission.*

they used for growing crops and raising livestock such as cattle and pigs. Most of the work on these estates—in the house and in the fields—was done by slave labor. In between the slaves and the patriarchs was a large class of poor peasants (laborers and small farmers), very few of whom could afford to own slaves.

Soldiers of misfortune The main sources of slaves in Homeric Greece were wars and slave raids (military expeditions for the purpose of taking slaves and precious goods). The heroes of Homer's tales were groups of Greek warriors who traveled abroad, usually by ship but sometimes by land, to seek their fortunes by battling and conquering foreign "barbarians." Greek raiding parties sometimes resorted to piracy (attacking and robbing unarmed travelers on the high seas) and kidnaping (taking captives for ransom).

If successful, the warriors returned to mainland Greece with prisoners, livestock, and precious goods, such as rare metals or jewels. They divided up the spoils and disposed of their "property" as they desired. The captured foreigners—mostly women and children, since the men were often killed in battle—were usually sold in the local slave market. Captives were sometimes sold abroad in exchange for supplies if the Greek raiding party was still traveling.

Domestic and agricultural slavery Wealthy landowners acquired slaves directly by force (as described above) or bought them from the local slave market. They used slaves on their estates for both domestic (household) and agricultural (farm) work. Female slaves generally performed household chores such as cooking, serving meals, cleaning, caring for children, and making clothes. Male slaves worked in the fields, tending the crops and looking after the livestock.

Slaves and the families they worked for often labored side by side, sometimes with hired help as well. Together they produced the food and clothing for everyone on the estate. Because of this system of shared labor, slaves in Homeric Greece were treated better than most slaves in ancient times. Slaves sometimes participated in religious rituals with their master's family and enjoyed some comforts, such as decent food and shelter.

A patriarch had the power of life and death over his slaves—and everyone else on the estate, including his wife and children. Slavery in Homeric Greece was permanent, with little chance for manumission. Children born to a slave mother and a free father, however, inherited the father's free status.

Archaic Greece (800–500 B.C.E.)

The slaveholding practices of the Greeks changed dramatically in the period historians call archaic (pronounced ar-KAY-ick; ancient) Greece (800–500 B.C.E.). In general, commerce and trade (the making and selling of goods for local and foreign markets) grew rapidly as Greece began to take part in the economy of the entire Mediterranean region.

The great farms of the patriarchs increased in size and began to grow products for market, such as olives for olive oil and grapes for wine. With less land available and less labor needed for these crops, many peasants were forced to move to find work and food. These changes in the Greek economy ultimately led to the rise of Greek city-states (independent political units consisting of a city and its surrounding countryside), as peasants moved from the country into the city.

These changes also spurred a period of colonial expansion (the movement of Greek people to new settlements in neighboring lands) from 750 to 550 B.C.E. To the east, in Asia, numerous Greek colonies developed along the shores of the Black Sea. Many of these new settlements maintained ties to an older Greek city-state. To the west, in Europe, Greek colonies could be found as far away as mainland Italy. To the south, Greek-speaking people dominated the entire Mediterranean coast of northern Africa.

The slave trade Greek colonists often took land by force, either killing, driving off, or capturing the natives. Those captured were frequently sent to the cities of central Greece, where they were sold as slaves. Sometimes slaves were sold through a prearranged contract between a colony and a sponsoring city-state.

Thus, the older Greek city-states became importers of slaves, and the colonies and their new city-states became exporters of slaves. The establishment of this trading network (which also included slave markets outside Greece) ultimately led to a rise in the number of slaves in central Greece.

The slave trade in Greece continued to grow in the sixth century B.C.E. (600–500 B.C.E.) because of two developments. First, slave trading became easier because of the introduction of money into the business world of the Mediterranean. Coinage (small, measured lumps of precious metal), not a shipload of manufactured or agricultural products, became all that was necessary to obtain slaves. Second, there was an increased demand for slaves in the old Greek city-states, especially in Athens (pronounced ATH-enz), ancient Greece's most important city-state. In 594 B.C.E., an elected lawmaker named Solon (pronounced SOLE-ahn) outlawed debt slavery for Greek citizens in Athens. This created a demand for foreign slaves who could do the work of the freed Greek debt slaves.

The birth of industrial slavery The growth of the slave trade in archaic Greece corresponded with a general increase in commerce and trade. The need for increased production of goods (such as textiles, pottery, armor, and weapons) for markets in Greece and abroad led to a higher demand for labor—specifically slave labor.

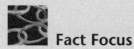

Fact Focus

- There were five so-called "slave societies" in the history of the human race. Ancient Greece and Rome produced two of them. (Brazil, Cuba, and the United States were the other three.)

- Slaves sometimes made up as much as 40 percent of the total population of ancient Greece and Rome.

- In ancient Greece and Rome, prisoners of war—the main source of slaves—were sometimes sold to slave dealers right on the battlefield. The captives were then sold as slaves (for a profit) in Greek and Roman slave markets.

- Ancient Greek and Roman economies were dependent on the output (mostly grapes and olives) of their enormous farms. Slaves did most of the work on these farms.

- At different times, Greece and Rome dominated trade and commerce in the Mediterranean region. Most of the work in producing items for export (such as pottery, olive oil, wine, and weapons) was done by slaves in small factories.

- In Greece and Rome the wealthiest landowners owned the most slaves, but even "poor" people owned a slave or two. The emperors of Rome (27 B.C.E.–476) owned the most slaves—boasting staffs of more than 20,000 slaves.

- Slaves held a wide variety of jobs in Greek and Roman society, from doorman to doctor. The worst fate for a slave was to be sent to the mines and quarries or to the plantations of Rome.

A female slave, who in Homeric Greece may have served her master on his farm estate by making clothes for the family, was in archaic Greece making clothes for market in a workshop (a small factory) with other slaves. This is known as industrial slavery. Male slaves continued to be the main source of farm labor for the big landowners, but a much larger number of male slaves were used in industries: in the mines, quarries, and workshops and in the building of cities, monuments, and ships. In 550 B.C.E., there were as many as 30,000 slaves in the silver mines alone.

Classical Greece (500–330 B.C.E.)

By 431 B.C.E., the city-state of Athens had so many slaves that historians consider it the world's first example of a

Illustration of slave girls at a fountain in ancient Athens. There were more slaves than citizens in Athens, the largest slave-holding city-state of classical Greece. *Archive Photos, Inc. Reproduced by permission.*

slave society. The number of slaves in Athens and central Greece in the historical period known as classical Greece (500–330 B.C.E.) was greater than anything the world had seen before. Of the 155,000 residents of the city of Athens, 70,000 were slaves, 60,000 were citizens, and 25,000 were metics (pronounced METT-icks; resident foreigners). Athens was Greece's largest slaveholding city-state, but other Greek city-states, such as Delphi (pronounced DELL-fie) and Delos (pronounced DELL-ohs), had similar numbers.

War and slavery Prisoners of war were the single greatest source of slaves in classical Greece. The fifth century B.C.E. was dominated by two very long wars. From 500 B.C.E. to 449 B.C.E., a series of wars were fought between the independent but allied Greek city-states and the invading Persians from the east. The Greeks eventually won. A second war, the Peloponnesian (pronounced pel-eh-po-NEE-zhen) War (431–404 B.C.E.), was a civil war between two Greek city-states—Athens and Sparta— which Sparta won. Both wars produced tens of thousands of slaves. For example, one Athenian commander who battled the Persians in 468 B.C.E. put 20,000 slaves on the market.

These wars not only produced great numbers of slaves, but they increased the demand for slave labor as well. More workers than ever were needed in the war industries, as makers of armor, shields, weapons, and so forth. In addition, wars naturally shrank the supply of free labor since many Greek citizens were needed for military duty. Slaves were not allowed to be soldiers.

These wars turned the slave trade into a very big business. Trading alliances developed among generals, admirals, pirates, and various middlemen who carved out territories and divided up the slave markets among themselves.

Who owned all the slaves? Private citizens owned most of the slaves in classical Greece. Unlike other ancient countries, which had kings, pharaohs, and emperors (see Chapter Two), Greece had no higher political authority than the government of the independent city-state. Conquering armies (often a group of allied city-states) rarely kept the slaves they captured. Instead they sold the slaves on the market, usually to slave traders, who would then sell them to private citizens.

The wealthiest private citizens owned most of the slaves. Slaves were considered an investment and could be used in a variety of ways: in households; on farms; or in mines, quarries, and workshops. Some of the wealthier Greeks purchased huge numbers of slaves and rented them out by the hundreds or even the thousands to mine operators, owners of industrial workshops (which made such items as pottery or beds), and government contractors. On the average, a rich household in classical Greece had about fifty slaves, and every free household that could afford it had between one and three slaves.

Destruction of the Athenian army by the Spartans in the Peloponnesian Wars, which produced thousands of slaves. *Archive Photos, Inc. Reproduced by permission.*

Some slaves were publicly owned. City-states often purchased slaves and used them for administrative tasks, or as court ushers, prison guards, and even police officers. In Athens, slaves were used in the minting of coins and the construction of roads and public buildings. Compared with private ownership, however, the number of public slaves was not very great.

Slave work and status There were two things that slaves in Greece could never do: participate in politics (only citizens had such rights) or be a soldier (only free men could serve in the military). All other occupations or professions were possible for a slave, from doorman to doctor.

The status of slaves, and the conditions under which they lived, depended in part on what kind of work they did. Some slaves received a formal education and training and managed to attain executive positions in business and industry. Some became professionals, such as doctors, nurses, teachers, or bankers. Slaves in domestic, agricultural, or industrial service could also attain positions of management and oversee the work of other slaves in the households, farms, and workshops of their owners.

Other slave jobs included butler, maid, cook, potter, prostitute, weaver, messenger, artisan, musician, and laborer. Some of the hardest work for slaves was in the farm fields, but the worst possible fate for a slave was to be sent to the mines, where the hours were long, the work was backbreaking, and the air wasn't fit to breathe. Slaves in the mines led shorter lives.

Opportunities for freedom No matter what type of work a slave did, he or she was still owned by someone else. Owners were allowed by law to beat and torture disobedient slaves. In classical Greece, slaveowners could not, however, kill their slaves without facing prosecution. Slaves faced severe punishment for disobedience, but if they did their work well they could be rewarded with a promotion to manager or foreperson.

An even greater incentive for a slave than promotion was the possibility of manumission. Although slaves could not own property, some slaves, especially in the cities, paid a rental fee to their owners and kept the rest of their earnings. Slaves who saved enough money could purchase freedom from their master for the market value of a slave.

A slave could also be granted manumission through the master's will after his death or by public declaration during the master's lifetime. Manumission of slaves, individually

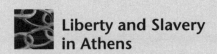

Liberty and Slavery in Athens

Athens, ancient Greece's most important city-state, is known as the world's first democracy (government by the people) *and* the world's first slave society. Historians have debated for years how it was possible to have a rapid growth in democratic liberty and an equally rapid growth in slavery at the same time (700–500 B.C.E.).

Some historians argue that the growth of slavery in Athens made democracy *possible* by providing slaveowners the time to participate in politics and government. For Athenian citizens, "freedom" meant freedom from having to work.

Other historians argue that the growth of slavery in Athens made the birth of democracy *essential*. The free people of Athens, the argument goes, pressed their lawmakers for certain rights and privileges that would distinguish them from the slaves who were all around them. Democracy, therefore, was invented in order to protect the majority of free people from being treated as slaves by the minority of rich and powerful landowners who had ruled Greece for generations.

or in groups, by private or public owners, occurred in archaic Greece but became more common in classical Greece.

In classical Greece, manumission of a slave officially made the ex-slave a freedman or freedwoman, a status somewhere between a slave and a freeborn Greek citizen. The freedperson gained liberty of movement and freedom from reenslavement but often remained obligated to serve their former master in some capacity, such as payments of fees or labor. Citizenship in an ancient Greek city-state, which entitled a person (males only) to vote and participate in politics, was reserved for the native-born or could be awarded to a foreigner for special services. Citizenship was rarely granted to freedpersons.

Slavery in Rome (509 B.C.E.–476)

One thousand years of government

The city of Rome, located in central Italy on the Tiber River (pronounced TIE-bur), was founded in 753 B.C.E. by the Etruscans (pronounced eh-TRUSS-kens), people from Asia Minor (a peninsula on the Mediterranean) who had migrated to Italy around 1200 B.C.E. In 575 B.C.E. the Etruscans made Rome the capital of their kingdom. Etruscan kings ruled over the many different tribes and peoples of Italy with the help of the Senate, a group of men chosen from the class of patricians (pronounced puh-TRISH-ens), the heads of wealthy and powerful landowning families.

In 509 B.C.E., the Senate overthrew the king and established the Roman Republic (a republic is a form of government that is run by elected representatives and based on a constitution). The patricians replaced the king with two magistrates (pronounced MAJ-iss-trates; the Roman word for "master"). The new heads of state were elected each year by the people but drawn exclusively from the Senate. In 471 B.C.E., the plebs (Rome's majority middle class) set up their own assembly of elected representatives and officers. In 287 B.C.E., the laws and decisions of the assembly of plebs were declared binding on the whole Roman people.

The last century of the Republic was marked by civil wars, economic crises, riots in the cities, and wars against pirates and rebellious slaves. Out of the political chaos emerged

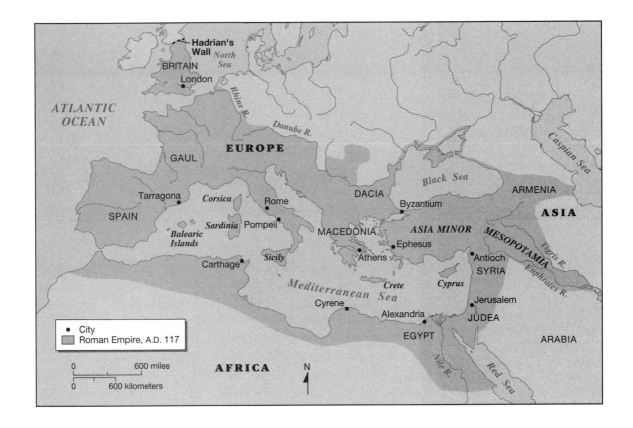

A map of the Roman Empire, c. 117 C.E.

the first emperor of the Roman Empire, Augustus (who reigned from 27 B.C.E. to 14). Under the Empire, the Senate and the assembly of plebs remained, but the real power belonged to the emperor. In 395, the empire of Rome was divided in two: the East and the West. The Western Roman Empire ended in 476. The Eastern Roman Empire, with its capital city of Constantinople, continued into the fifteenth century.

Ancient Rome's slave society

Slavery under the Roman Republic and the Roman Empire was so widespread that ancient Rome is known as one of the five "slave societies" in the history of the human race. The other slave societies were ancient Greece, Brazil, Cuba, and the United States. Rome's slave population in Italy (not necessarily in all Roman-occupied lands), from about 200 B.C.E. to about 200, is estimated to have made up between 30 and 40 percent of the total population.

Virtually everyone in Roman society in this period owned slaves, from the peasants (who had a few) to the very wealthiest (who owned hundreds or even thousands). The abundance of slaves at all levels of Roman society—from the lowest laborers to the highest executives—meant that the slave experience in ancient Rome was as diverse and complex as Roman society itself. Slaves had opportunities to lead lives ranging from great comfort (some slaves achieved significant wealth and power) to utter despair (many slaves worked in chain gangs, groups of workers chained together at the ankles, on huge farms or in the mines).

Slave sources

War The greatest source of slaves under the Roman Republic was prisoners of war. During the fourth century B.C.E. (400–300 B.C.E.), Rome fought many wars of territorial expansion with its neighbors in central and southern Italy. The number of slaves rose greatly as the Romans perfected their method of warfare for territorial gain and profit: capture a city, divide its lands among Romans, and sell its entire population into slavery or hold them for ransom (a payment in return for their safety). These wars sometimes produced tens of thousands of slaves.

Rome fought many overseas wars in the second half of the Republic (264–27 B.C.E.). These wars of expansion produced hundreds of thousands of slaves for central Italy. In the first of Rome's three wars against Carthage (pronounced CAR-thidj; a city in northwest Africa), one battle in 256 B.C.E. produced 20,000 slaves. The third war against Carthage ended in 146 B.C.E. with the enslavement of 55,000 Carthaginians. In 102 to 101 B.C.E., a Roman general fighting the Germans put 150,000 captives on the slave market. Julius Caesar (pronounced JOO-lee-us CEE-zer; Roman general and statesman, 102–44 B.C.E.) reportedly captured more than 500,000 prisoners in his nine years in Gaul (France).

Even though Rome's first emperor, Augustus Caesar, ended Rome's wars of expansion, warfare continued to be an important source of slaves in the first two centuries of the Roman Empire. When the Jews rebelled in 66, the Romans responded by destroying the city of Jerusalem in 70, taking 97,000 prisoners for the slave market. In 198, a Roman em-

peror enslaved 100,000 prisoners after the destruction of just one city in a border war in the eastern part of the empire.

Slave trade The Roman government technically owned all prisoners of war, but the commander in the field had the authority to dispose of captives as he saw fit. Captives were sometimes sold on the battlefield to slave dealers who trailed the armies or held for ransom if that would be more profitable. Under the Republic, the profits from selling prisoners of war usually went to the public treasury in Rome. Under the Empire, the profits mostly went to increase the emperor's personal wealth.

In addition to selling prisoners of war to slave dealers, Rome also bought significant numbers of slaves from the international slave market. For example, there is evidence to suggest that from around 200 B.C.E. to the end of the Republic (27 B.C.E.), Rome exchanged Italian wine for as many as

A scene from the Third Punic War, in which the Romans destroyed Carthage and took 55,000 Cathaginians as slaves, 146 B.C.E. *Archive Photos, Inc. Reproduced by permission.*

15,000 slaves a year from Gaul. Slaves from distant lands continued to pour into Rome for many centuries, having been sold as captives by foreign rulers or forced into slavery by their extreme poverty.

Piracy Victims of piracy were another significant source of slaves for ancient Rome, more so under the Republic than under the Empire. Piracy on the open seas was a fact of life in ancient times, but by 150 B.C.E., the raiding and looting of coastal cities in the eastern Mediterranean Sea had become an organized and profitable business. Delos, a tiny island in the eastern Mediterranean, was the largest of several markets where pirates could sell their captives from eastern lands such as Asia Minor, Syria, and Egypt to Roman slave dealers for sale in Italy. Before Delos was destroyed in a civil war in 88 B.C.E., its huge docks could receive and send out 10,000 slaves a day.

Pirates became so powerful that in 69 B.C.E. they even raided Rome's own port town of Ostia (pronounced AH-stee-uh). In 66 B.C.E., the Romans waged a short, successful war against the pirates. In forty days the Romans killed 10,000 pirates (and captured many more alive), seized 377 pirate ships, and liberated 120 cities and fortresses under pirate control. Piracy was not completely wiped out, however, and it continued to provide small numbers of slaves to Rome for centuries.

Natural reproduction Another major supply of slaves for Rome, beginning in the last two centuries of the Republic (c. 227–27 B.C.E.), was natural reproduction among the existing slave population. Under Roman law, a child born to a slave mother was considered a slave, even if the father was free. Before Rome's wars of the third century B.C.E., there were more male slaves than female slaves, primarily because male slaves were needed in greater numbers for farming and herding.

By the second century B.C.E., the movement of Rome's rural population (rich and poor) to the cities created the need for more female slaves for domestic work. Accordingly, female slaves became more numerous on the slave market. (The destruction of Carthage in 146 B.C.E. produced 25,000 female slaves, for example.)

Under the Roman Empire, when warfare and piracy declined as steady sources of slaves, natural reproduction became an extremely important source of new slaves. It became legal to sell the newborn infants of slave mothers, and the practice of breeding slaves for profit rose significantly.

Ownership

Private After Rome's wars of the third century B.C.E. flooded Italy and Sicily (pronounced SISS-ill-ee; a large island off the southern tip of Italy) with slaves, private slave ownership increased significantly. Even some of Rome's poorest citizens—its peasants, army privates, and laborers—owned a slave or two. A Roman of only moderate wealth probably owned as many as 400 slaves. The son of the Roman general and statesman Pompey (pronounced POM-pee; 106–48 B.C.E.), sent 800 slaves as a gift to his father's army in Greece. Crassus (pronounced CRA-suss; c. 115–53 B.C.E.), another Roman general and statesman, owned as many as 20,000 slaves, whom he hired out to industries, such as mining.

Imperial The number of slaves owned by private individuals remained very high under the Roman Empire, but few could boast of owning as many as the emperors. A staff of 1,000 or more slaves was common for some of the more powerful Romans, but the emperors were known to have staffs of 20,000 or more slaves to serve their needs. Imperial slaves (slaves owned by the emperor) catered to his every domestic need, from polishing eating utensils to tending to every aspect of his appearance. Imperial slaves also served as clerks, record keepers, and financial agents in the administration of the empire and as craftspeople (such as weavers, carpenters, goldsmiths, and jewelers). Occasionally, imperial slaves rose to important posts in government and business, achieving great wealth and power.

Public Roman cities and towns also owned slaves. Public slaves worked in such jobs as clerks, secretaries, and tax collectors. They also worked with priests in the state-run temples and shrines, helping with ceremonies and upkeep. Other functions of public slaves included building and repairing roads, fighting fires, and maintaining the public baths and water supply.

Work

Agricultural Slavery Rome's wars of conquest made some of its citizens very wealthy, especially those who had the means to invest in land and slaves. By the second century B.C.E. (200–100 B.C.E.), farming and ranching estates were huge. Most had more than 1,000 acres of land and used thousands of slaves to work the land and to herd livestock. Life for a slave on one of these giant estates was often brutal. Slaves were forced to live in barnlike housing (locked in at night), given minimal rations of food, and often worked the fields in chain gangs. In the last two centuries under the Republic, slaves were so numerous on these giant estates—the world's first plantations—that one historian estimates it was the greatest concentration of slave labor in ancient times.

By the time of Augustus, there were many of these plantations in Italy, Sicily, Sardinia (pronounced sar-DIN-ee-uh; the second-largest island in the Mediterranean), and on the coasts of North Africa. Massive numbers of slaves worked in the vineyards and olive groves. Slaves by the thousands, often branded with their owner's mark, tended the enormous herds (hundreds of thousands) of sheep, goats, oxen, and cows that grazed on plantation pasturelands.

Industrial slavery Hundreds of thousands of slaves worked in horrible conditions in mines scattered throughout the Roman

Empire. Great wealth in the form of precious minerals such as copper, gold, and silver continuously flowed to Italy from mines in Spain, Britain, Gaul, and Egypt. The silver mines in Spain alone (in the second century B.C.E.) had more than 40,000 slaves. The Greek historian Diodorus (pronounced DIE-oh-door-us) wrote about the conditions he observed in the mines of Spain and Egypt of the first century B.C.E. Men, women, and children, he wrote, many of them without shoes or clothing, were kept in chains and forced to work under threat of the lash (a whip). Thousands of slaves also worked in the many stone quarries of the Roman Empire in conditions similar to the slave miners.

Slaves were also present in large numbers in other industrial enterprises. By the beginning of the first century, production of goods outside the home became an important part of the Roman economy. Slaves were used to manufacture such items as pottery and bricks, and in the workshops that produced bronze and copper. Many slaves were trained artisans and worked in the gold and silver workshops.

Domestic slavery Slaves were used extensively in Roman households under the Republic and the Empire. For legal purposes, they were divided into two categories: rural (country) slaves or urban (city) slaves. Rural slaves worked either in the household or in the fields of an estate. Their jobs were often defined very precisely. Slave jobs in the rural household had such names as maidservant, water carrier, valet, kitchen maid, sweeper, and furniture supervisor. Slave jobs in the fields of a rural household had such names as plowman, tree pruner, poultry keeper, pig breeder, and goatherd.

Urban slaves worked in households in the city and had such jobs as cook, waiter, secretary, weaver, barber, tailor, gardener, and groom. Some of the wealthier urban households had slaves with such jobs as architect, singer, comic actor, silversmith, doctor, servant in charge of statues, and pedagogue (teacher of children).

Many of Rome's wealthy citizens considered politics, farming, and soldiering as honorable occupations, while occupations involving the business world and marketplace were

beneath their status. Thus, by the time of Augustus, Roman commerce was conducted in large part by slaves who acted as agents for their owners. Slaves also managed their masters' businesses, farms, workshops, and offices. The menial jobs necessary for the master's business were done by slaves as well, sometimes alongside free, hired labor. Slaves were also bakers, porters, fishermen, shipbuilders, shoemakers, and shop clerks (selling meat, fish, bread, or wine).

Slave conditions

Legal status Slaves under the Roman Republic had no legal rights. They were not allowed to marry or own property. A slaveowner could whip, beat, maim, torture, and even kill a slave without being prosecuted. However, if a slave killed his or her master, all the slaves of the household were, by law, condemned to death. If caught, runaway slaves could face crucifixion (being nailed or bound to a cross until death). If not killed, runaway slaves were branded or made to wear a slave collar with their master's name inscribed on it. Roman law did not protect slaves, male or female, from sexual assault by their masters. Disobedient slaves could be left out to starve or sent to die in the arena fighting gladiators (men trained in fighting; see "*Spartacus*" box, on pages 54-55).

Slaves under the Roman Empire slowly acquired some legal rights. Augustus restricted the practice of taking legal testimony from slaves under torture (a common practice in ancient times). The Emperor Claudius (who ruled from 41–54) made it a crime to murder a slave or to turn a sick slave out to die. Other emperors continued the trend: selling female slaves into prostitution was banned (c. 75); mutilating slaves was prohibited (c. 88); and killing slaves except by judicial authority (with the court's permission) was outlawed (c. 127).

It should be noted that the more humane laws of the Empire did not necessarily mean that slaves were treated well. The most important factor in that regard was still the character of the slaveowner, for a master still had tremendous power over the day-to-day life of a slave.

Manumission Manumission of slaves in ancient Rome was a common practice. The manumission of a slave officially made the ex-slave a freedman or freedwoman, a status somewhere between a slave and a freeborn Roman. Under the Republic, Roman law did not grant full citizenship rights to the freed slave for two generations, which meant that the grandchildren of ex-slaves were the ones who finally gained the status and privileges of the freeborn. Under the Empire, freed slaves were granted immediate and full citizenship in Roman society, which for male ex-slaves included the right to vote and participate in politics (females were not allowed to vote in any ancient society).

Spartacus and the War of the Gladiators

When *Spartacus* was made in 1960, it was the most expensive movie ever made. The film is a fact-based tale of a slave rebellion in ancient Rome led by a gladiator named Spartacus. The movie is a very good dramatization of what slavery might have been like in Rome. Director Stanley Kubrick provides a stark view of the cruelty and violence of Rome's slave-based society.

The historical records tell us that Spartacus was born to a slave mother in Thrace, a region of southeast Europe. Spartacus was eventually brought to Rome and sold, along with his wife, to a slave trader who ran a training school for gladiators. As early as 400 B.C.E., gladiators in ancient Rome fought each other—and sometimes wild beasts—to the death in huge arenas. One of the larger arenas, the Colosseum in Rome, could hold 50,000 spectators. Gladiators were chosen for their potential fighting abilities from slaves, war captives, and

criminals. "Death in the arena" was the sentence for crimes such as murder, treason, and robbery.

In the spring of 73 B.C.E., Spartacus led a breakout of about seventy gladiators from their training school. The rebels set up a base camp near Mount Vesuvius (pronounced veh-SOO-vee-us; a volcano in southern Italy), and attacked nearby towns, freeing slaves and killing slaveowners, sometimes by forcing them to fight each other to the death. As word spread, the gladiator-led revolt attracted thousands of runaway slaves to the rebel camp. By the time Rome sent a small military force to Vesuvius to end the rebellion, they faced thousands of liberated and runaway slaves. The Romans were soundly defeated.

For two years the rebels roamed Italy, first to the Alps, a mountain range in the north, and then to the very southern tip of the country. They fought and defeated

A slave could be granted manumission by the owner's declaration, either during the master's lifetime or through the master's will. Often slaves were allowed to purchase their freedom from their master as a reward for good service, the price being the market value for a slave. Even though a slave could not legally own anything, some slaves saved what was called peculium (pronounced peh-COOL-ee-um). Peculium was money, such as wages, tips, or gifts, that slaves earned by doing extra jobs; they were allowed to keep it after giving their master part of the income.

Actor Kirk Douglas (center) plays the Roman gladiator/slave revolt leader Spartacus in the 1960 Universal film. *The Kobal Collection. Reproduced by permission.*

the Romans in battle after battle, gaining wealth from looting cities and country estates along the way. In 72 B.C.E., disagreements among the rebel leadership (Sparta-cus was only one of three leaders) led to a split in the rebel forces and the defeat of one faction of 20,000 slaves by the Romans.

In the winter of 72 to 71 B.C.E., Spartacus and his followers found themselves trapped on the southern Italian peninsula by the Roman army. Having been betrayed by pirates who were supposed to supply a fleet of ships for their escape off the mainland, the rebels were forced into a decisive battle with the Romans. By the spring of 71 B.C.E., Spartacus and most of his 70,000 followers were killed by a massive Roman force—ten legions (each one made up of 3,000 to 6,000 foot soldiers with a cavalry) under the command of Marcus Crassus, and the armies of Pompey and Lucullus (recalled from foreign wars to fight Spartacus). The 6,000 surviving rebel slaves were crucified alongside the road that led from Capua (where the revolt began) to Rome.

Manumission became so commonplace that Augustus made laws restricting the number of slaves that could be set free at one time by one master (no more than 100). At the same time, Augustus granted more rights to freedmen and freedwomen, such as the right to marry or to hold high office, a trend that emperors would continue for centuries.

However, even though many slaves were freed and integrated into Roman society, not all slaves had the same opportunity for manumission, nor were most slaves ever set free.

And, for every slave who was freed from bondage, a new slave probably took his or her place, until the third and fourth centuries, when freed slaves were more likely to be replaced by the cheap labor of the poor and plentiful peasant class.

Western Europe in the Middle Ages (500–1500)

Serfdom: A new form of slavery

Slavery in western Europe changed dramatically after the fall of the Roman Empire in 476. As it was practiced in Italy, France, Germany, and England under Roman rule, slavery was a very organized institution, with distinct differences in society between slaves and free people. Slaves basically had no legal rights, and their lives were controlled by someone else. Free people were citizens who could live and work where they chose and who had access to public courts of law and the right to participate in politics.

During the Middle Ages, the distinctions between free people and slaves were a lot less clear. Over time, slaves came to live more like free people, and free people, in a way, lived more like slaves. A new class of people arose called serfs. "Serf" is a French word derived from the Latin word "servus," which means slave. Technically, serfs were not slaves, but they were often treated that way, and what few rights they had were mostly ignored.

French peasants mowing, raking, and stacking hay on the outskirts of Paris; from the fifteenth-century manuscript of the *Tres Riches Heures* of Jean, Duke of Berry. *The Granger Collection, New York. Reproduced by permission.*

A new world order

The Germanic tribes that took over much of the former Roman Empire by the year 600 brought with them their own form of government. For example, a Germanic tribe called the Franks established a vast kingdom in Gaul (France) and western Germany. The king owned all the land but could not possibly govern and defend it without help. In exchange for a pledge of loyalty and military service, the king gave parts of the kingdom to the highest nobles (wealthy families of landholders). These nobles were called dukes and counts. The dukes and counts, in turn, divided their land among lower nobles, or lords. Dukes, counts, and lords constantly fought one another—and sometimes even the king—over land and power. The services of knights (trained soldiers who fought on horseback) became very important to the nobles as these conflicts became more numerous.

Lords ruled at the local level, meaning that the vast majority of people were under their direct control. In times of

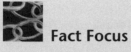

Fact Focus

- The masses of Germanic peoples who settled on the territories of the old Roman Empire had no written version of their tribal languages.

- In a period called the Dark Ages (500–750), there was no central government. Kings were supposed to be in charge, but dukes and counts were often more powerful.

- About 80 percent of the population were peasants. About half of the peasants were serfs. Serfs were like slaves but had a little more personal freedom.

- Slaves made up about 10 percent of the population in the Middle Ages.

- In general, whoever held the land ruled it. In western Europe the nobility and the church held the most land.

- The people of western Europe in the Middle Ages, from kings to slaves, were almost all Christians.

- The largest armies of the Middle Ages were assembled in the Christian "holy wars" known as the Crusades.

- Around 1350, a plague known as the Black Death killed as much as one-third of the population of western Europe— nobles and peasants alike.

- About two-thirds of all children in the Middle Ages died before the age of ten.

peace, peasants lived and worked on small plots of land on the lord's manor (the castle and surrounding land). In times of war they sought the protection of the lord's army and castle. How these peasants were treated depended on the customs and laws of the manor, and on their status as free, serf, or slave.

Free and unfree peasants

Free peasants received a plot of land from the lord in exchange for "rent" (part of their harvest, or work on the lord's fields, bridges, or castle). Free peasants could move off the manor, control their possessions, and marry. If a free peasant had a dispute with his lord or another person, he could take his case to the court of the manor and have it judged by the lord and his vassals (other, lower nobles who had pledged loyalty and services to the lord).

Unfree peasants, or serfs, received a plot of land from the lord in exchange for part of their harvest and work on the lord's fields as well. Serfs did not serve in the lord's army. By law they were not allowed to leave the land where they worked. If serfs ran away and were caught, they were punished severely, by whipping and branding. If the land changed hands, the serfs stayed, "bound" to the soil. A lord controlled a serf's private property, and his permission (usually gained by paying a fee) was needed for marriage. A serf could not sue his lord directly but could bring other disputes to the manor's court of justice. Serfdom was hereditary: the children of serfs became serfs at birth.

Hutted slaves and peasants

Beneath this huge class of peasants were a small number of slaves—probably around 10 percent of the population. Some slaves worked in the lord's household, doing jobs like cooking and cleaning. Some slave families actually lived in their own huts and farmed a plot of land owned by the lord. The lord took most of their harvest, leaving the slaves a small portion for their own consumption. Whatever their jobs, slaves had to work where and when their lord desired. Slaves were considered the lord's property and could be sold, given away, or inherited independent of the land the slaves worked on. By law, slaves had no rights. The lord was a slave's judge, jury, and executioner. Slaves could marry, but only with their master's permission.

Slaves, serfs, and free peasants all had a hard life. Together, they produced the entire food supply for the nobles, the priests, and themselves. Their work was rough and their tools were crude. They lived in small, one-room, wooden huts with dirt floors and thatched roofs. Windows were openings in the walls stuffed with straw in the winter. There was enough room in the hut for a fire pit and a straw bed, where the whole family slept together for warmth. Their food was poor; it was illegal for them to hunt or fish on the lord's manor (and breaking the law could cost them a hand), so there was little or no meat. Life was particularly hard for the young. About two-thirds of all children died before the age of ten.

Europe's religious unity

In a period of the Middle Ages known as the "Dark Ages" (500–750), western Europe was a patchwork of competing kingdoms, duchies (pronounced DUTCH-ees, the territories of dukes), and counties (the territories of counts). The masses of Germanic peoples who settled on old Roman territories had no written version of their tribal languages. There was no central government and very little trade and commerce between the kingdoms. Kings ruled the land only in theory; in practice, the dukes and counts had bigger armies and controlled more land. But the kings, dukes, and counts were too busy fighting one another and fending off foreign raids and invasions to conquer and unify Europe politically.

The people of Europe in the Dark Ages, however, were united in their common belief in Christianity. From kings to slaves, people converted to Christianity in large numbers and looked to the church for guidance on how to live a Christian life. Some of the actions of the church contributed to the perpetuation of slavery and serfdom, and some helped lead to slavery and serfdom's eventual decline.

The church as feudal landlord

In the Middle Ages, the general rule was whoever held the land ruled it. The largest landholders in Europe were the nobility and the church (which received most of its land from the nobility). The leaders of the church, like the feudal nobles, became landlords. The church's authority, also like that of the feudal nobility, was set up as a chain of command, with the pope (the bishop of Rome and head of the Roman Catholic church) at the top. Bishops and abbots (rulers of monasteries—churches and residences for monks and nuns) served the pope. Monks and priests served the bishops and abbots.

Not only did the church not oppose slavery in the Middle Ages, but the church itself also owned many slaves. The church often received slaves as gifts from the French king and nobles. Pope Gregory I (590–604) used hundreds of slaves on his estates. Like the nobles, the church used a combination of free, serf, and slave labor on its manors. Early in the eighth century, one monastery in France had 8,000 slaves; another had 20,000. Under King Charlemagne (pronounced SHAR-leh-mane; ruled 768–814), each priest was allowed two slaves, one male and one female.

Christianity's contradictions

Some of the church's teachings seemed to support the practice of slavery as part of the natural order. In the Bible's New Testament, Jesus says in one of his parables (stories with a moral): "Blessed is the slave whom his master, returning, finds performing his charge." In other words, slaves should obey their masters at all times. The Bible does not portray Jesus as an abolitionist (someone who favors banning slavery), and neither were the leaders of the church. In 630, for example, the church declared that any slaves fleeing their master were to be denied communion (a holy ritual) until they were returned to their owner. Christians in the Middle Ages considered slavery God's will and part of a divine plan to serve his ends.

At the same time, the church was influential in making day-to-day life easier for slaves by preaching about the brotherhood of man and how people should treat others as they would like to be treated themselves. In other words, slaves should be treated as humans, not animals. Some of the church's rules also contributed to the decline of slavery. The most important church law about slavery was that Christians should not enslave other Christians, which severely limited the source of slaves, since almost everyone in western Europe was a Christian. The church also opposed the enslavement of Christians by non-Christians but did not object to Christians enslaving non-Christians. The church encouraged slaveowners to free their slaves, promising they would be rewarded in the afterlife.

War and slavery

Throughout ancient times, war captives were the main source of slaves. The ancient Greeks and Romans had huge empires, waged many battles, and enslaved millions of prisoners of war. In general, wars in the Middle Ages were on a much smaller scale, with much of the fighting taking place between lower nobles over small parcels of land. And although some captives were turned into slaves, their numbers were very low compared with those in ancient Greece and Rome.

The average manor in Europe did not find slave labor profitable because of the large population of serfs (see "Free and unfree peasants," earlier in this chapter). When land was conquered in battle, the victor also won the right to rule over the people who lived there. Slaves and serfs were considered too valuable to kill, and it made no sense to move them off lands where their work produced a profit. The powerful simply occupied the land and ruled over the weak, meaning that slaves remained enslaved and serfs remained enserfed. Often, free peasants lost their land to the new lord and were reduced to serf status.

Charlemagne and the Holy Roman Empire

Not all battles in the Middle Ages were local or small, but even larger wars sometimes failed to produce a

Charlemagne (742-814), king of the Franks and founder of the Holy Roman Empire. *Courtesy of the Library of Congress.*

new supply of slaves and serfs. When King Charlemagne united the different Germanic tribes of Europe into the Holy Roman Empire, he conquered and Christianized a huge area that included France, Italy, most of Germany, Austria, Czechoslovakia, and Hungary, yet the conquests produced few slaves.

King Charlemagne, a Frank, viewed his conquest of the other Germanic tribes—the Saxons, Burgundians, Bavarians, and Lombards—as his Christian duty. Some of these conquered tribes worshiped non-Christian gods. Charlemagne gave them a choice: convert to Christianity or die. On one Christmas Eve, he had 4,500 rebel Saxons beheaded for refusing to be baptized.

On Christmas Day in the year 800, the pope of the Roman Catholic church declared Charlemagne the first emperor of the Holy Roman Empire. Charlemagne shared his power with the church, dividing up control of the empire between the nobility and the clergy. Charlemagne also gave nearly two-thirds of the lands he conquered to the church. The church set up an extensive network of abbeys (huge monasteries), and in 787 Charlemagne ordered that they be turned into schools for his subjects—not just for the nobles, but for serfs and free peasants as well.

Rise of the knights

In 869, Charlemagne's empire was broken into two parts—the Frankish kingdom (modern-day France and Belgium) and the German Empire (Germany, part of Italy, and Austria). Louis the German, Charlemagne's grandson and the German emperor, enjoyed the support of the Roman Catholic church and the stability it brought to his rule.

But in the Frankish kingdom, with Charles the Bald (another of Charlemagne's grandsons) as king, a period of feudal conflict that would last more than 300 years was just beginning. Feuds between nobles over land and invasions and raids by Vikings from the north, Hungarian warriors from the east, and Muslims (members of a religion called Islam) from the south made for very violent times and led to significant changes in medieval society.

By the year 900, knights became very important. Every lord in France was fighting over land, and they all needed knights for their armies. Lords began to recruit knights by awarding them land to rule over in exchange for their military skills. Knights began to appear in the courts of justice of the great lords—the dukes, counts, and viscounts—and were recognized as members of the ruling class. As lords of small estates (villages of less than 100 people), knights also held their own courts, usually to settle disputes among peasants.

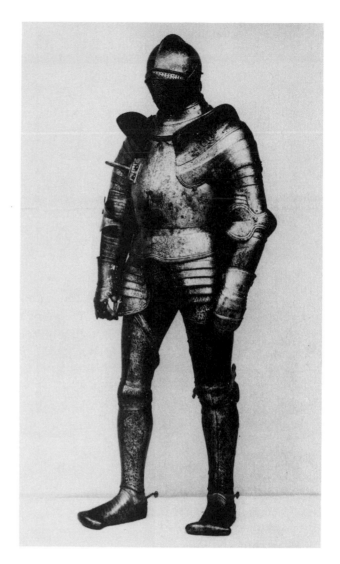

Armor worn by a French or Italian knight in 1527. A great deal of battling and feuding took place during the Middle Ages. Although knights did the actual fighting, peasants and serfs were victimized by the wars. *AP/Wide World Photos. Reproduced by permission.*

Land of burning huts

Historians estimate that by the year 1000, as many as 80 percent of Europe's peasants were living on feudal estates. One-half of those peasants were free, able to live and work where they chose; the other half were serfs, legally bound to the land they worked. There is no telling how many slaves there were, but their numbers were very low, as descendants of slaves, through the years, had risen to the level of serfs.

Lords came and went, but the peasants—free or unfree—stayed. Tied to the land for generations, they were at the mercy of more powerful forces around them. Though

peasants did little, if any, of the actual fighting, they were greatly affected by the constant warfare. As one eleventh-century knight quoted in Timothy Levi Biel's book *The Age of Feudalism* said: "When two nobles quarrel, the poor man's thatch [hut] goes up in flames."

Anglo-Saxon England

Germanic tribes known as the Angles and Saxons invaded England in 449. After defeating what was left of the Roman occupiers and enslaving or enserfing much of the native Celtic population, the Anglo-Saxons set up a system similar to the early Frankish kingdoms. The king ruled over landowning nobles known as earls and thanes. Like the dukes and counts of Germany and France, earls and thanes owed military service and counsel (service in the courts of justice) to the king. The thanes ruled over the churls (free peasants), the serfs, and the slaves.

Slaves in the Anglo-Saxon era (449–1066) tilled the land alongside the serfs and the free peasants. Slaves also performed specific jobs such as herdsmen, dairymaids, blacksmiths, weavers, cooks, carpenters, and tailors. Slaves could be flogged for minor offenses and mutilated or executed for major crimes. Slaves guilty of thieving faced death: males by stoning and females by burning. Some of the slaves were descendants of the native Celts. Some were captives from petty wars between England's nobles. Most, however, were free people who were being punished for certain crimes or for failing to pay fines or debts.

English feudalism

Anglo-Saxon kings ruled until 1066, when an army from France, led by Duke William of Normandy, invaded England. Normandy, an area of northwest France, was the land of the Normans (or Norsemen), who were descendants of people from the north we call Vikings. The Vikings came from Scandinavia—what is now Norway, Sweden, and Denmark. The Vikings had been raiding the coasts of England and northern France for more than a century when in 911, fearing that the Vikings might overtake his whole kingdom, the French king made Rollo, a great Viking chieftain, the first Duke of Normandy. In time, the dukes of Normandy became more powerful than the kings of France.

Duke William of Normandy, later known as William I, the Conqueror (c. 1027–1087), and his soldiers. *Courtesy of the Library of Congress.*

On Christmas Day in 1066, after Duke William's army had defeated the Anglo-Saxons in battle, William I was crowned king of England. One of the first things the new king did was take stock of his conquered territory. When the census, known as the Domesday Book, was finished in 1085, it showed that 9 percent of the population in England were slaves, or "personal serfs."

Personal serfs were bound to their masters by blood: their parents were slaves and their children were slaves. As on the European continent, most of the people in England were peasants, and about one-half of the peasants were "tenant serfs," bound to their land (see "Free and unfree peasants," earlier in this chapter). By 1200, there were very few slaves left on England's farms. Most of the field work was done by serfs and free peasants, and what few slaves remained worked mostly in the lords' households.

The Peasants' Crusade. As Crusade fever hits Europe in the twelfth century, peasants by the thousands follow the troops to war in Jerusalem. *Picture Collection, The Branch Libraries, The New York Public Library.*

The Crusades

Three major religions influenced medieval Europe: Christianity, Judaism, and Islam. Christians considered Jews and Muslims to be "infidels" (a disrespectful word for non-Christians). Pope Urban II began the First Crusade in 1096 when he called for a "holy war" by Christians to liberate the city of Jerusalem from Muslim control. Jerusalem, a city in Palestine on the eastern shores of the Mediterranean Sea, was considered a "holy city" by all three religions. The nobles of England, France, Germany, and Italy rallied around the pope's call, and the largest army of feudal times was assembled.

In the Third Crusade (1189-92), Richard I, the Lionheart, watches the execution of Muslims after taking the city of Aker in the Holy Land, 1191. *Archive Photos, Inc. Reproduced by permission.*

The pope traveled France for nine months recruiting his army for the holy war. He promised, in the name of the church, to protect the lands of any nobles who joined the Crusade. The pope also permitted serfs to be soldiers in the army, attracting thousands of peasants who had been bound to their land for generations. The pope forgave taxes and debts and pardoned (set free) criminals. All people had to do was sign up to march on Jerusalem.

A force of 30,000 Crusaders, mostly peasants who were untrained in war, left France in 1096. In 1099, 12,000 reached Jerusalem (many Crusaders died during the long march). Still, the Crusaders easily captured the city and proceeded to massacre thousands of local Muslims—men, women, and children. The pope had promised the Crusaders something else: to kill infidels, or to be killed fighting infidels, was a sure ticket to heaven. But by 1150, all the lands conquered by the First Crusade were taken back by Muslim armies.

By 1204, there had been four major Crusades. All of them failed to secure Jerusalem under Christian control for any great length of time. The great lords of Europe, however, founded and abandoned several feudal kingdoms in Palestine and Syria. The nobles returned to Europe with new tastes for eastern products such as silks, sugar, and spices, for which they traded English wool, German steel, and Italian fabrics.

The decline of serfdom

Rapid changes followed the Crusades. Some lords—including many knights—returned to Europe to find that wealthier and more powerful nobles had taken over their lands. Some lords found their villages without serfs because many of them had joined the Crusades or had moved to cities to take jobs making goods for trade with the east.

One historian estimates that in 1200, 90 percent of the population in France and southern Germany were rural peasants, and more than half of those were serfs. By 1300, only 70 percent of the people were living in rural villages, and most of them were free.

By 1300, Europe was emerging from the feudal era. The laws and customs of the villages were being replaced by the common law of an entire kingdom. For example, the Magna Carta, signed by King John of England in 1215, guaranteed everyone in the English kingdom "due process of law." Kings still had dukes and counts, but they were no longer relied on to raise an army or to help with governing the land. Instead, kings hired soldiers and public servants and paid them with money.

The end of serfdom

Another factor in the decline and eventual end of serfdom in western Europe was the Black Death. The plague started in central Asia, and in 1348 it found its way to Italy and the rest of western Europe in a shipment of rat-infested grain. A disease for which there was no medicine or cure, the Black Death killed from one-quarter to one-third of the population—nobles and peasants alike. Sometimes whole villages were wiped out. Many rich estates fell into ruin. The economy of Europe took a downturn. With an extreme shortage of labor and fewer goods being produced, prices on almost everything rose.

Peasant workers were now in great demand in both rural areas and cities. Landlords even welcomed runaway serfs, illegally granted them freedom, and leased them land made vacant by death. Likewise, peasants were welcomed in depopulated towns, where their status—free or serf—was not challenged.

The Peasant Wedding, **painting by Flemish painter Pieter Bruegel (c. 1525–1569).** *Photograph by Erich Lessing. Reproduced by permission of Erich Lessing/Art Resource, NY.*

As more and more serfs tasted freedom and realized how important their labor was to society, they became less and less likely to accept the traditional limits and duties forced upon them by the ruling nobles. In England in 1380, when landlords tried to impose harsh and unfair taxes, the peasants responded with armed rebellion. That revolt and another one in 1450 failed. But the idea that all people should be free had taken seed, and in 1574, the queen of England abolished serfdom.

The cry for freedom was heard throughout Europe, and over time, serfdom slowly disappeared. The number of serfs in Italy declined steadily beginning in the twelfth century, and by the fifteenth century serfdom had virtually vanished. In Germany, serfdom ended in the eighteenth century. And in France, serfdom officially ended with the revolution in 1789.

Africa and the Atlantic Slave Trade

The impact of slavery

Both slavery and the slave trade existed in Africa long before the Portuguese and Spanish began their explorations by sea of Africa's Atlantic coast in the mid-1400s. Most historians agree that the Africans practiced a milder form of slavery than the ancient Romans or Greeks, and nowhere near as harsh as what awaited Africans in the European colonies of the Americas (South and North America).

For centuries before African slaves were shipped across the Atlantic Ocean, the peoples of West Africa had exported slaves, gold, and other goods by way of overland trade routes (through the Sahara Desert) to European and Near East (a region of southwest Asia that includes the Arab nations) countries. The peoples of East Africa also traded slaves and other goods to the Arabs and to merchants from other eastern destinations, such as India.

It was the common people of West Africa who suffered the most from the effects of the Atlantic slave trade. Their rulers, on the other hand, grew rich. They exchanged slaves mostly for such luxuries as guns, liquor, fine fabrics,

Muslim traders transporting
captives to coastal ports.
*Archive Photos, Inc. Reproduced
by permission.*

and other items for their own benefit, not for the improvement of their subjects' lives. The European slave traders, especially the British, also grew incredibly rich from the transport and sale of millions of Africans to New World colonies.

Africa

Slavery in the Middle Ages

In the absence of any records, there is no way of knowing for sure how many slaves there were in West Africa in the Middle Ages (500–1500), but there were probably relatively few. Prisoners of war were the main source of slaves, and wars were infrequent and mostly local and small. There were exceptions, of course, as African empires (a number of united kingdoms) waged war on each other from time to time. In addition to losing prisoners taken in battle, conquered tribes were often forced to pay a tribute (a periodic tax for losing) in the form of slaves or goods.

People guilty of crimes, and people rejected from their tribes for various reasons, were another source of slaves. Slaves were usually considered the property of the chief of the tribe or the head of the family. Some slaves were kept for domestic and farming work, some were sold and exported to

Fact Focus

- Prisoners of war were the most common source of slaves in West Africa in the Middle Ages.

- By 1500, the Portuguese were importing 3,000 slaves a year to Europe from West Africa.

- Africans who lived on the coast were rarely enslaved.

- Guns played a major role in increasing the number of slaves obtained through raids and warfare between African tribes.

- The first slaves to cross the Atlantic Ocean on European ships were Indians, not Africans.

- In 1492, there were 300,000 Indians in the Spanish colony on the Caribbean island Christopher Columbus named Hispaniola. By 1548, a mere 500 were alive.

- By 1600, about 367,000 African slaves had crossed the Atlantic to the Americas.

- The voyage from West Africa to the West Indies, known as the Middle Passage, took about two months. Many slaves died at sea from the brutal conditions on ships.

- From 1451 to 1870, at least 11 million African slaves were imported to the Americas.

other countries, and some were sacrificed (killed in a religious ceremony) by kings in the worship of their royal ancestors.

Not all slavery was on a small scale. In one kingdom in Benin (pronounced beh-NIN), the ruler forced slaves to work on large plantations in conditions similar to New World slavery. In southeastern Nigeria the Ibo (pronounced EE-bo) tribe used an organized slave-labor force for growing crops. Their neighbors to the west, the Ashanti (pronounced ah-SHON-tee), also used slaves on their farms and demanded a tribute of 2,000 slaves a year from one defeated tribe.

Slaves in society

Slaves, as usual, did the hardest work in African society. But Africans enslaved by other Africans during the Middle Ages did not lose all of their rights and were not denied a place in society. Traditions allowed slaves to marry and have families, with the opportunity for those families to become

Captives, yoked and chained, in a forced march from the interior to the coastal markets. *The Granger Collection, New York. Reproduced by permission.*

part of their master's extended household. Though they could never be as close as kin (people related by blood), slaves were, in a sense, "adopted" into families and sometimes rose to be leaders—chiefs, kings, and even emperors.

R.S. Rattray, a historian who studied the Ashanti noted that among these forest-dwelling people, "a slave might marry; own property; himself own a slave; swear an oath; be a competent witness; and ultimately become heir to his master." The historian as quoted in Milton Meltzer's *Slavery: A World History* also found that "an Ashanti slave, in nine cases out of ten, possibly became an adopted member of the family; and in time his descendants so merged and intermarried with the owner's former kinsmen that only a few would know their origin."

Slave trading: It takes two

In the 1500s, the growth of plantations in the New World colonies of Spain, France, England, and Denmark fueled the demand for African slaves. The profits that could be earned by supplying slaves to satisfy that demand—by both Europeans and Africans—transformed the slave trade into a very big business. Wars between African tribes in-

The Fort of Judah, or Ouidah, founded by the French to protect the slave trade and hold captives before transporting them overseas. The fort was destroyed in 1726 by the army of the king of Dahomey (now Benin). *The Granger Collection, New York. Reproduced by permission.*

creased. They were no longer minor local skirmishes over land or honor but major battles for slave-taking and profit.

Most of the slaves taken to the Americas came from West Africa. Europeans built forts and trading posts along a 3,000-mile stretch of Africa's Atlantic coast, from Senegal in the north to Angola in the south. About 70 percent of the slaves taken from West Africa came from north of the Congo River and south of the Sahara Desert. The coastal countries now known as Benin, Ghana, and Nigeria supplied a large share of the captives.

At first, the trade was a cooperative effort between the European merchants and the coastal African tribes. The Europeans built their trading posts only with permission from the African rulers who controlled the coastal lands. The Europeans also had to pay rent to the Africans on their trading posts and forts.

Draining Africa's heartland

Africans who lived on the coast were rarely enslaved. Instead, coastal tribes, through warfare, raids, and trade, obtained slaves from other tribes located farther inland. In turn, those tribes took slaves from tribes even farther from the coast. Most raids and wars for the purpose of capturing slaves took place within 500 miles of the Atlantic coast.

For example, on Africa's Gold Coast (a region of West Africa on the north shore of the Gulf of Guinea), the Europeans rented their trading posts from the local Fanti (pronounced FAN-tee) or Akan tribes. The Europeans traded for slaves from the Fanti, who, through warfare or trade, took slaves from the Ashanti to the north. The Ashanti in turn obtained slaves by warfare or trade with their up-country neighbors.

More guns, more slaves

Most of the common people of Africa, the small family farmers, did not own slaves and were too busy bartering with their neighbors for the necessities of daily life to care much about the slave-trading business. It was the rich people of Africa, the royal courts of nobles and lords who lived in the cities, who wanted the European goods that the slave trade provided. The list of items brought into Africa was long and included such things as wine, brandy, bars of iron, glass beads, tobacco, hats, linen, carpets, silks, satins, kettles, pans, dishes, plates, knives, and fishing hooks.

There were two other items that Africans traded slaves for that took the slave trade to a higher level: guns and ammunition (gunpowder). Africans sold slaves for guns and used those guns to take even more slaves. Guns played a major role in increasing the number of slaves obtained through raids and warfare between tribes. Africans without guns were forced to trade slaves for weapons to defend themselves.

In addition to more frequent raids and wars, Africans were increasingly enslaved by other traditional means. African chiefs and kings expanded the list of crimes punishable by enslavement to include thievery, adultery by women, and even "plotting against the king."

By the end of the 1600s, Africans were commonly kidnaped by roving gangs of both black and white slavers. Whole villages sometimes fell victim to these kidnappers, but it was mostly women and children who were stolen in this fashion. Faced with occasional famine, and frequent warfare

en aan d'andre zyde.

This Dutch line engraving of 1704 depicts Elmina, a Portuguese slave-trading fortress on the African Gold Coast, taken by the Dutch in 1637. *The Granger Collection, New York. Reproduced by permission.*

and violence, poor African families were sometimes forced to sell themselves or their children into slavery.

The Atlantic slave trade

Building the network

The development of the network for shipping slaves from Africa to the New World began in 1441 with the arrival of fourteen African slaves in Lisbon, Portugal. The slaves were brought as a gift to Prince Henry the Navigator (1394–1460), the son of the king of Portugal. The Africans had been captured in a raid on one of the many voyages Portuguese explorers had made along Africa's Atlantic coast.

Being a Christian, Prince Henry sought the pope's approval for more raids. The pope not only approved more slave raids, but in 1455 he also gave Portugal blanket permission to enslave all "heathen" (a disrespectful word for non-Christian) people.

Without a great need for additional labor on the continent, European traders were at first more interested in African gold, ivory, leather, spices, and perfumes than in slaves. Initially, Arab traders of the south Sahara Desert acted as middlemen. The Arabs traded horses, silks, and silver for slaves, gold, and other goods from black African rulers. The Arabs then traded the slaves to the Portuguese for more gold, silks, and silver.

By the late 1400s, the Portuguese were importing about 1,000 West African slaves a year from the port of Arguin (an island off the West African coast). By 1500, the Portuguese were taking 3,000 slaves a year from Africa's Atlantic coast, from as far south as Angola. By then, the Portuguese were trading directly with African coastal tribes. The slaves, having been captured in raids or warfare or by trade between tribes, were marched to the coast from inland Africa, bound together and carrying such items as ivory, gold, iron, and spices. The slaves and goods were sold to the tribe in charge of the coastal lands, who in turn traded them to the Portuguese.

The Portuguese were great explorers at sea. In the fifteenth and sixteenth centuries, they financed many of their naval expeditions from the profits they gained by using large amounts of African slave labor on their island sugar plantations off the coasts of Europe and Africa. Some African slaves were imported to the European mainland and were mostly used for domestic work in the households of the rich. By 1552, there were 10,000 African slaves in Lisbon, a city of 100,000 people.

A failed experiment

The first slaves to cross the Atlantic Ocean on European ships were "Indians," not Africans. On October 12, 1492, Christopher Columbus (an Italian explorer, 1451–1506) reached Watling Island in the West Indies (a group of islands on the edge of the Caribbean Sea between North and South Ameri-

ca). Believing he had sailed far enough west from Spain to have reached the eastern shores of India (which is what he set out to do), Columbus declared the people he found to be "los Indios," or the Indians. The three ships of his first voyage, the *Niña*, *Pinta,* and *Santa Maria,* also visited Hispaniola (pronounced hiss-pan-YO-la; an island in the West Indies) and Cuba.

In 1493, Columbus sailed on a second voyage to the New World with a fleet of seventeen ships. He explored Puerto Rico and parts of the Leeward Islands and established a Spanish colony on Hispaniola. In 1494, Columbus sent a dispatch to his Spanish sponsors, King Ferdinand and Queen Isabella, proposing to send Indian slaves back to Spain. Despite their lack of enthusiasm for the idea, Columbus captured 1,500 islanders, picked what he considered to be the "best" 500, and sent them to Spain. When the ship arrived in 1495 there were only 300 Indians left alive. The surviving slaves were sold but most of them died within a short period of time. France and England also tried unsuccessfully to profitably import Indian slaves to Europe from the West Indies.

Christopher Columbus with Indians in Hispaniola during an eclipse of the moon. Columbus sent 500 Indians to Spain as slaves in 1494. *Archive Photos, Inc. Reproduced by permission.*

Genocide in the West Indies

Ferdinand and Isabella made Columbus an admiral and the governor general of all new lands in the Spanish colonies. Columbus oversaw the distribution of land and villages to Spanish soldiers and colonists and granted them rule over the inhabitants. Columbus and the colonists forced the conquered Indians to pay them a tribute in the form of gold dust, which could be mined from the island's riverbeds. The work needed to produce the large sums demanded by the colonists was brutal. Many Indians revolted or fled. Some took poison. Diseases brought to the island by the Europeans also killed many of the Indians. Most, however, probably died from working under such horrible conditions.

The Spanish conquest of Hispaniola was disastrous for the native population. When the Spaniards invaded the island and captured cities and villages, they slaughtered all in their path—men, women, and children. They then enslaved the survivors, forcing the men into fourteen-hour workdays in the mines and making the women and children household slaves or putting them to work on the farms. Historians estimate that in 1492, when Columbus arrived, there were 300,000 Indians on Hispaniola. By 1494, one-third of them had died. In 1508, only 60,000 Indians were left, and in 1548, a mere 500 remained.

Africans replace Indians

With most of the native population of the West Indies wiped out, the colonists needed a new source of slaves for their plantations, mines, and households. They turned to West Africa. In 1518 the first cargo of slaves from the Guinea coast of West Africa arrived in the West Indies.

The full-scale use of African slaves instead of Indian slaves was due in part to the efforts of a Dominican missionary named Bartolomé de Las Casas. In 1510, Las Casas became the first priest to be ordained in the New World. Like other Spaniards, he owned Indian slaves. Las Casas traveled throughout the islands and witnessed the destruction of the Indians at the hands of the Spanish colonists. He gave up his own slaves and appealed to the Spanish king to spare the remaining Indians by bringing African slaves to the colonies.

In 1517, the king of Spain formally granted permission for colonists to import twelve African slaves each. By 1540, the West Indies were receiving 10,000 African slaves a year, and still more were going to Mexico and South America. By 1600, about 367,000 African slaves had crossed the Atlantic to the Americas. Europe's demand for sugar skyrocketed in the next century, leading the Dutch, French, and British to establish colonies and sugar plantations in the West Indies. By 1700, another 2.75 million African slaves had been imported to the Americas.

The network for slave trading in the Atlantic was now complete. Cheap manufactured goods from Europe were shipped to Africa and traded for slaves. Slaves were shipped across the Atlantic to the colonies where they were traded for sugar, tobacco, cotton, and minerals. Finally, the produce of the colonies was shipped back across the Atlantic to the markets of Europe. Slave trading in this manner became very prof-

African slaves working on a sugar plantation in the Spanish West Indies. *Copper engraving, 1596, by Theodore de Bry. The Granger Collection, New York. Reproduced by permission.*

itable, with each voyage delivering and picking up goods—and thereby generating profits—in three different ports.

Sharing the New World

Shortly after Columbus claimed the islands of the West Indies for Spain, the Portuguese began competing with Spain for control of the slave-shipping trade to the colonies. Since both countries were Christian, their rulers turned to the pope to resolve the dispute. In 1493, the pope granted Spain sole shipping rights to the New World, and Portugal was forced to confine its naval commerce to Africa.

In the 1500s, Spain dominated the Atlantic slave trade. The Spanish were the main supplier of slaves to all the European colonies at the time. In the course of the century they brought hundreds of thousands of slaves to the West Indies, Brazil, Colombia, Argentina, Peru, Mexico, and Panama. In the 1600s, the Dutch, Danes, French, and English started to compete with the Spanish, all wanting a part of the riches of the New World and the profits from supplying it with slaves.

Slave factories

In 1481, the Portuguese built the first European fort on the Gold Coast of West Africa at Elmina (pronounced el-MEEN-a; "the mine"). By the 1700s there were more than forty European forts and other outposts on the coasts and nearby islands of West Africa.

The forts had little military value. They were built only with the permission of whichever African ruler was in charge of that part of the coast and could not have withstood a determined military attack. The forts were essentially trading posts—slave factories—with dungeons capable of holding thousands of captured Africans awaiting the next ship to the Americas. Not all slaves were processed through the European trading posts. Some were simply sold from shore, held there by a coastal tribe and paddled out in canoes to the buyers' ships.

British dominance

In the seventeenth and eighteenth centuries most of the great ship owners of Europe made fortunes in the trans-

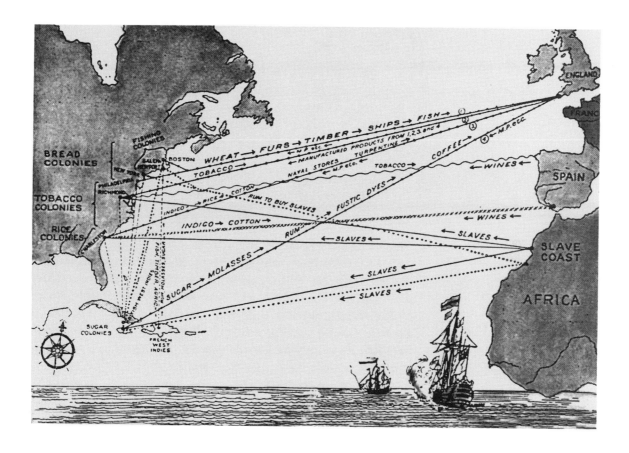

WHEAT → FURS → TIMBER → SHIPS → FISH →

MANUFACTURED PRODUCTS FROM 1,2,3 and 4

TOBACCO

NAVAL STORES TURPENTINE

COFFEE →

M.P. etc

← WINES ←

TOBACCO →

RICE → COTTON

RUM TO BUY SLAVES

FUSTIC DYES →

← WINES ←

INDIGO → COTTON →

RUM

← SLAVES ←

← SLAVES ←

SUGAR → MOLASSES →

← SLAVES ←

← SLAVES ←

BREAD COLONIES

FISHING COLONIES

BOSTON

NEW YORK

PHILADELPHIA

RICHMOND

TOBACCO COLONIES

RICE COLONIES

CHARLESTON

SUGAR COLONIES

FRENCH WEST INDIES

ENGLAND

FRANCE

SPAIN

SLAVE COAST

AFRICA

Atlantic slave business. The monarchy, the church, the government, and the public approved of the slave trade. Almost everyone had a stake in the slave trade—kings, dukes, earls, countesses, lords, knights, bishops, mayors, and even some of the general public. In slave-trading port cities, it generated thousands of jobs. Slave trading was a fact of life, and most of European society was invested in it, in one way or another.

It was the British, however, who ended up dominating the Atlantic slave trade. In the late 1600s, the city of Liverpool became the largest port in the world and the home base of ten companies that controlled two-thirds of the Atlantic slave-trading business. The largest of those companies, the Royal African Company, was chartered by King Charles II in 1672. The Royal African Company became the number one slave trader in the world by securing, under a thirty-year agreement with Spain, the exclusive

Map of the "Triangular Trade" between England, its American colonies, and Africa in the seventeenth and eighteenth centuries. *The Granger Collection, New York. Reproduced by permission.*

rights to ship West African slaves to the Spanish colonies in the Americas.

By 1800, Liverpool-based trading companies were shipping 35,000 African slaves a year across the Atlantic. The 120 British ships sent annually carried about 90 percent of the slaves exported from Africa. The profit margins on each voyage ranged from 30 percent to 100 percent—a fantastic amount of money. Liverpool, and much of England's commercial wealth in this period, was built on the enormous profits from the Atlantic slave trade.

The Middle Passage

The British were able to make such huge profits because they were willing to cut corners on costs, no matter what the human consequences were. The voyage from Africa to the Americas was called the "Middle Passage" because it was the middle stretch of the slave-trading triangle that connected Europe to Africa, Africa to the Americas, and the Americas back to Europe. In pursuit of higher profits, the British overloaded their ships with slaves, packing in as many Africans as possible for the two-month voyage.

Most of the time, the slaves were kept in the ship's hold. They were allowed on deck for only a few minutes a day for fresh air and forced exercise. Otherwise, they were chained and locked belowdecks in extremely small spaces. The space for an adult male slave was five-and-a-half feet long, sixteen inches wide, and two to three feet high—in effect, smaller than a coffin. Sometimes there was only eighteen inches of vertical space between slave decks. The British Parliament (legislative body) tried to limit the number of slaves allowed on ships, but their rulings were mostly ignored.

Merchants of death

The conditions aboard the ships were so bad that many slaves died before they ever reached the other side of the Atlantic. On the voyage, slaves were fed just enough to keep them alive (if they survived the trip, they were fattened up before being put on the market). Spoiled food; stagnant water; diseases such as smallpox and dysentery; and dark, damp, and dirty quarters all took their toll. For example, from

1680 to 1688, the Royal African Company picked up 60,783 slaves from Africa but only delivered 46,396 in the Americas. The Middle Passage, in eight years, claimed the lives of 25 percent of the slaves—14,387 Africans. Over the next century the number of slaves killed during the Middle Passage fell from 25 percent to 12.5 percent.

Slaves did not always cooperate with their masters. There is no telling how many slaves committed suicide by jumping off ships at sea or by refusing to eat. Slave revolts aboard ships were not uncommon either, with at least fifty-five recorded from 1690 to 1845.

African slaves faced the possibility of death at every stage of the forced migration from their homeland to the New World. Some died as fresh captives on the march from the central forests to the coasts of Africa. Still more died while being warehoused on the Atlantic coast waiting for slave ships. Of those slaves who survived the Middle Passage, 4 to 5 percent died in the harbors of the New World, waiting to be

An 1850s engraving of a scene in the hold of the slave ship *Gloria*, in the Middle Passage. *The Granger Collection, New York. Reproduced by permission.*

unloaded and sold. Thirty-three percent of those slaves who made it ashore died before they became "seasoned" (broken in) workers. One historian estimates that no more than half of the slaves who were taken from Africa ever became "effective" workers in the New World.

How many African slaves did the Europeans bring across the Atlantic? For the period from 1441 to 1880, historians calculate that the Europeans made more than 54,000 voyages, transporting more than 11 million Africans to their colonies in the Americas. Roughly 95 percent of all slaves taken from Africa, or about 10.5 million slaves, went to Spanish, French, Dutch, Danish, and Portuguese colonies in Latin America (the West Indies, Mexico, and Central and South Americas). The other 500,000 slaves were taken to mainland North America—the United States.

Colonial Latin America

Slaves come to the Americas

The first African slaves arrived in the Americas (North and South America) in 1518, shortly after the king of Spain granted Spanish colonies in the West Indies permission to import 4,000 Africans. The Spanish brought slaves to Guatemala as early as 1524, and by the end of the century they had shipped at least 60,000 Africans to Mexico. The Portuguese colonies in Brazil began importing African slaves in 1538. The Spanish settlement in Saint Augustine, Florida, used slaves since its founding in 1565.

Twenty-five years after the arrival of the first slave ships, Africans were being shipped to the Americas at a rate of 10,000 a year. By the end of the century, according to one historian, a total of 367,000 African slaves had been brought to North and South America—mostly to Latin America.

In the 1600s, other countries in Europe—England, France, Denmark, and the Netherlands—joined Spain and Portugal in seeking riches in the New World. The Europeans established gigantic farms in their colonies that depended on large-

Latin America

Latin America is made up of the countries of South and Middle America where Romance languages (languages derived from Latin) are spoken. Geographically, it includes almost all of the Americas south of the United States—Mexico, Central America, South America, and many of the islands of the West Indies.

Spanish is the dominant language of Latin America. The Spanish-speaking countries of Latin America are Argentina, Bolivia, Chile, Colombia, Costa Rica, Cuba, the Dominican Republic, Ecuador, El Salvador, Guatemala, Honduras, Mexico, Nicaragua, Panama, Paraguay, Peru, Puerto Rico, Uruguay, and Venezuela. Latin America also includes Portuguese-speaking Brazil, French-speaking Haiti, and the French West Indies.

scale production and huge amounts of cheap labor to make a profit. For the most part, colonists succeeded in growing sugar, tobacco, cotton, coffee, indigo (a plant used for making dyes), and cacao (pronounced ke-KAY-oh; a bean used for making chocolate). An increased appetite for those products in Europe (especially sugar) led to a steep rise in the number of slaves needed. By 1700, an additional 1.8 million slaves had been taken from Africa and brought to the Americas.

With European colonies and their plantations in place throughout Latin America, and with the growing presence of the British in North America by 1675 (see Chapter 7), African slaves poured into the colonies in the next two centuries. One historian estimates that in the 1700s, 6.2 million more slaves arrived from Africa. In the 1800s the number of imported slaves totaled 3.3 million. From 1500 to 1900, an estimated total of 11.67 million Africans were brought across the Atlantic Ocean as slaves for the New World colonies of Europe.

The West Indies

Up for grabs

In the 1600s, Spain lost control of many of its island colonies in the West Indies. Denmark, Holland, France, and England all wanted a piece of the New World and moved into the West Indies with their government-supported slave-trading companies. The Dutch West India Company, the French Company of the Islands, and the Royal African Company (of England) established colonies on behalf of their mother countries and imported African slaves to work on their plantations and in their mines and homes.

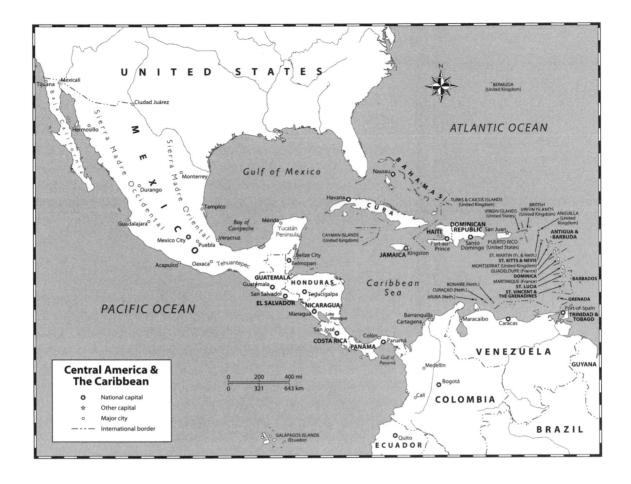

Map of Central America and the Caribbean in modern times.

In 1655, the Spaniards lost Jamaica, the "jewel" of the West Indies, to the British. And a 1695 treaty between Spain and France gave the western part of Hispaniola (pronounced hiss-pan-YO-la) to the French. The Spanish were left with Cuba, Puerto Rico, and the eastern part of Hispaniola, now known as the Dominican Republic.

Sugar islands

At first, slaves worked on tobacco plantations. But when the European markets became flooded with tobacco by 1639, prices dropped, and the planters turned to cotton and indigo. It was sugar, however, that proved to be the biggest moneymaker; European markets just couldn't get enough of it. More sugar plantations meant more slaves. In British Barbados, the first of the islands to grow sugarcane, the

A sugar plantation, probably in what is now Haiti, depicting the main house and the slave quarters on the right. *The Granger Collection, New York. Reproduced by permission.*

African slave population increased from a few hundred in 1640 to 20,000 in 1650, and to more than 80,000 by 1700.

The next two centuries saw an even greater growth of sugar plantations and slave populations in the West Indies. For most of the 1700s Haiti was the world's greatest producer of sugar and its by-products, rum and molasses. By the middle of the century the island had more than 600 sugar plantations and was importing about 10,000 African slaves a year. In 1787 alone, Haiti brought in 40,000 slaves. By the 1790s, no other place in the New World had as many African slaves in such a small area of land.

Cruelty was common in Haiti, and the living conditions in general were very poor. Slaves lived in windowless huts and were given small rations of rice or oatmeal, herring (from New England, and usually spoiled), crackers, and molasses. Slaves and poor people in Haiti did not know how to read or write because neither their French masters nor the Catholic church made an effort to teach them (see "Catholic colonies," later in this chapter). Manumission (a formal release from bondage) was rare in Haiti, and few slaves could afford to buy their freedom.

At the end of the 1700s, Cuba became the number one sugar producer in the West Indies. The effect on the slave population was dramatic. In 1763, there were about 60,000 slaves on the island. By 1790, another 40,000 had arrived. From 1791 to 1825, at least 320,000 more slaves were imported to the island. In 1836 alone, 60,000 slaves were brought to Cuba. Not all the slaves stayed in Cuba. The greatest sugar island in the West Indies also became the largest slave market in the New World, supplying African slaves to colonies far and wide.

Worked to death

One of the reasons planters in the West Indian colonies overpopulated their islands with slaves is that many of the slaves were eventually shipped to other European colonies on the mainland. The islands served as a kind of training ground, a place where slaves were broken in and made accustomed to their new, harsh way of life—or where they were killed by it. The death rate for slaves in the West Indies in their first three to four years was as high as 30 percent in some places. The terrible working conditions—poor diet, diseases, a new climate, and severe and frequent floggings—took their toll.

Slaves worked on the sugar plantations six days a week, from daybreak to sundown, with a two-hour period set aside for light labor during the hottest part of the day. At harvesttime, they worked eighteen-hour days—twelve hours at the sugar mill's boiling house (where the sugarcane was processed into sugar) and another six hours in the fields.

Male and female slaves were required to work the same hours in the fields and mills and were subject to the same punishments if they failed in their duties. Pregnant women (who were forced to work until they gave birth) and women caring for their children in the fields were lashed with cart whips like everyone else if they failed to keep pace with the other slaves.

The law of the whip

On many islands of the West Indies, black African slaves far outnumbered the white colonists. In Jamaica in 1724, for example, there were 32,000 slaves and 14,000 colonists. In St. Christopher, by 1700 the population was more than 20,000, with blacks outnumbering whites twenty

A seventeenth-century line engraving of African slaves working at a sugar mill in the West Indies, probably on a Dutch-owned island. *The Granger Collection, New York. Reproduced by permission.*

to one. The ratio of black slaves to free whites made the colonists uneasy. The fear of mass slave rebellions or breakouts in the West Indies led to the passage of some of the most severe slave codes in history. The passage of the "Act to regulate the Negroes on the British Plantations" in 1667 gave planters the legal power to control their slaves "with strict severity."

Under the code, slaves could not, for any reason, leave the plantation on Sundays (for many slaves their only day off work). During the workweek, leaving the plantation required a pass. Slaves were not allowed to carry weapons, and they could be severely whipped if they struck a white Christian. A second offense was punished by branding the slave on the face with a hot iron. Slave owners, however, faced neither a fine nor imprisonment if they "accidentally" whipped a slave to death.

Spain, Portugal, and France had similar laws that were designed to prevent slaves from revolting or running away. The codes allowed the planters to control the slave population with the cruelest punishments imaginable for the slightest disobedience or crime. Slaves were commonly flogged—lashed with a whip made of braided cowhide—for the slightest offenses (100 lashes for petty thievery, for example). Making slaves fear punishment, the Europeans thought, was the best way to keep them in line.

A nineteenth-century wood engraving depicting the flogging of a slave in the West Indies. *The Granger Collection, New York. Reproduced by permission.*

Rebels and runaways

Slave codes reserved the worst punishments for slaves who revolted. In one French colony in the 1790s, slaves found guilty of planning an uprising had all their bones

Slaves in Haiti revolt against plantation owners. *The Granger Collection, New York. Reproduced by permission.*

broken with clubs and then were fastened to a wheel, faceup to the sun, and left to die. Finally, their heads were cut off and put on public display.

Despite the horrible price of failure, there were runaway slaves and revolts on almost every island. When the British took over Jamaica from the Spaniards in 1655, many slaves ran away to the mountains. Other fugitive slaves joined the rebels, known as Maroons. They stole from

Fact Focus

- For most of the 1700s, Haiti was the world's greatest producer of sugar. It also had more slaves, for its size, than any other colony in the New World.

- The death rate for slaves in the West Indies in their first three to four years was as high as 30 percent in some places.

- On many islands of the West Indies, black African slaves far outnumbered white European colonists.

- In the 1700s, the highest concentrations of slaves in mainland Spanish America were in Panama, Colombia, and Venezuela.

- In Haiti in 1791, what started as a slave uprising led to a revolution, the aboli-tion of slavery in 1794, and the island's independence from France in 1804.

- From 1538 to 1828, the Portuguese im-ported at least 5 million African slaves to Brazil.

- On coffee plantations in Brazil, a slave's workday began at three o'clock in the morning and lasted until at least nine o'clock at night.

- The longest-running slave rebellion in the New World took place in Brazil. It lasted almost seventy years, from 1630 to 1697.

- The Catholic church had great influence in Latin America. It demanded that all African slaves be baptized within a year of their arrival in the Americas.

planters, traded goods with slaves (a crime), and encouraged other slaves to run away.

Even though they faced the possibility of being burned, whipped, or hanged if caught, in 1733 slaves in the Danish is-lands seized a fort of the Danish West India Company. For several days, the slaves murdered all the whites they could find be-fore the local army brought the rebellion under control.

In Haiti, thousands of slaves constantly ran away to the forests and mountains to join groups of other fugitives. By 1700, there had been at least six recorded slave revolts. The seventh rebellion, in 1791, turned into the largest and most significant slave uprising in the West Indies. Led by a slave named Toussaint L'Ouverture (pronounced too-SAHN loo-ver-chur, c. 1743–1803), the revolution resulted in the abolition of slavery on the island in 1794 and ultimately to

Haiti's Slave Revolution

There had been slave uprisings in Haiti before—four in the 1500s and two in the 1600s—but nothing like what happened on August 14, 1791. The rebellion had been brewing for some time. In September 1789, the National Assembly of France had granted independence to the whites of Haiti, giving them control of their own government and taxes. In 1791, the rights granted to the whites were also given to Haiti's mulattos (pronounced muh-LAH-toes; persons of mixed white and black ancestry) and free blacks—but not to the slaves.

Hundreds of years of pent-up hatred for their brutal masters exploded on that August night in 1791. Rebellious slaves torched everything: the cane fields, the sugar mills, and the properties and homes of the planters. Armed with machetes and knives,

they killed white men, women, and children. France responded by sending 6,000 troops to the islands to try to restore order.

The slave uprising was a genuine revolution, led by Toussaint L'Ouverture, the grandson of a West African king. Toussaint's father, a slave, had been captured in a war in Africa and sold to Haitian planters. Toussaint was a baptized Catholic who, encouraged by his master, read history, politics, and military science. Toussaint built a small army of 600 men and with them fought the French and the planters in fierce battles. Under Toussaint's leadership, the slave army became better at fighting and grew larger as every battle hardened the troops and attracted new recruits. In a short time, the rebel army grew to a force of 100,000 soldiers.

Haiti's independence from France in 1804 (see "Haiti's Slave Revolution" box).

Spanish and Portuguese America

Spanish America

Spain colonized many parts of the Americas and imported millions of African slaves into the New World. Slaves arrived in Spanish ports in the West Indies (see above), Mexico, Panama, Colombia, Argentina, and Peru, where they were used locally or taken to Spain's many other colonies in North and South America.

Throughout Spanish America, slaves were mostly agricultural workers on the many plantations that grew sugar, to-

Toussaint L'Ouverture, Haitian general and liberator, engraving, 1805. *The Granger Collection, New York. Reproduced by permission.*

The revolution was won when, on February 4, 1794, the French Assembly abolished all slavery in their colonies. Toussaint was eventually appointed governor-general of the island, marking the first time an African slave had won power in a European colony. In France, however, the dictator Napoleon I Bonaparte (1769–1821) came to power. He sent 20,000 veteran troops to retake Haiti, and in 1802, Toussaint was captured, taken to France, and thrown in a mountain dungeon where he died on April 7, 1803. Toussaint had the last word, however, when on the last day of 1804, Haiti declared its independence from France. The French, having lost 60,000 troops, gave up and went home.

bacco, cacao, maize (corn), cotton, and indigo. Most of the plantations were located in the Atlantic and Pacific coastal regions. Some slaves were sent inland to work on plantations, cattle ranches, or gold mines. Others performed domestic services in cities, where the wealthier planters kept them for their own households or hired them out to others. Some slaves in the cities worked in small household workshops producing goods for market.

From Mexico to South America

By 1700 the Spanish had imported more than 200,000 slaves to Mexico and Guatemala, part of an area known as the Viceroyalty of New Spain. Slaves were not a large part of the colonial population, but they played an important role on the region's indigo plantations and cattle ranches.

Map of South America in modern timess.

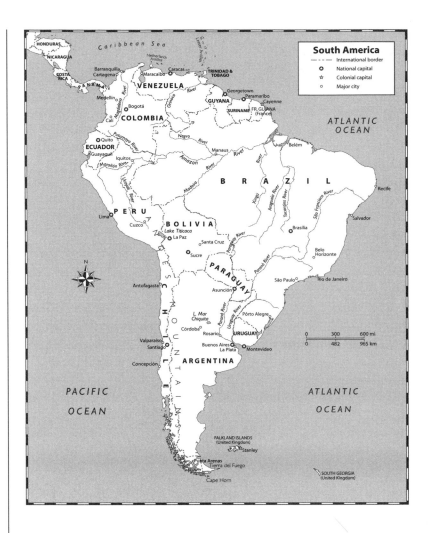

The largest concentration of slaves in continental Spanish America was in the Viceroyalty of New Granada—the modern states of Panama, Colombia, Venezuela, and Ecuador. In the 1700s, the ports of Caracas (pronounced ka-RAH-kus; a city in Venezuela), Cartagena (pronounced kar-ta-GAIN-ah; a city in Colombia), and Panama became some of the largest slave markets in the world.

The Viceroyalty of New Granada was divided into three parts. Census figures from 1810 show that in the combined area of Panama and Colombia, there were 210,000 blacks and mulattos, both slave and free, in a population of 1.4 million. In Venezuela, there were 493,000 blacks and mulattos in a population of 900,000. And in Ecuador, blacks and mulattos numbered 50,000 in a population of 600,000.

In the Viceroyalty of Peru (modern-day Chile and Peru), some slaves came directly from Africa on ships that sailed around Cape Horn (the southern tip of South America) and up the west coast. Other slaves were shipped in from the north, from Panama and Cartagena. Peru's port of Lima (pronounced LEE-ma) became a large slave market for planters and ranchers from all over Venezuela, Ecuador, Chile, and Peru. A 1791 census showed that in Peru, in a population of 1.25 million, there were 40,000 blacks and 135,000 whites. The rest of the people were Indians and mestizos (pronounced meh-STEE-soes; people of mixed Indian and European ancestry). In Chile, there were 30,000 blacks and mulattos in a population of 500,000.

The Spanish also brought many slaves to the Viceroyalty of La Plata (modern-day Uruguay and Argentina). There are no reliable census figures for this region, but Montevideo (pronounced mon-te-ve-DAY-oh; a city in Uruguay) and Buenos Aires (pronounced bway-nus-AR-ees; a city in Argentina) were both major ports of entry for slave traders. By 1805, an estimated 2,500 slaves were imported yearly through these cities.

Portuguese America

The Portuguese brought slaves from the coasts of Africa to their colonies in Brazil as early as 1538. Once sugar plantations were established in 1540, the number of slaves increased steadily. In 1585, there were 14,000 slaves in the colony out of a total of 57,000 people. By 1625 there were 121 sugar plantations, and Brazil was supplying Europe with most of its sugar. In the 1600s, according to one estimate, 44,000 slaves were imported annually. The number rose to 55,000 a year in the 1700s.

The first reliable figures come from a 1798 census. In a population of 3.25 million, there were 1.58 million slaves and 406,000 free blacks. Twenty years later, the African slave population had risen to 1.9 million. There were also 585,000 freed blacks in a total population of 3.8 million.

How many slaves were brought into Brazil altogether? Estimates for the years 1538 to 1828 vary from a high of 18

million slaves to a low of 5 million slaves. Brazil declared its independence from Portugal in 1822, abolished the slave trade in 1850, and emancipated all slaves in 1888.

Brazil's slave machines

In Brazil, five out of six slaves worked on plantations growing sugar, coffee, cotton, and cacao. On coffee plantations a slave's workday began at three o'clock in the morning and lasted until at least nine o'clock at night. The aim of the Portuguese planters was to get as much profit from their slaves' labor in the shortest period of time possible. To that end, the field bosses used their whips constantly to make the slaves work harder and faster. The result was a very high death rate for the overworked and underfed plantation slaves. If twenty-five out of one hundred slaves lived longer than three years, the planters figured they were doing well.

After gold was discovered in Brazil in 1695, plantation owners rented out a large number of their slaves to mine operators in the interior regions of the huge colony. Slave miners were treated, housed, clothed, and fed poorly. Many died of diseases. The mine operators expected their male slaves to survive about twelve years, but one missionary estimated that slave miners were lucky to live for seven.

Slaves mining diamonds in eighteenth century Brazil. *Iconografico SA, Archivo. Reproduced by permission.*

A small number of slaves worked in the cities. Slaves in Rio de Janeiro (pronounced REE-oh-day-juh-NAIR-oh) and Sáo Paulo (pronounced sow-PAW-loh) worked as servants in homes and shops and were sometimes rented out for services and errands. Some slaves hauled crates of produce and 200-pound sacks of coffee beans, finding their work on a freelance basis and paying their master a set fee. If a slave was able to read and write, and some could, they could earn fairly good wages. By scrimping and saving, some of these slaves eventually earned enough money to buy their freedom.

Catholic colonies

Cruel and inhumane treatment of slaves was common in the colonies of Spain and Portugal. The two countries, however, shared something that made a huge difference in the everyday lives of their slaves: the influence of the Roman Catholic church. The Catholic church demanded that all African slaves be baptized within a year of their arrival in the Americas. As Catholics, slaves attended mass and participated in all of the holy rituals and sacraments of the church, including marriage.

The Catholic church, in effect, gave the slaves something in the eyes of their owners that the Anglican church (the Protestant Church of England) denied them: a soul. The result was that Spanish and Portuguese colonists thought of their slaves as more human.

In general, racism was less extreme in the Spanish and Portuguese colonies than in the British colonies. Marriages and unions between the different peoples—the African slaves, the European colonists, and the native Indians—were more numerous and generally more accepted by society. Children of mixed unions, often between slave women and free men, were also treated better by the Spanish and Portuguese than they were by the British colonists in North America (see "Religion and race," Chapter 7).

Easing the burden

In the process of trying to make good Catholics out of the slaves, the church, through its many missionaries (such as the Dominicans, Franciscans, Jesuits, and Carmelites), taught some slaves how to read and write. Slaves with these basic skills could often escape the hard physical labor of the plantations, gold mines, and urban workshops. These slaves worked as teachers (mostly of white children), merchants, dentists, barbers, architects, cooks, musicians, and entertainers.

The church also lightened the burden of slavery in other ways. Masters were not allowed—though some did anyway—to work their slaves on Sundays or on certain Catholic holy days (about thirty days a year). In Brazil, the church strongly encouraged slaveowners to grant their slaves manumission, telling them that freeing slaves was a generous act of a holy person. Slave women's children who were fathered by a member of the household (sometimes the master himself) were usually set free in the master's will. Devoted nurses, favorite personal servants, and, by custom, slave women who had given birth to at least ten children were also set free.

"The Apostle of the Negroes," Saint Peter Claver (1581–1654), a Spanish Jesuit missionary who worked with recent captives from Africa at the slave trade center of Cartagena, Colombia, helping the sick and converting and baptizing the new slaves into the Catholic church. *Corbis-Bettmann. Reproduced by permission.*

Spanish and Portuguese laws and customs, together with the policies of the Catholic church, resulted in large numbers of freed Africans in Spanish and Portuguese colonies. Freed black slaves, including those who managed to raise the money to buy their own liberty, were immediately entitled to the same rights and privileges as free whites. Freed slaves could serve in their country's army, become wealthy, own slaves themselves, and become leaders in government and the church. By the eighteenth century, Brazil had African priests and bishops.

Masters of cruelty

The policies of the Catholic Church did not always have a positive effect on slavery in colonial Latin America, however. The church never formally opposed slavery. In

Brazil's Independent Slave Republic

One of the most successful examples of slave resistance in all of the Americas was the establishment of the Republic of Palmares (pronounced paul-MAR-ays) in northeastern Brazil between 1630 and 1697. Fleeing coastal towns and plantations, slaves settled in communities in the area's heavy inland forests. They lived in clusters of huts, designed as fortresses against attack. They were ruled by a king who lived in Cerca Real do Macaco, the republic's capital city. The king was assisted by ministers of justice, guards, and civil and military servants.

Palmares was a magnet for fugitive slaves and at its peak had a population of about 20,000. The rebel slaves developed their own system of laws in which murder, robbery, and adultery were punishable by death. They traded agricultural products such as bananas, sugarcane, and beans with neighboring villages for utensils, arms, and ammunition.

Palmares was destroyed twice—first by the Dutch in 1644, as they attempted to occupy that part of Brazil, and again in 1676 by the Portuguese army. Each time, the communities quickly rebuilt. Finally, in 1696, Portuguese soldiers laid siege to the capital city. The longest-running slave rebellion in the New World ended in 1697 when soldiers finally penetrated the city's walls and the king and his closest advisers jumped to their death from a cliff rather than face capture.

fact, the same religious orders that taught slaves to read and write (see above) all owned large amounts of land and many slaves. Their slaves were housed and fed better than most, and they were rarely sold, which meant that slave families were not broken apart and life in general was more stable. Still, the burden of slavery was heavy, and some slave masters of the church were as cruel as any in Latin America.

Slaves in the Spanish and Portuguese colonies were in general treated very poorly. They worshiped the same god as their masters, but for the most part they were treated no better than animals. Slaves had few rights. They were considered the property of their owners and could be bought, sold, given away, inherited, or rented out for use by others. Slaves lived in small, crowded huts and were given minimum amounts of food and water. They were punished for any sign of fatigue, laziness, or illness—flogged, branded, mutilated, burned, and generally abused at the whims of their masters.

In the Spanish colonies, many of the harshest laws were designed to keep slaves from running away or revolting. Laws in place by 1536 in Lima forbade African slaves to be on the streets at night unless they were with their master. The first offense was punishable by 100 lashes and the second offense by mutilation. Slaves who ran away for less than six days were mutilated. Those gone for a longer period of time were often hunted down and killed (for a reward).

In Portugal's colony of Brazil, slaves on the plantations were worked the hardest and treated the worst. They were constantly under the threat of being whipped by their white overseers in the fields. Though there were laws to protect slaves from cruel masters, they were mostly ignored. The Portuguese invented unique devices and ways to punish and torture their slaves. One such device was made of wood or iron and was designed to restrict the arms and legs of slaves for several days. Other cruelties included a punishment where a slave was tied facedown and beaten for nine (*novenas*) or thirteen (*trezenas*) consecutive nights.

An illustration of the Brazilian slave trade around 1850. The plantation owner, seated in his home, looks over prospective slaves a man if offering for sale. *Corbis-Bettmann. Reproduced by permission.*

Breaking the chains

Despite the terrible price if they were caught, slaves in the Spanish and Portuguese colonies ran away from their masters as often as possible. Sometimes they fled to the cities, hoping to find work and blend in with the population of freedpeople. Slaves also fled to the mountains or other remote regions to join groups of other fugitive slaves. Some groups of runaway slaves established organized communities. They harassed the colonial planters and encouraged other slaves to run away or revolt.

In Santa Maria, Colombia, in 1550, slaves burned the city and terrorized the white population. A few years later an African slave calling himself a king led a violent uprising of slaves. Both rebellions were crushed, and a series of laws and royal decrees were enacted to try to keep slaves in order.

The greatest slave rebellion in Brazil lasted almost seventy years (see box titled "Brazil's Independent Slave Republic"). From 1630 to 1697, runaway slaves lived in organized communities in the forests of northeastern Brazil. They had their own government, legal system, and friendly trading relations with neighboring villages. The Portuguese army destroyed them in 1697.

Colonial America

Slaves come to North America

African slaves first came to the North American mainland in 1526 when a Spanish explorer tried to colonize some land in what historians believe was South Carolina. He brought with him 500 Spanish settlers and 100 African slaves from Haiti (an island in the West Indies). The expedition's leader soon died, the slaves revolted, and the colonists fled to Haiti. The earliest example of an established colony using slaves on the mainland was in Saint Augustine, Florida, which the Spanish settled in 1565.

Slaves did not come to the British colonies of mainland North America in great numbers until the last quarter of the seventeenth century (1675–1700). After having unsuccessfully tried different sources of labor—Indian slaves and white and Indian indentured servants—the colonists ultimately turned to African slaves. The New World planters reasoned that the supply of Africans was plentiful, they were easily identified by the color of their skin if they ran away, they were cheap to buy and maintain, they could be controlled, and they were bound to serve for life.

Indentured Servants

Indentured servants worked under a contract, bound to their masters for terms between two and fourteen years (the average term was from four to seven years). For the white servants, the terms of service were part of the deal that paid for their passage from England to the New World. Upon completion of their contract, indentured servants were promised their freedom and perhaps some food, clothing, tools, or land.

Indentured servants were part of the labor force in every colony. The whites who came to the New World as indentured servants were a mixed group, mostly from the poor and rural classes of England. Many of them were unemployed farmhands, convicted criminals, or prison-ers taken in English wars against the Irish and Scots. Others had been kidnaped by men who specialized in the trade, much like the raiders of West Africa's coasts had been doing for years (see "Draining Africa's heartland," Chapter 5). Sometimes sheer poverty drove whole families—men, women, and children—into selling themselves into servitude.

The trip across the Atlantic for white indentured servants was not much different from the Middle Passage endured by black slaves shipped from Africa (see "Merchants of death," Chapter 5). The same things that killed many African slaves on their Atlantic voyage—rough seas, overcrowding, lack of safe (uncontaminated) food and water, un-

The southern colonies needed as much labor as possible for their large-scale tobacco, rice, and indigo (a plant used for making dyes) farms. (Cotton did not become an important crop until 1800.) The middle and northern colonies, especially New England, were more interested in slaves as commodities—things to be bought and sold for a profit—than their labor potential. Thus the greatest concentration of slaves in the British colonies of mainland North America was on the plantations of the South. The southern colonies, where black slaves often outnumbered the white colonists, had much harsher slave codes than the northern colonies.

Southern colonies

Virginia

In 1619 Jamestown, Virginia, was the first English colony to receive Africans. The twenty blacks a small Dutch

This certificate of indenture terminates after eleven years, five months, and twenty-five days.
Archive Photos, Inc. Reproduced by permission.

sanitary conditions in general, and disease—also killed many whites. The death rate for whites on the trip from England to the colonies was sometimes as high as two-thirds of the passengers.

Whether white, black, or Indian, once they reached the New World, indentured servants were treated like slaves in many ways. They received no wages, only room and board and maybe the chance to learn a trade. They had no control over their working hours or conditions. Punishments were determined by their masters and included beatings, whippings, branding, and chaining.

warship left at Jamestown technically were not slaves. The first Africans in Virginia were, like about one-half of the white immigrants at that time, indentured servants (see box titled "Indentured Servants").

By 1650, there were only 300 blacks in Virginia. Records show that some of the blacks were free and had been granted land after completing their terms of indentured service. As Africans trickled into the colony in those early years, their status as equals with the white servants began to change. In 1640, a black servant was sentenced to life service for running away, a punishment never before used on white servants. After 1640, contracts with black indentured servants, if they existed at all, started to define the length of their service as "perpetual," or "for life," and included their future children as well. By 1661, laws in Virginia recognized the legality of hereditary lifetime service, or slavery, for blacks.

Fact Focus

- Massachusetts, not Virginia, was the first colony to legally recognize slavery as an institution.

- The first Africans in the colony of Virginia were indentured servants, not slaves.

- The death rate for white indentured servants on the voyage from England to America was sometimes as high as two-thirds of the passengers.

- New England slave traders controlled most of the slave trade in the New World from 1700 to 1750.

- In 1765, there were 90,000 slaves in South Carolina, or about 69 percent of the colony's total population of 130,000.

- Thomas Jefferson was the first highly regarded thinker of the era to put in writing the idea that black Africans were biologically inferior to white Europeans.

- Of the 300,000 American soldiers who fought in the War of Independence, 5,000 were black.

- George Washington, during his two terms as president, held 317 slaves on his vast tobacco plantation, Mount Vernon.

From 1675 to 1700, slave importation into Virginia increased sharply. At the close of the century, African slaves were arriving at a rate of more than 1,000 per year. By 1708, there were 12,000 black slaves and 18,000 white colonists. In 1756 there were 120,156 black slaves and 173,316 white colonists. Slaves at that time made up about 40 percent of the colony's population and actually outnumbered colonists in many of Virginia's counties.

As in the West Indies (see "The law of the whip," Chapter 6), where slaves also far outnumbered the colonists, by 1700 a strict slave code was enacted in Virginia to try to keep the large slave population in line. Slaves were not allowed to leave their plantation without a pass. Slaves guilty of murder or rape were hanged. Robbery of a house or store by a slave was punishable by sixty lashes from the sheriff. After the whipping, the slave was placed in a pillory (a wooden frame used to confine prisoners) with his or her ears nailed to the post for a half-hour. Then their ears were cut off. Petty offenders were routinely whipped, maimed, or branded.

South and North Carolina

Settlers were encouraged to bring slaves to the Carolinas from the beginning. In 1663, planters were offered twenty acres for every African male slave and ten acres for every African female slave they brought into the colony. The business interests in the Carolinas of several members of the African Royal Company, England's government-supported

An illustration of the introduction of African slavery into Virginia. *Archive Photos, Inc. Reproduced by permission.*

slave-trading company, also contributed to the colony's use of slaves. These very powerful colonial investors sought profits from both the slave trade and the use of slaves on their own plantations.

In 1708, the population of the Carolinas was split almost equally between free and slave: there were 4,100 black slaves and 4,080 white colonists. In 1715 there were 10,500 black slaves and 6,250 white colonists. In South Carolina in 1739, the slaves outnumbered the whites by almost four to

A male slave confined in stocks in Florida. *Courtesy of the Library of Congress.*

one: 35,000 slaves compared with only 9,000 colonists. In 1765, the slave population was 90,000, while the colonists numbered only 40,000. Slaves at that time made up about 69 percent of the colony's population.

Beginning in 1686, Carolina's colonial legislature passed laws that ensured the domination of black slaves by their white masters. In time, the slave code of the Carolinas became a model for much of mainland North America. Blacks were not allowed to engage in trade of any sort with whites. Slaves were not allowed off their master's property between sunset and sunrise without a pass. In 1722, white patrols were granted the authority to search and whip blacks deemed to be a threat to peace and order.

For slaves, crimes punishable by death included murder, burglary, arson, robbery, and running away. For stealing things like hogs or chickens, slaves were branded on the face with the letter "R." A thief caught for a second or third time faced the death sentence.

North and South Carolina shared the same slave code until North Carolina broke away and in 1741 enacted its own laws concerning slaves and servants. In 1756, the population of North Carolina included 19,000 slaves and 60,000 whites. The presence of Quakers, a religious group opposed to slavery, and the lower number of slaves compared with colonists made slavery in North Carolina a little less harsh. The colony's slave code at least tried to establish procedures by which slave offenders were tried. Even though the panel of jurors consisted of four slave owners and two justices (nothing close to the modern concept of a jury of peers), it was a step forward in the protection of slaves from their masters' crueler abuses.

Maryland

It is unclear how many slaves were in Maryland in the early years of the colony, but records indicate their presence as early as 1638. In 1663, Maryland legally recognized the institution of slavery. The slave population increased at a rate of a couple of hundred each year in the first decade of the 1700s. By 1750, however, there were about 40,000 black slaves in the colony's population of 140,000. In 1790, there were 100,000 black slaves and 200,000 white colonists. Slaves were about one-third of Maryland's population.

Just as everywhere else where slaves were present in great numbers, Maryland enacted strict laws to try to maintain order. Special punishments—whipping, branding, or death—were reserved for blacks guilty of such crimes as murder, arson, burglary, theft, associating with whites, and disorderly conduct.

Georgia

The southernmost colony, Georgia, had a unique beginning. Its earliest settlers were Englishmen who were released from prison in order to help their mother country develop the New World. The colony's trustees forbade three things: free land titles, alcoholic beverages, and slaves. Georgia was supposed to supply England with goods such as silks, oils, dyes, and drugs—products that did not require a slave-labor force.

The Georgian colonists, however, only had to look to their northern neighbor, South Carolina, to see how profitable it was to own slaves. In 1750, after many pleas and petitions from the planters of Georgia, the prohibition on slaves was lifted and free land titles were granted (alcohol had been allowed in 1742). By 1760, there were 3,000 black slaves and 6,000 white colonists. In 1773, there were 18,000 white colonists and 15,000 black slaves. Slaves at that time were about 45 percent of the colony's population.

Georgia's slave code, like many of its new colonists, came mostly from South Carolina. In Georgia, no more than seven blacks were allowed to congregate unless a white person was present. Slaves could not possess canoes, horses, or cattle. Under no conditions were slaves to be taught to read or write. And finally, as a gesture to protecting their health, no slave was to work more than sixteen hours a day.

Middle colonies

New York

Before the English captured New Netherland and re-named it New York in 1664, the area was mostly controlled by the Dutch and their government-supported slave-trading firm, the West India Company. The Dutch brought a steady supply of black slaves from Africa and Brazil to work their farms in the Hudson River valley. The Dutch colonists in New Netherland treated slaves relatively well. There were few restrictions on their movement, and manumission (a formal release from bondage) was possible as a reward for their good services.

The Dutch apparently never got around to developing a slave code. The English, however, passed laws in 1665 and 1684 that made slavery an accepted legal institution. New York's slave code was similar to the codes of the other colonies. Laws passed in 1702 prohibited any trade between colonists and black slaves. Slaves were not allowed to meet in groups of more than three. And a "common whipper" was ap-pointed to carry out sentences of the courts.

In a short time, New York City, with its excellent har-bors, became an important slave market for the region. The city's merchants competed with the English traders for the slave trade's profits. The result was that the number of African slaves rose steadily. In 1698, there were 2,170 African slaves in New York's population of 18,067. By 1771, the number of slaves climbed to 19,883 in a total population of 168,007. Slaves at that time were about 12 percent of the colony's population.

The New York colonists used slaves in a variety of ways—on farms, in households, and in small factories. A very wealthy landowner might own between twenty-five and sixty slaves. Small farmers, tradespeople, and craftspeople might own a slave or two. Slaves earned their keep in a variety of ways. Many slaves became skilled craftspeople, capable of doing any kind of work a city or rural area needed. They

Slaves appear in court in New York, defending themselves against charges of being involved in arson in a slave uprising in 1741. Although there was no hard evidence, eleven slaves were burned and eighteen were hanged. *Courtesy of the Library of Congress.*

sometimes competed with white artisans for work as carpenters; masons; blacksmiths; weavers; goldsmiths; and makers of shoes, sails, brushes, and candles.

The skilled slaves in New York enjoyed a few benefits and liberties that were denied to their mostly unskilled counterparts in the southern colonies. They had better food, clothing, and medical care. Some slaves could acquire private property. The more slaves were valued by their masters, the greater their bargaining power was in seeking freedom through a fixed term of service. Some slaves saved enough money to purchase manumission from their masters.

New Jersey

New Jersey had the second-highest slave population of the middle colonies, next to New York. In 1726, there were 2,581 black slaves in a total population of 32,422. By 1745, there were 4,606 black slaves and 56,797 white colonists. At that time slaves made up about 8 percent of the population. By 1790 New Jersey had 11,000 slaves. Slaves worked on New Jersey's farms, mines, lumberyards, shipyards, ports, and docks.

The colony's early Dutch and Swedish settlers had very few black slaves. When the English took over in 1664, they granted new settlers seventy-five acres of land for every slave or servant brought into the colony. The English also brought with them some very strict laws and harsh punishments for slaves. Petty theft was punished by whipping and grand larceny by branding; rapists were castrated, and murderers were put to death.

Pennsylvania and Delaware

African slaves were present in Pennsylvania as early as 1639, but only in small numbers. The German, Dutch, and Swedish settlers had little use for slaves on their small farms, and white laborers resented the competition for work that slaves would bring. There was also considerable antislavery sentiment in the colony for moral and ethical reasons (questions of right and wrong). Pennsylvania's influential population of Quakers voiced their religious opposition to slavery as early as 1688.

The slave population grew slowly in the 1700s. In 1721 there were an estimated 2,500 to 5,000 blacks in the colony. In 1751, there were about 11,000 blacks in Pennsylvania, with 6,000 in Philadelphia alone. And in 1790, out of 10,274 blacks in the colony, 3,737 were slaves and 6,537 were free, attesting to the strength of the Quakers' persistent pleas for the manumission of slaves.

In 1700 slavery was recognized in a code of laws very similar to New Jersey's. Despite laws restricting their movements, blacks in Pennsylvania moved about freely to visit with friends. Pennsylvania's slaves were fed, clothed, and housed better than most colonial slaves. The Quakers taught many slaves to read and write in the course of providing religious instruction.

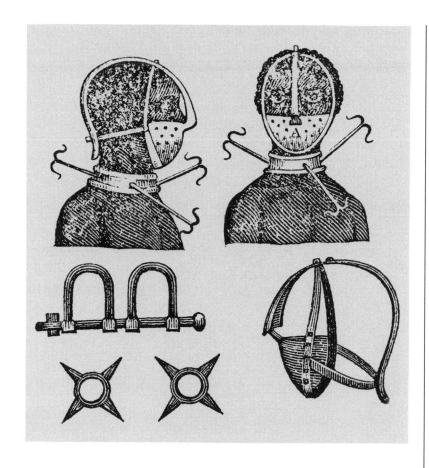

Delaware was part of Pennsylvania until 1703, and much of its early history of slavery is tied to its larger neighbor. In 1722, Delaware enacted its own slave code, which was very similar to the other middle colonies'. Over the years, however, without a large number of Quakers in the colony, Delaware became more like its southern neighbors than its mother colony.

Northern colonies

New England's slave traders

As a group, the northern colonies of Massachusetts, Rhode Island, Connecticut, and New Hampshire are known as New England. In 1638 a Salem ship named *Desire* unloaded New England's first cargo of African slaves at Boston Harbor.

The slaves were brought from Haiti, where they had been "seasoned" (broken in) on the island's plantations. The *Desire* also unloaded other goods from the West Indies, including cotton, salt, and tobacco.

The *Desire* was the first of many ships to sail into New England's harbors carrying slaves and goods from Africa and the West Indies. Once the slave trade began in earnest near the end of the 1600s, Massachusetts became the leading slave-trading colony of New England, ahead of Rhode Island, Connecticut, and New Hampshire, in that order. New England's slave traders had smaller ships than their European competitors, such as England's Royal African Company, but they managed to control most of the slave trade in the New World from 1700 to 1750.

Ships left the harbors of New England loaded with items such as beans, peas, corn, fish, dairy products, horses, hay, lumber, lead, steel, iron, shoes, candles, dry goods, and muskets (guns). They sailed to the West Indies, where they traded most of their cargo for rum. The "rum boats," as they were called, then sailed to Africa, where they traded the liquor, along with iron bars, beads, and cheap jewelry, for slaves (in 1756, a male African slave was priced at 115 gallons of rum and a female at 95 gallons). The ships then sailed back to the West Indies, where they traded some, if not most, of the freshly captured African slaves to the sugar islands for "seasoned" slaves, more rum, sugar and molasses (to make yet more rum), cocoa, and other products of the islands.

From the West Indies, the ships sailed up the Atlantic coast to New England's major slave ports: Boston, Salem, Marblehead, Newburyport, Portsmouth, New London, Newport, and Bristol. The slaves were sold in the local markets, where New Englanders bought some of them to work in their fields, forests, shipyards, workshops, and households. Most of the slaves brought to New England ports, however, were purchased by southern planters and transported to their tobacco and rice plantations in Virginia and South Carolina.

Fewer slaves, less punishment

The land, climate, and soil of the northern colonies were not suited for large-scale farming, and thus only a small number of slaves were needed compared with the South. In 1700, when New England's total population was around 90,000, there were only about 1,000 slaves in the region. The black population of Massachusetts, the largest slaveholder in the area in 1764, was only 5,235 compared with 218,950 whites. In Connecticut in 1756, there were 3,587 black slaves and 128,212 white colonists. Rhode Island had the highest percentage of slaves compared with colonists in the region, but they amounted to no more than 5 percent of the population. New Hampshire, as late as 1773, had only 674 slaves.

In 1641, Massachusetts was the first colony—even before Virginia—to recognize the legal institution of slavery. In the last quarter of the century, the other New England colonies followed suit. Rhode Island actually passed a law banning slavery in 1652, but it was ignored.

Slave codes did not appear in New England until the late 1700s, and they were not nearly as harsh as in the southern colonies. As in almost every colony, whites were forbidden to trade with blacks and restrictions were placed on the movement of blacks. However, few crimes were punishable by a death sentence, and branding and maiming were seldom used. Instead, whippings were the punishment of choice for most of New England's masters and colonial officials.

Education and marriage

The slaves of New England were probably the best educated and best-trained in all the colonies. In the early years, the Puritans (Protestant settlers) taught slaves and Indians to read the Bible. Some Puritans, such as Cotton Mather (1663–1728; a clergyman and author), opened small schools

CAUTION!!

COLORED PEOPLE OF BOSTON, ONE & ALL,

You are hereby respectfully CAUTIONED and advised, to avoid conversing with the **Watchmen and Police Officers of Boston,**

For since the recent ORDER OF THE MAYOR & ALDERMEN, they are empowered to act as

KIDNAPPERS

AND

Slave Catchers,

And they have already been actually employed in KIDNAPPING, CATCHING, AND KEEPING SLAVES. Therefore, if you value your LIBERTY, and the *Welfare of the Fugitives* among you, *Shun* them in every possible manner, as so many *HOUNDS* on the track of the most unfortunate of your race.

Keep a Sharp Look Out for KIDNAPPERS, and have TOP EYE open.

APRIL 24, 1851.

A handbill posted in Boston in 1851 warning black people, free or enslaved, to watch out for slave catchers. *Courtesy of the Library of Congress.*

with evening classes for the general instruction of Indians and blacks. The New England Quakers supported the education of young blacks and opened small schools for them as well.

Blacks, slave or free, were not just allowed to marry in New England, they were required to do so just as any other persons who wanted their union to be legal. The institution of marriage made life more stable for New England's slaves, and it was a law that blacks did not seem to mind obeying, given the many records of marriages between black couples, black-Indian couples, and even a few black-white couples.

Race and slavery

Law and race

The twenty Africans traded for food and supplies by a Dutch warship in Jamestown, Virginia, in 1619 were most likely stolen at sea from Spanish slave traders. As captives of the Spanish, the Africans had been baptized as Roman Catholics and given Christian names. As Christians, these first Africans in the American colonies, by custom, could not be enslaved for life. They were, like most of the rest of America's first immigrants, made servants for a fixed period of time, usually four to seven years (see "Indentured Servants" box on page 110).

From the time the first Africans arrived to the time each colony made slavery a legally defined practice, the definition of who could be enslaved slowly changed. Beginning with the first black indentured servant who was sentenced in Virginia to a lifetime of servitude in 1640, the laws in the colonies started shifting. Faced with a severe shortage of permanent workers—for indentured servants did not stay long—the colonists basically decided that being a baptized Christian no longer saved black Africans from lifelong enslavement.

Religion and race

The change in the legal status of blacks over the years reflected a belief among the British colonists that black Africans were inferior to white Europeans. As Christians, some colonists turned to the Bible to justify their prejudices. Christian legend taught that Ham, the son of Noah, fathered the African peoples. In the Bible's Old Testament, Ham incurred the curse of his father for being disrespectful. The descendants of Ham and Ham's son Canaan, according to Noah, were to be servants of all men. It was therefore right and proper, reasoned some British colonists, to enslave people of a race already condemned by Scripture to servitude.

Unlike the colonists of Latin America, who were influenced by the Roman Catholic church, the Protestant British were under no obligation to baptize their slaves in the New World. Slaves were not allowed to worship with their masters in the British colonies until the 1800s. Although baptism into the Christian faith did not save black Africans from lifelong enslavement in Latin America, it at least resulted in Spanish and Portuguese slave masters seeing their slaves as human beings—people with souls, and equal before the eyes of God (see "Catholic colonies," Chapter 6).

Marriages between whites and blacks, more frequent and accepted by society in Latin America, were very rare in colonial North America. In Latin America, a child born to a black slave woman and fathered by a white man (usually the master or a member of his household) was often treated well; some were even sent to Europe for a formal education. In colonial North America, mulatto (pronounced muh-LAH-toe; of mixed white and black ancestry) children were often sold by their ashamed masters with little hesitation.

Of course, not all British colonists were mean or evil people who ignored their Christian convictions in order to make profits from the sweat of other human beings. Most colonists, in fact, did not even own slaves. The influence of religious movements, such as the Quakers and the Puritans, was important in some of the American colonies and lessened some of the harsher effects of racial slavery.

Biology and race

The British colonists viewed Africans not only as morally inferior but biologically inferior as well. Africans were seen as physically a lesser breed than white Europeans. To many white colonists, black Africans were alien and foreign, even mysterious and threatening. The pigment of their skin, the shape of their faces, and the texture of their hair all set Africans apart to the whites and fueled their contention that Africans were a race that was somehow suited to enslavement.

Thomas Jefferson (1743–1826), the principal author of the Declaration of Independence and the third president of the United States, was the first highly regarded thinker of the colonial era to put in writing the idea that black Africans were biologically inferior to white Europeans. In a 1793 book entitled *Notes on the State of Virginia,* Jefferson also put forth the idea that blacks and whites were too different from one another, by nature, to be able to live together in peace.

The American Revolution

Cry for freedom

By 1750, slavery was a fact of life in colonial America. There were few slaves in the North, but the profits of the slave trade were essential in developing thriving industries connected to the trade, such as shipbuilding, iron foundries, sawmills, rum distilleries, and sail making. In the South, where a vast majority of the slaves lived, slavery on the plantations was a way of life for Africans, from cradle to grave and from generation to generation. About two-thirds of the slaves in the colonies at this point had been born on American soil.

In the Declaration of Independence, published on July 4, 1776, Thomas Jefferson wrote, "All men are created equal." At the time, neither the writer nor the Declaration's signers intended those five words to apply to anyone but an elite group of landowning colonists who sought their independence from England. Yet the notion of equality, the cry for freedom from oppression, was heard and understood by the hundreds of thousands of African slaves as well. At the same time that the colonists were demanding their freedom from King George III of England, the slaves repeatedly petitioned the colonial assemblies and courts for their freedom, asking simply: How can you shout "Liberty or death!" while holding at least half a million human beings in slavery?

Fighting for freedom

Blacks were involved in some of the earliest battles of the American Revolution. On March 5, 1770, a forty-seven-year-old runaway slave named Crispus Attucks was the first man to die for the cause in a hail of British bullets known as

the Boston Massacre. In the spring of 1775, blacks fought alongside the white militia in the battles of Lexington and Concord, the first examples of armed resistance to the British.

Also in the spring of 1775, General George Washington (1732–1799) formed the Continental Army on the outskirts of Boston. In November 1775, Washington decided not to allow the enlistment of blacks—free or slave—into his troops. A few days earlier, however, the British governor of Virginia, Lord Dunmore, had declared that all slaves who joined the British side would be set free. When Washington learned of Dunmore's Proclamation, he reversed course, and in January 1776, blacks were allowed to enlist.

Dunmore's Proclamation had an almost immediate effect on the huge slave population of the South. Slaves ran away by the thousands. In 1778, an estimated 30,000 slaves ran away from their masters in Virginia. South Carolina lost about 25,000 slaves between 1775 and 1783. And by the end of the war, 11,000 of Georgia's 15,000 slaves had fled. Hundreds of

Crispus Attucks, an escaped slave, led a group of angry colonists in taunting British soldiers. One soldier panicked and opened fire; Attucks and four others died in the Boston Massacre, on March 5, 1770. *National Archives and Records Administration.*

Revolutionary war hero Peter Salem (c. 1750–1816) standing behind Lieutenant Grosvenor in a painting of the Battle of Bunker Hill (1775). Salem, a Massachusetts slave, turned the tide of the battle when he shot and killed the commander of the British troops as they advanced on the colonists. *Associated Publishers. Reproduced by permission.*

slaves joined Dunmore, who formed all-black fighting units in what he called his "Ethiopian Regiment." Their motto: "Liberty to Slaves."

By the end of the war, all the states except Georgia and South Carolina had enlisted slaves and free blacks in their state and Continental armies. The slaves joined with the understanding that they would have their freedom after three years of service. The government compensated their masters with money for their "loss." Of the 300,000 American soldiers who fought in the War of Independence, 5,000 were black. Blacks served alongside whites in the army as well as the navy and were engaged in almost every military battle between 1775 and the British surrender at Yorktown in 1781.

The aftermath

There is no doubt that blacks helped colonial America gain its independence from the British. At the war's end,

however, most of America's blacks were still not free. Black soldiers in the North and South went home with their personal freedom but little to show for their effort. Many fugitive slaves from the South were rounded up and returned to their plantations (with help from the northern authorities). Still, tens of thousands of slaves made it to freedom; how many is impossible to know. At least 13,000 blacks made it onto British ships as they retreated from Charleston, Savannah, and New York in 1782, but some of those were reenslaved in the West Indies.

The immediate effect of the Revolution on the South was to increase the number of slaves that were needed on the plantations due to wartime losses. The importation of slaves, which had been banned as a wartime measure in 1776, was resumed with a vengeance as the planters of Virginia, South Carolina, and Georgia sought to refill their plantations with African slaves.

George Washington with slaves and an overseer at Mount Vernon, his tobacco plantation in Virginia. *The Granger Collection, New York. Reproduced by permission.*

By 1787, when delegates from twelve of the thirteen colonies met in Philadelphia for the Constitutional Convention, many of the northern states had already outlawed slavery in their own constitutions. On the federal level, however, the largest slaveholding states of the lower South prevailed on the issues of slavery. The slave trade could continue for at least twenty more years, three-fifths of the slave population could be counted toward determining the number of each state's Congressional representatives, and all states were required to return fugitive slaves to their owners. The federal Constitution was ratified on June 21, 1788.

Founding Fathers

On April 30, 1789, the person who had presided over the Constitutional Convention, General George Washington, was sworn in as the first president of the United States. At the time, one in five Americans were living in bondage. Ninety percent of the country's 700,000 slaves lived in the South. The president's home state of Virginia led the nation with a slave population of 304,000. The president himself, during his two terms in office, held 317 slaves on his vast tobacco plantation, Mount Vernon.

In 1793 Thomas Jefferson, the writer of the famous words "All men are created equal," was secretary of state and the owner of more than 130 slaves on his Virginia farming estate, Monticello (pronounced mon-te-CHELL-oh). In his eighty-three-year lifetime, Jefferson freed just three of his slaves. When he died on July 4, 1826, he granted freedom to five more.

There is little doubt that the black slave population of America did not benefit from the bloodshed of the American Revolution in the same way as their white masters. Although slavery was on the decline in the North and legally abolished in many places there, in 1790 there were still slaves in every state except Massachusetts and Vermont. The promises of the American Revolution, and the rights guaranteed in the federal Constitution—freedom and equality—were still denied to all but a few black Americans. The goals of the antislavery forces were strengthened by the Revolution but would have to wait many more years before bearing fruit.

Slave Life in Antebellum America

8

Turn of the century

The era between 1800 and the beginning of the Civil War (1861) is known as the antebellum period (pronounced an-teh-BELL-um), which means "before the war." The early 1800s was a time of great change brought on by the invention and use of various machines in the workplace. The Industrial Revolution in England (a period of great economic changes in the late 1700s) had a major effect on the newly created United States and, ultimately, on the large population of slaves in the South. The invention of weaving and spinning machines in England dramatically changed the textile industry by making it easier to produce cotton goods. Consequently, the price of cotton products went down and the demand for cotton—raw and processed—significantly increased.

The planters in the southern United States had experienced hard times in the decade since the American Revolution (1775–1783). The markets were not as strong for their staple crops of tobacco, rice, and indigo (a plant used for making dyes), and they were eager to switch to cotton. England's textile mills would buy as much as they could grow and pay a fair price for it. There remained a problem, however. Separating the fragile cotton fibers from the seed—a process known as ginning (pronounced JIN-ing)—could only be done by hand, which made it labor-intensive and costly.

The machine that changed everything

Eli Whitney (1765–1825), a young white schoolteacher from the North, found the solution in 1793. While visiting a plantation in Georgia, Whitney learned of the planters' desperate need for a machine that could separate cotton fiber from seed. In a matter of days he made a model, and in a matter of weeks he worked out the mechanical difficulties and began making plans to manufacture his invention. With just two people working it, Whitney's cotton gin cleaned as much cotton as 100 workers could by hand, thus freeing up laborers for the cultivation of the crop.

The invention of the cotton gin led to a tremendous increase in cotton cultivation on the plantations of the Deep South and to the rise of an industrial economy in the North centered on the manufacture of cotton products. U.S. cotton production increased from 3,000 bales in 1793 to 178,000 bales in 1800. In 1825, American plantations were producing 500,000 bales of cotton a year, and by 1840, three-fourths of the world's cotton was coming out of the South.

At the beginning of the nineteenth century, the Carolinas and Georgia grew most of the cotton (Virginia continued to grow tobacco), but the area of cotton cultivation pushed westward as people migrated by the thousands into Alabama, Mississippi, and Louisiana by 1820. By 1840, the cotton belt stretched from the Atlantic coast to Texas. In 1834, Alabama, Mississippi, and Louisiana were producing almost two-thirds of the cotton grown in the United States.

Cotton and slavery

The rise of cotton as the number one crop of the nation had a tremendous impact on the institution of slavery and the lives of slaves in the American South. In 1790, there were fewer than 700,000 slaves in the United States. In 1830 there were more than 2 million slaves; less than 3,000 lived

in the North. And in 1850, the U.S. census chief estimated that of the 2.5 million slaves producing staple crops, 1.8 million, or almost three-fourths, were in cotton. About 350,000 slaves were in tobacco, 150,000 in sugar, 125,000 in rice, and 60,000 in hemp. In 1860, on the eve of the Civil War, there were just under 4 million slaves in the United States. Seven out of eight slaves, or around 3.5 million, lived and worked on the farms and plantations of the South.

Women cotton workers in the South. *Archive Photos, Inc. Reproduced by permission.*

The emergence of cotton farming and its westward expansion affected slavery in two important ways. First, it immediately increased the number of African slaves imported into the South. With help from New England slave traders, in 1803 alone South Carolina and Georgia planters imported 20,000 African slaves to work their new cotton fields. Second, the demand for slaves to work the ever-growing number of cotton farms created a slave trade between the states and forced the migration of hundreds of thousands of slaves from the upper South states of Maryland, Virginia, and the Carolinas into the Deep South and west—into Georgia, Alabama, Mississippi, Louisiana, and Texas.

The African slave trade

The U.S. federal government's official abolition of the African slave trade in 1807 did little to stop the importation of African slaves, the growth of slavery, or its westward expansion in the cotton belt of the South. The main problem with the law was that it was poorly enforced, and consequently ignored by the people who profited most from the trade—the New England shipowners, the Middle Atlantic merchants, and the southern planters. The main effect of the prohibition, says one historian, was the creation by slave traders of the first underground railroad, a secret network for illegally transporting blacks—in this case, newly imported Africans—into slavery.

In spite of the 1807 law, the African slave trade persisted and, at times, flourished right up until the Civil War. There is evidence that in 1836 as many as 15,000 Africans were being shipped annually on American vessels from Africa through Havana, Cuba, to Texas. Bay Island, in the Gulf of Mexico, sometimes held as many as 16,000 newly arrived Africans waiting to be taken to markets along the southern U.S. coast—to ports in Florida, Mississippi, Louisiana, and Texas.

The domestic slave trade

What little, if any, decrease there was in the importation of slaves from Africa was made up for by the rise of the

domestic—or interstate—slave trade. The large numbers of settlers who migrated west starting in the 1810s were desperate for laborers to clear the lands and cultivate cotton, and they were willing to pay good prices for slaves. With the plantation economy of the upper South in decline, the farmers of Maryland, Virginia, and the Carolinas found themselves with a surplus of laborers and became the main suppliers of slaves to the cotton belt.

A slave coffle, or a group of people chained together, passes the United States capitol. *Archive Photos, Inc. Reproduced by permission.*

Fact Focus

- In 1840, three-fourths of the world's cotton was grown in the American South.

- In 1860, there were almost 4 million slaves in the U.S. South. Seven out of eight slaves lived and worked on farms and plantations.

- The official abolition of the African slave trade in the United States in 1807 did little to stop the importation of African slaves.

- Slave trade between states generated millions of dollars annually for the U.S. economy.

- Virginia, Maryland, and Kentucky were known as "slave-breeding" states.

- In 1860 one out of four southern families owned slaves. Of those who owned slaves, 88 percent owned fewer than twenty.

- In the Black Codes of the South, crimes such as running away or talking back to a white person were punishable by a whipping of 300 to 500 lashes.

- In the cities of the South, it was common for slaves to hire themselves out and pay their master a set fee or portion of their wages.

- Marriages between slaves were not legal.

- In the deep South, it was against the law to teach slaves how to read and write. Ninety percent of slaves were illiterate.

- By 1835, religious services for blacks, slave or free, had to be presided over by a white minister.

- Christmastime was a weeklong holiday for both plantation and city slaves.

One of the reasons the upper South was able to continually supply slaves to the Deep South was that some slaveholders practiced the systematic breeding of slaves. Slave girls often became mothers at thirteen and fourteen years of age. Rewards, prizes, and even freedom were promised to slave women who bore the most children for their master. In 1832, an estimated 6,000 slaves per year were being exported from Virginia as a result of breeding. Maryland and Kentucky were also known as "slave-breeding" states.

The slave trade between the states generated millions of dollars annually for the U.S. economy. Some of the slave trade was handled by companies and their agents who specialized in the business. Slave traders constantly traveled

the countryside in search of good deals on slaves. The traders then took the slaves into a nearby town or city where they were housed in the local slave pen. Slave pens were typically converted chicken coops, stables, or warehouses and served as secure holding areas for slaves awaiting public auction or private sale. Businesses that sold farm supplies and animals also advertised slaves. Slaves were also sold at auctions, at county fairs, and through newspaper advertisements.

Major slave-trading centers in the older states of the South included Baltimore, Washington, Richmond, Norfolk, and Charleston. Slaves were transported from as far north as

Philadelphia and New York all the way to the cotton-belt cities of Montgomery, Memphis, and New Orleans. If it was spring or summer, slaves were chained together and marched over land to their destinations. In the fall and winter, slaves were loaded on ships for an ocean voyage to the Deep South and West.

Ownership

In 1860 there were about 4 million slaves in the United States, 90 percent of them living in the rural South. In the same year there were about 1.5 million free families in the South (in a total white population of 8 million). One-fourth, or 385,000 free families, owned slaves. The average white southern farmer did not own slaves but worked his small farm with his family and maybe some hired help. Of those families who owned slaves, 88 percent owned twenty or fewer slaves. Owners of more than fifty slaves were in the minority, and only 3,000 families owned more than one hundred slaves. More than 200,000 owners, or just over half, held five or fewer slaves. Contrary to popular myth, the slave-owning South was not full of large plantations with pillared mansions run by aristocratic gentlemen with hundreds of slaves.

The number of large slaveholders was small, but their cotton production and public influence on life in the South were enormous. In 1860, the United States was producing more than 5 million bales of cotton annually. The four states that produced 70 percent of the cotton—Mississippi, Alabama, Louisiana, and Georgia—were also at the top of the list in the number of large slaveholders. And, compared with blacks in other parts of the South, blacks in these states did not live as long or have as many children.

Field hands

The men, women, and children who slaved in the fields of the South were rated according to their ability to work. Children, who were often sent into the fields at age five or six to help their mothers, were rated as "quarter-hands." As

they grew older and stronger, slaves were rated as half-hands, then three-quarter-hands, and finally full-hands. As slaves' productivity declined with age or poor health, their ratings went back down the scale.

At harvesttime, many of the plantations required their field hands to pick a minimum amount of cotton each day. Masters, depending on their level of greed or cruelty, demanded from 100 to 300 pounds of cotton per day from each slave (150 pounds was generally considered a good day's work). If the quota was not met, a slave could expect a whipping as punishment. If slaves picked more than their quotas, there was a good chance that their minimum daily loads would be increased for the next workday.

One former plantation slave, Solomon Northrup, wrote in his 1853 autobiography (see "Fruit of the vine,"

Weighing in the cotton. On cotton plantations, whippings were the standard punishment for slaves who did not pick enough cotton to meet the quota for the day. *Archive Photos/Lass. Reproduced by permission.*

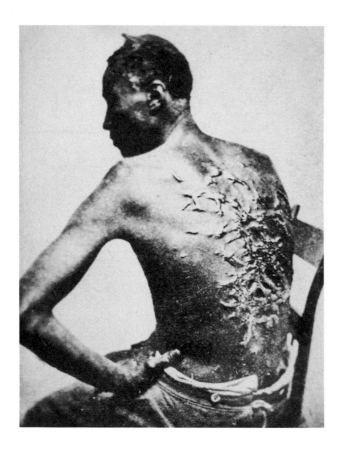

A slave shows the scars left on his back from being whipped. *National Archives and Records Administration.*

Chapter 9) about the constant sound of the whip at night during cotton-picking time (which lasted from late August through January): "It was rarely that a day passed by without one or more whippings. This occurred at the time the cotton was weighed. The delinquent, whose weight had fallen short, was taken out, stripped, made to lie upon the ground, face downwards, when he received a punishment proportioned to his offense. It is the literal, unvarnished truth, that the crack of the lash, and the shrieking of the slaves, can be heard from dark till bedtime, on Eppes' plantation, any day almost during the entire period of the cotton-picking season."

Clearing the fields, planting, weeding, hoeing, picking, ginning, and baling the cotton were all done by slaves. The pattern was the same whether the plantation grew cotton, tobacco, sugar, rice, or hemp. Slaves were forced to work very hard from daybreak to nightfall, from "can-see to can't-see," often working sixteen to eighteen hours a day. If work on the farm was slow because of the season, masters kept their field hands busy by hiring them out for a fee for short periods.

House slaves

Trained slaves were also used for the many nonfarming jobs of the plantations. Both men and women worked as domestic servants, or slaves trained for household service. They held such jobs as cook, nursemaid, butler, seamstress, coachman, laundress, and waiter. Slaves were also carpenters, mechanics, brick makers, blacksmiths, shoemakers, weavers, stonemasons, architects, and engineers. House slaves had much more day-to-day contact with their masters, which could be good if their owners were kind and not so good if otherwise (see "Slaves of color," later in this chapter).

Masters apprenticed out some slaves to nonslaveholders at an early age so that they might learn a skill. Training for some slaves was provided by the skilled slaves on the plantation. Slaves who had skills were considered more valuable and, in general, enjoyed a higher status and better food, clothing, and housing than the plantation's field hands. On small farms, some slaves might work as field hands for half the day and domestics the other half. At harvesttime, on small farms and plantations alike, both house and field slaves worked together for very long hours to bring in the crops.

Black Codes

As slavery took hold throughout the South in antebellum America, there emerged bodies of law that governed almost every aspect of slaves' lives, known as Black Codes. Each state had its own variations, but the general view was that slaves were nothing more than chattel (pronounced CHAT-el;

Wash day at the plantation.
Archive Photos, Inc. Reproduced by permission.

In the antebellum years, slaves were restricted from meeting in groups without supervision of whites. Meetings were often held in secret, where the slaves could hear their own preachers, worship, sing, and talk freely. *Corbis-Bettmann. Reproduced by permission.*

property). As such, slaves had little standing in the eyes of the law except as property owned by their masters. A slave could not give testimony in court (except against other slaves or free blacks), be a party in any lawsuit, or have a jury trial. Slaves could not make contracts, own any property but a few personal items, make a will, or inherit anything.

In some states, slaves were tried in regular courts for breaking the law. Other states had slave tribunals or trials by juries of slaveholders. Punishments were generally harsh and inflicted in public. Petty offenses were punished by "mild" whippings of twenty-five lashes. Crimes such as running away or talking back to a white person were punishable by 300 to 500 lashes. More serious crimes called for branding, imprisonment, or death. Arson, rape of a white woman, and conspiring to revolt were capital crimes.

As in colonial times (see Chapter 7), slaves were prohibited from a host of activities and behaviors. Slaves could

here their enemies had themselves; dashed up the airways and out upon the fs, and compelled the in- Mexicans to fling down rms and beg for mercy. ia, the commander, was the honors of war, and

A SLAVE-HUNT.

evacuated the city and back toward the capital. capture of Monterey w brilliant victory for the A cans.

General Taylor now ceived notice that the can authorities were abo make overtures for

not leave the plantation without permission, visit the homes of whites or free blacks, or have such people visit them. Slaves were not allowed to meet in groups unless a white person was present. Slaves could not hire themselves out for work or conduct themselves in any way as free people. In some communities, slaves were not allowed to carry arms, gamble, smoke or swear in public, blow horns, beat drums, or make "joyful demonstrations."

After the slave revolts led by Denmark Vesey (pro-nounced VEE-zee) in 1822 and Nat Turner in 1831 (see "Major uprisings," Chapter 10), the Black Codes became even more restrictive. In the 1830s, for example, Virginia banned nighttime religious meetings for slaves. Slaves could go to church only in the day, with their masters, to hear only white preachers. By 1835, the right for blacks, slave or free, to assemble in groups for any purposes without a white person present was denied throughout the Deep South. Of course, blacks met anyway, in secret, at so-called "hush-harbor" meetings where they could hear their own preachers.

Frontier justice

In the cotton-belt states of the South, where slaves often outnumbered their masters, plantation owners divided their counties into districts and paid local patrols to enforce the Black Codes. All white men were expected to serve in the patrols for periods of one to three months (failure to serve resulted in a fine). The patrols were mounted, armed, and equipped with dogs to track down missing or runaway slaves. Patrols punished offenders on the spot—usually by a whipping—and were empowered to search slave quarters for weapons or evidence of planned rebellion and to break up any gatherings of slaves.

Most of the time, however, what passed as law and justice for slaves was determined by the master of the plantation or, in his absence, his overseer. For a slave owner to subject one of his slaves to the public court system might mean the loss, through imprisonment or death, of his "property." Whenever possible, especially when dealing with daily discipline, plantation owners acted independently as judges, juries, and sometimes executioners.

The lash—or cowhide whip—was a brutal weapon in the skilled hands of a master, overseer, or driver (the person in charge of the slaves in the field, often a black). It was the same kind of whip that ranchers and farmers used to control bulls and horses. Slaves, both men and women, received whippings ranging from a few to 500 lashes on their bare backs while they were tied to a tree, bent over a barrel, or tied

to stakes on the ground. Special paddles, with holes drilled through the heads to inflict the greatest pain, were sometimes used instead. Stocks (a wooden frame with holes for the hands and feet) were also a common form of punishment and a whipping site as well.

In testimony before a congressional commission in 1863, Robert Smalls, an ex-slave from South Carolina, described some of the punishments he had witnessed in this passage from John Blassingame's *Slave Testimony: Two Centuries of Letters, Speeches, Interviews, and Autobiographies:*

> I have had no trouble with my owner but I have seen a good deal in traveling around on the plantations. I have seen stocks in which the people are confined from twenty-four to forty-eight hours. In whipping, a man is triced up to a tree and gets a hundred lashes from a raw hide. Sometimes a man is taken to a blacksmith's shop, and an iron of sixty pounds weight is fastened to his feet, so that when it is taken off he cannot walk for days ... I have seen a man owned by John Verdier wearing an iron collar with two prongs sticking out at the sides like cow's horns ... I have heard of whipping a woman in the family way [pregnant] by making a hole in the ground

Slaves on large plantations were often subjected to supervision of overseers hired by the owner. Many overseers wielded the whip on a regular basis. *Courtesy of the Library of Congress.*

for her stomach. My aunt was whipped so many a time until she has not the same skin she was born with.

There is no way to quantify the collective cruelty or kindness of southern slave owners. Historians point out that a great majority of planters owned twenty or fewer slaves and worked alongside them in the fields on their small farms. Under such conditions, they argue, brutality was less likely. Still, hundreds of thousands of slaves lived on plantations that were too large for them to be under the direct supervision of their owners. Life on plantations with absentee owners was extremely harsh, as overseers were notorious for their abuse of power and their violence against slaves.

Bare necessities

When it came to the necessities of life—food, clothing, housing, and health care—slaves were generally given the bare minimum. Some of the larger plantations had a central kitchen, but most did not, and slaves were responsible for making their own meals. The food was rationed to slaves on a daily or weekly basis. On average, adult slaves received about three pounds of meat (salt pork) and a peck (eight quarts) of cornmeal a week. Sometimes slaves also got rations of sweet potatoes, peas, rice, syrup, and fruit. If they had any time or energy left after their work duties, slaves could add to their diet by hunting, fishing, raising chickens, or growing their own small vegetable gardens.

Domestic servants not only had better food than field slaves (even if it was only their masters' leftovers), but they also had better clothes (even if they were mostly their masters' castoffs). Many of the women slaves made their own fabrics and clothing. The men wore cotton jeans and shirts of coarse cloth. Shoes were provided only for the winter months. The amount of food provided to slaves might affect their productivity, the slave owners reasoned, but they saw no connection between a slave's clothing and a possible rise in their personal profits.

Slaves were housed in small huts, or cabins. Most had no windows or floors and very little furniture. Slaves slept on boards, or blankets and quilts spread over beds of

straw. A well-furnished cabin might have some cooking pots, a chest, a stool, and a bed. To let the smoke out from cooking, the cabins and huts had small holes in their roofs or crude chimneys, sometimes made of mud. To keep costs down, owners crammed as many slaves as possible into each cabin. On one Mississippi plantation, 150 slaves lived in only twenty-four huts, each measuring fourteen by sixteen feet.

Several generations of a slave family outside a cabin on a plantation in South Carolina in 1862. *Photo by I. H. O'Sullivan. Courtesy of the Library of Congress.*

City Slaves

In 1860, on the eve of the Civil War, there were about 4 million slaves in the United States. One out of eight slaves lived and worked in the towns and cities of the South. In general, they did the hardest and dirtiest work. Slaves built the streets, railroads, and bridges. They worked in the mines and quarries; they cut and milled the timber. Slaves worked on the riverboats and waterfronts and toiled in the shops and factories. They made turpentine, iron, cotton jeans, and tobacco products. With training from their masters or other slaves, many blacks found work as carpenters, masons, mechanics, shoemakers, painters, and cabinetmakers.

Life in the city provided more opportunities for slaves—especially slaves with marketable skills—to gain some small measures of freedom. On plantations, owners often hired out their slaves in return for a fee. In the city, the arrangement was taken a few steps further. It became common for slaves to hire themselves out and pay their master a set fee or a portion of their wages. This freed the master from having to provide food, clothing, health care, and even housing for his slave, as some owners allowed their hired-out slaves to live out as well. In turn, slaves gained more control over their own work and leisure time.

Many slaves in the city worked as domestic servants. Women, with help from their children, did most of the household chores. Their days began at 5:00 A.M. and lasted until late at night, with rarely a Sunday off. Men served as butlers, valets, coachmen, gardeners, and the like. Slave quarters were usually located behind the master's house. Typically, they were long, narrow two-story brick buildings, with small, windowless rooms. They were run-down, unfurnished, and terribly overcrowded. Compared with plantation slaves, however, city slaves in general had better housing, food, and clothing.

While the white patrols were the enforcers of the Black Codes in the rural South, in cities, the job belonged to the police force. The city of Charleston in the 1850s, for example, spent more money on their police force than on anything else in their budget; there were 281 police officers, 25 of them mounted. The city had a 10:00 P.M. curfew for blacks, and after that hour armed patrols of twenty to thirty police officers marched through the streets, looking for violators. A northern journalist who passed through the city in 1857 wrote that Charleston at night looked like a city at war.

When slaves became ill, it was their masters' responsibility to provide medical treatment. If a slave was hired-out at the time, then the temporary master was obligated to seek a doctor. Slaves who needed hospitalization were

forced into segregated wards of the white hospitals or, if one existed, sent to the area's hospital for blacks. The quality of care that slaves received sometimes depended on how valuable they were to their masters. Many slaves distrusted the white man's medicine and preferred to treat their own illnesses with folk remedies, using the healing qualities of herbs and roots.

Slave quarters on a South Carolina plantation, 1860. *Archive Photo, Inc. Reproduced by permission.*

A family on the block at a slave auction in Charleston, South Carolina, 1861.
Corbis-Bettmann. Reproduced by permission.

Family life

Given the conditions of slavery in the South, it is hard to imagine more difficult circumstances in which to raise a family. The very nature of slavery, which viewed enslaved blacks as property rather than human beings, denied to slaves the basic rights and freedoms necessary to form secure and stable families. Though many slaves were married, the Black Codes never recognized the legality of their marriages. When slaves were sold, families were often divided—husband from wife, parents from children—with little regard given to keeping a family together if higher profits were possible by selling them separately.

The invention of the cotton gin had a profound effect on family life for slaves of the upper South. In the first quarter of the nineteenth century, hundreds of thousands of slaves were uprooted and forced to migrate to the new cotton fields of the Deep South and West (see "The domestic slave trade," earlier in this chapter). Many families were divided in the process. The breeding of slaves and the selling of children eight to twelve years of age also tore apart many families. The practice also increased the number of runaway slaves, as husbands and wives sought to be reunited or parents fled from their masters in search of their children.

The master's absolute power made it nearly impossible for slaves to develop relationships and responsibilities considered typical of a healthy family structure at the time. A male slave had none of the traditional authority or prestige as breadwinner that was usually granted to a husband or father. The master was in charge of his labor and could exploit the slave's wife sexually or punish his children at will. A female slave, too, was denied her customary role as wife, mother, and homemaker. She had little choice, as she was forced to serve her master first. She also was worked too hard to have much time or energy left for her husband or children. Children, though obeying their parents, learned from an early age that their parents had very little ability to protect them from the master.

Marriage

"Marriages" between slaves were often arranged by their masters (mostly for the purpose of breeding more slaves). As with many other aspects of their lives, slaves could either go along with their masters' wishes or face severe punishments, including being sold away and forced to leave loved ones. For slaves who were able to choose their own spouses, marriage was sacred and obviously more stable in the long run, although no less likely to be broken up by sale than arranged marriages. Caroline Johnson Harrison, an ex-slave from Virginia, described her marriage experience on the plantation, which appears in John Blassingame's anthology *Slave Testimony:*

> "Didn't have to ask Marsa or nothin'. Just go to Ant Sue an' tell her you want to get mated. She tell us to think 'bout it hard for two days, 'cause marryin' was sacred in the eyes of Jesus. After two days Mose an' I went back an' say we done thought 'bout it an' still want to get married. Then she called all the slaves after tasks to pray fo' the union that God was gonna make. Pray we stay together an' have lots of children an' none of 'em gets sold away from the parents. Then she lays a broomstick 'cross the sill of the house we gonna live in an' join our hands together. Fo' we step over it she ask us once mo' if we was sho' we wanted to get married. 'Course we say yes. Then she say, 'In the eyes of Jesus step into the holy land of matrimony.' When we step 'cross the broomstick, we was married."

Some married slaves were able to stay with their mates for life. Some slaves lived in the same place all their lives, raised families, and had grandchildren like most folks, despite the tremendous odds against them. As parents, slaves educated and protected their children the best they could. Mothers and fathers taught their daughters and sons what they knew about life and survival, such as how to hunt, fish, and trap food, or how to build canoes and make clothes.

Slaves of color

Some historians point to the large number of mulattoes (muh-LAH-toes; people of mixed white and black ancestry), slave and free, as a sad testimony to the sexual abuse of black women slaves in antebellum America. In 1850 there were 246,000 mulatto slaves in a total slave population of 3.2 million. By 1860, the mulatto slave population had increased to 411,000 out of a total of 3.9 million slaves.

There is no way of telling how many children born to black slave women were the result of consensual relations or rape. There is, however, ample testimony from female slaves that their white masters forced sexual relations on them. A whipping or beating was often the punishment for slaves who resisted, and many slave women carried the scars of their defiance to the grave.

Mulattoes were considered blacks with light complexions. As such they were victimized by the same racial prejudices that held that all blacks, slave or free, were inferior to whites. Mulatto children born to slave mothers, however, were the offspring of white fathers and therefore more likely to receive somewhat better treatment than children born to black slave parents. Relations between white men and free black women, and the manumission of mulatto slaves by their white fathers, accounted for the 159,000 free mulattoes in the United States in 1850.

Organized religion

Slave owners in the South tried to control every part of a slave's life, no matter how personal it was: where and how they worked and lived, who they married and had families with, how they were supposed to behave, and whether they were to be punished. If it was up to the slave owners, they would have controlled their slaves' spiritual lives as well—not that they didn't try.

After the abolitionists started their radical antislavery campaign in the 1830s, many states in the Deep South made it illegal for black preachers to hold services without at least one white person present. By 1835, religious services for blacks, slave or free, had to be presided over by a white minister. In urban areas, slaves were invited to attend the white churches, only to find themselves seated in the balconies or the back pews. On the plantations, owners brought in white preachers for Sunday services, which they attended along with their families. In the name of providing slaves with moral and spiritual guidance, slaves were fed a steady diet of sermons on why they should always obey their masters, work their hardest, and never steal or destroy things.

Slaves in the cities and towns of the upper South, and those states that bordered on the North, were sometimes able to attend separate black churches. There they found a safe forum, free from their white masters, for their religious and political expressions. Blacks, slave or free, could worship and have their children attend Sunday Bible schools with their own community (see "Organized religion," Chapter 9).

A Letter from Emily

Although the law classified slaves as property rather than human beings, slaves lived, loved, married, raised children, worked, worshiped, socialized, and generally did their best to rise above their degraded positions in life. A letter in Blassingame's anthology from a North Carolina slave named Emily to her mother in 1836 illustrates the predicament and suffering of a woman separated from her family by forces beyond her control:

> A cloud has settled upon me and produced a change in my prospect, too great for words to express. My husband is torn from me, and carried away by his master. Mr. Winslow, who married Miss Little, although he was offered $800 for him that we might not be parted, he refused it. I went to see him—tried to prevail on him not to carry my husband away, but to suffer him to be bought for $800, that we might not be separated. But mother—all my entreaties and tears did not soften his hard heart—they availed nothing with him. He said he would 'get his own price for him.' O! mother, what shall I do? The time is fast approaching when I shalt want my husband and mother, and both are gone!

Sacred space

Slaves conducted their own religious services long before they were outlawed in the Deep South in the 1830s, and

First African Baptist Church, founded in 1779, Savannah, Georgia. *Archive Photos, Inc. Reproduced by permission.*

they continued to meet in secret long after they were forbidden to do so. Slaves may have sat patiently with their masters in Sunday services, nodding their heads and saying "Amen" for emphasis every now and then, but they were not blind to their masters' attempts to control them with the fear of God. Nancy Williams, an ex-slave from Virginia (whose words appear in Deborah Gray White's *Let My People Go*), wasn't fooled: "Dat ole white preachin' wasn't nothin'. Old white preachers use to talk with dey tongues widdout sayin' nothin'. But Jesus told us slaves to talk wid our hearts."

Slaves were able to create, through their own religious practices, songs, music, families, and folk beliefs, a sacred space that was untouchable by their white masters. Slaves seemed to be in control of at least one thing in their lives—their own souls. And for guidance, many slaves turned to the Bible. They found comfort in the Old Testament stories of God's deliverance of the Israelites from slavery, and the punishment of the Egyptians for their treatment of his chosen people. Slaves also found comfort in the story of Jesus, a "servant" who suffered from great persecution as well. For slaves, contrary to their masters' designs, the Bible confirmed what they felt in their hearts: the slaveholder, not the slave, was the sinner.

Education

On the plantations of the Deep South, very few slaves received an education. It is estimated that 90 percent of slaves were illiterate (unable to read or write). Officially, no one was allowed to provide any organized instruction of any kind to blacks, slave or free. Occasionally people brave enough to break the law attempted to open schools for blacks, but they were always shut down. If slaves were caught with books or writing materials, they were whipped.

Some slaves, however, did learn to read and write, often with help from their owners. Frederick Douglass (1817–1895), writer and abolitionist, was the most famous example of a slave who learned to read and write from his owner's wife, the mistress of the house (see "Fruit of the vine," Chapter 9). Other slaves somehow managed to learn the basics, perhaps from the white children of the house or other slaves, and then secretly educate themselves.

In the cities and towns of the South, especially the upper South, slaves had a much better chance of learning to read and write, and maybe even receive some schooling. Slaves were constantly exposed to newspapers, books, and pamphlets. Some cities in the upper South even had schools for blacks (see "Education," Chapter 9). In 1847, one such school in Louisville, Kentucky, admitted slaves as students—with their master's permission, of course.

Recreation

Only as very young children did slaves have much time they could truly call their own. In their earliest years slave children on plantations played with the white children. Once slave children reached the age where they could do minor tasks in the fields or around the house (around five or six years old) they were left with little time for playing. As slave children grew into teenagers and young adults, their playing time disappeared altogether, as did their social contact with white children.

Even if slaves found the time, there were very few recreational opportunities available on the plantation. Fishing and hunting were sometimes possible, but the need to bring home something to eat probably made it less relaxing. Some slaves were given permission to attend certain community events, such as fairs and races. Elections and militia gatherings were also occasions for relaxing the rules. Even if most slaves did not go to any of these events, there was often a festive spirit of singing, dancing, and socializing on the plantation on those special days.

The Christmas holiday meant a week off from work—except for cooking and washing duties—for both plantation and city slaves. It was a chance for slaves to visit with family and friends and to celebrate together with singing, dancing, socializing, and presents. Plantation slaves could also look forward to a slow period in the summer, between spring planting and fall harvesting, when their workloads were greatly reduced. Weddings, anniversaries, birthdays, and the like also provided occasions for gatherings and celebrations among slaves.

Free Blacks in Antebellum America

The conditions of freedom

The era between 1800 and the Civil War (1861–1865) is known as the antebellum period (pronounced an-teh-BELL-um), which means "before the war." Life for free black persons in this time period became increasingly harder as tensions mounted between the proslavery South and the antislavery North and the country moved slowly toward civil war. What few rights free blacks had in the colonial and revolutionary periods were for the most part gone by 1835. By the time of the Civil War, especially in the South, the conditions under which free blacks lived were very similar to the conditions of slavery that many thought they had escaped from or, in the case of freeborn blacks, hoped that they would never know.

Free blacks had little claim to the basic rights of citizenship enjoyed by whites. Free blacks were not permitted to move about freely or live where they chose, and they faced harsh penalties for violating those laws. Free blacks were sometimes limited as to what occupations they could pursue. And free blacks found little justice in courts of law, unable even to testify if the case involved whites. Forbidden to vote in almost every state, free blacks had very little power or influence in the political arena as well.

For blacks, the conditions of freedom resembled the conditions of slavery because free or slave, North or South, blacks in antebellum America were treated in a prejudiced way by whites because of the color of their skin. The beliefs and laws that made slavery in America an institution based solely on race pervaded the entire society. Many whites believed that blacks were inferior in every way—physically, morally, spiritually, and intellectually. Deemed unfit for freedom and viewed with hostility and suspicion by whites, blacks trying to attain the same status and prosperity as whites had every possible obstacle placed in their path.

Where free blacks lived

In 1790 there were 59,000 free blacks in the United States: 32,000 in the South and 27,000 in the North. The number of free blacks increased sharply in both the North and the South in the next two decades. From 1810 to 1860, however, that trend was reversed. Laws were passed that made it harder for owners to free their slaves, and the increased profitability of slaves in the cotton belt (see "Cotton and slavery," Chapter 8) also made freedom less likely, as slave owners desired to get the most work possible out of their "investments."

In 1830, there were 319,000 free blacks in the United States. About 16,000 lived as far west as Ohio, Michigan, Indiana, and Illinois. By 1860, there were 488,000 free blacks: 224,000 in the South Atlantic states, 215,000 in the North, and 49,000 in the South Central states and the West. Not surprisingly, the fewest number of free blacks were found in the states that produced the most cotton and held the most slaves—Georgia, Alabama, Mississippi, and Louisiana. Maryland had the most free blacks of any state (83,900), followed by Virginia (58,000) and Pennsylvania (the state's entire black population of 56,000).

Free blacks tended to live in cities, where economic and social opportunities were greater for blacks, free and slave (see box titled "City Slaves," Chapter 8). In 1860 there were 25,600 free blacks in Baltimore, 22,000 in Philadelphia,

Fact Focus

- In 1860, there were 488,000 free blacks in the nation. About half lived in the North and half in the South.

- If found guilty of certain crimes, free blacks were subject to public whippings and the possibility of enslavement, fates that no whites were forced to endure.

- In the North, only five states, four of them in New England, permitted free blacks to vote. Free blacks could not vote anywhere in the South.

- Every state had laws requiring free blacks to be employed. If found guilty of not working, or "loitering," free blacks could be sold into slavery.

- A very small number of free blacks were wealthy business owners and planters. Some even owned slaves.

- In 1794, Richard Allen founded the first independent church for blacks in America, the Bethel African Methodist Episcopal Church (Bethel AME, for short).

- In the last decades before the Civil War, organized religion in the South became one of the strongest allies of the slaveholders.

- In the states of the Deep South, after 1830, it was against the law to educate blacks, free or slave.

- In 1860, there were 32,629 blacks in schools in the United States out of a total population of almost 500,000 free and 4 million enslaved blacks.

- Marriages between free blacks were legal. A free black wishing to marry a slave needed permission from the slave's master.

12,500 in New York, 10,600 in New Orleans, and 3,200 in Charleston. In the South, one out of three free blacks lived in towns or cities.

Paths to freedom

There were a number of different ways for blacks to obtain their freedom, few of which were easy. One way was to be born free. In the slave period in America, the status of the mother—free or slave—determined the status of her children, even if the father was a free man. A small number of free blacks were the offspring of free black women. Some slaves acquired their freedom through manumission (a formal release from bondage) by their owners for having served them well. This was usually done in a master's will at the time of his or her death.

Slaves were sometimes able to buy their own freedom or the freedom of family members. The price depended on the circumstances, but it was usually set at what the slave would cost on the open market. It is not known how many slaves made enough money, through earning extra wages as hired-out laborers, to take advantage of this opportunity. In an 1863 interview with a congressional commission investigating slavery included in Blassingame's *Slave Testimony*, Mrs. L. Strawthor, an ex-slave from Kentucky, described how she and her family bought their freedom:

> I reckon it is about fifteen or sixteen years since I bought myself. I paid $800 for myself and two children. This house belongs to me, but the ground is leased. I pay $51 a year for the ground. My house was burned about eight years ago and was not insured. I make my living at washing: I had a husband when I got my freedom. He bought me for $300 ... and then we went to work and bought the children.

The most radical path to freedom for slaves was to run away from their owners. The chances of getting caught were high, and the penalties were harsh. One historian estimated that each year about 1,000 slaves chose this option. Many fugitive slaves fled to the cities of the South where they hoped to blend in with the crowd and pass as free blacks. Some made longer journeys and escaped to the free soil of the northern states, the western frontier, or Canada.

Free but not equal

A free black person in antebellum America enjoyed few of the rights and privileges usually associated with freedom. Citizenship for whites at this time, it should be noted, was limited to white males. It meant the right to vote, to be elected, to serve on juries, to conduct one's business and move about freely, to be educated, and to serve in militias. If the freedom of free blacks were measured against these standards, their status appears to have been just slightly better than the enslaved black population.

For a short period of time, free black males could vote in Maryland, North Carolina, New York, and Pennsylvania.

A newspaper depiction of a fugitive slave, 1837. Although the odds were stacked against them and the penalties were terrible, many attempted to escape from slavery; some succeeded.

Their state constitutions had been written during the country's revolutionary period and influenced by the ideals of the times—equality and liberty. By 1838 all of these states had taken away the voting rights of free blacks. In the North, only five states, four of them in New England, permitted free blacks to vote. Without widespread voting rights, free blacks' right to be elected was beyond consideration.

In courts of law, free blacks could not serve on juries. They were not even allowed to testify in court if the case involved whites. Yet the courts permitted slaves—who had no legal standing in courts otherwise—to testify against free blacks. The punishments for free blacks convicted of the same crimes as whites were always more severe. Free blacks were subject to public whippings and the possibility of enslavement, fates that no whites were forced to endure. Courts of law, especially the higher courts, did provide some degree of protection to free blacks. In one such case, the North Carolina Supreme Court ruled that a free black had the right to strike a white in self-defense.

Unfree to move

Nowhere in the South could a free black move about without restrictions. In North Carolina, for example, free blacks could not legally travel farther than the next county from where they lived. Registration was required for free blacks in Virginia, Tennessee, Georgia, and Mississippi. In Florida, Georgia, and a few other states, free blacks had to have a white guardian who would vouch for their good behavior. Throughout the South, free blacks were required to have passes; without the proper certificate or official identification, free blacks were assumed to be fugitive slaves. In Charleston, both freed blacks and slaves were required to wear identification badges that indicated their status.

Some states also limited the movement of free blacks coming into and leaving the state. Many states required freed slaves to leave the state once they had been manumitted. In Georgia, a free black who left the state for sixty days or more was not allowed to return. Georgia, as well as most of the southern and several of the northern states, also had laws prohibiting the migration of free blacks. Penalties for breaking these laws were severe, usually a stiff fine that was impossible to pay, which then resulted in the free black being sold into slavery.

Even in the nonslaveholding states of the North and West, states placed restrictions on free blacks' movements that were designed to discourage or prevent them from moving into the state. As in the South, free blacks were required to register their certificates of freedom with the county clerk. In some communities, they also had to pay a bond of $500 or $1,000 as a guarantee that they would not disturb the peace or become wards of the state.

Losing freedom

Free blacks were always in danger of losing their freedom. Freeborn blacks and ex-slaves were constantly challenged to prove that they were not slaves. For black people, having the proper official papers to prove their free status helped, but it did not guarantee that they would remain free. Such was the case of Solomon Northrup, whose story of being kidnaped by slave dealers was told in an 1863 *New York Times* article. Northrup, born a free black in the state of New York in 1803, was on business in Washington City in 1841 when he fell ill in a hotel room. The article told the story of his kidnaping and enslavement:

> While suffering with severe pains some persons came in, and, seeing the condition he was in, proposed to give him some medicine and did so. That is the last thing of which he had any recollection until he found himself chained to the floor of Williams' slave pen in this City, and handcuffed. In the course of a few hours, James H. Burch, a slave dealer, came in, and the colored man [Northrup] asked him to take the irons off of him, and wanted to know why they were put on. Burch told him it was none of his business. The colored man said he was free and told where he was born. Burch called in a man by the name of Ebenezer Rodbury, and the two stripped the man and

laid him across a bench, Rodbury holding him down by the wrists. Burch whipped him with a paddle until he broke that, and then with a cat-o'-nine tails [a whip with nine knotted cords], giving him a hundred lashes, and he swore he would kill him if he ever stated to any one that he was a free man. From that time forward the man says he did not communicate the fact from fear, either that he was a free man, or what his name was, until the last summer.

Solomon Northrup was sold to a plantation in Louisiana, where he spent nearly ten years as a slave—a field hand and carpenter. He regained his freedom, with much legal help from his friends in New York, when a court ruled that Northrup was a victim of an illegal kidnaping.

Work

Every state had laws requiring free blacks to be employed. If found guilty of not working, or "loitering," free blacks could be sold into slavery for periods of time as the courts saw fit. If the guilty party had children, they were put into the custody of white persons, who usually put them to work. Many states had rules that restricted the ways that free blacks could make a living. Some states prohibited free blacks from buying or selling certain goods, such as corn, wheat, tobacco, and alcohol, without special licenses. In South Carolina, free blacks could not be clerks; in Georgia, they could not be typesetters.

Free blacks seeking work, especially ones with skills, often faced strong and organized opposition from whites. White artisans tried to get laws passed that prevented blacks from working in certain trades. Where that failed, white tradespeople used violence and bullying tactics to secure work and eliminate competition from free blacks. White workers everywhere, in the North, South, and West, refused to work next to blacks. This forced white employers to turn away qualified black workers or risk having their entire white workforce walk off the job.

Still, free blacks found employment in the towns and cities where many of the white workers had left for the western frontier. Free blacks worked in many different skilled trades and professions; some were carpenters, architects,

druggists, photographers, barbers, tailors, jewelers, furniture makers—even teachers and dentists.

Free blacks seeking employment who had no special skills, and that was most of them, had an even harder time finding work. Even those who made it to the North found

Levee roustabouts (laborers) on the Mississippi River in New Orleans unloading barrels from a ship. *Archive Photos, Inc. Reproduced by permission.*

that many of the unskilled jobs, such as ditchdigger, street cleaner, and porter, were taken by poor German and Irish immigrants. The vast majority of free blacks ended up working for substandard wages as agricultural workers and in the cities and towns as common laborers. Some unskilled free blacks found work in the lowest-paying jobs in urban-based industries of the South, such as tobacco factories, paper mills, and iron foundries.

Property and prosperity

Free blacks were allowed to own property in every state. In 1837, free blacks owned $1.5 million worth of real estate in New York City and had more than $600,000 deposited in savings accounts. In 1860, free blacks in Virginia owned more than 60,000 acres of farmland and city real estate valued at almost $500,000. In New Orleans, free blacks owned more than $15 million worth of property.

Some blacks were able to acquire their first home or piece of land with financial help from organizations such as the Society of Friends (Quakers), the Pennsylvania Society for the Abolition of Slavery, or the North Carolina Manumission Society. Some blacks acquired property from their masters at the time of their manumission. Still others accumulated enough money through sheer hard work and thrifty lifestyles to buy a small piece of land or house.

Some free blacks became wealthy property owners and businesspeople. A fortunate few became successful hotel owners, grocers, sail makers, and even plantation owners. Some free blacks even owned slaves. Instances were known of free blacks in the Charleston area and around New Orleans who owned estates with as many ninety-one slaves. More often, if free blacks owned slaves, they did not own many of them and they usually had some personal connection to their "property." Husbands, wives, children, relatives, and friends sometimes purchased each other or were bought from white owners by wealthy free blacks.

It must be stressed that free blacks who acquired property or prosperity were not typical. Most free blacks barely scratched out a living, and what little property or housing

they might possess most likely really belonged to the creditors and banks.

Benevolent societies

Wherever possible, in both the North and the South, free blacks formed organizations, independent of churches and dedicated to the betterment of their people. They formed so-called benevolent societies (benevolent means "good") and fraternal organizations (fraternal means "brotherly"). These organizations were supported by dues from their members, who received such benefits as burial expenses, yearly incomes for widows and orphans of deceased members, and a form of unemployment insurance for disabled workers.

Benevolent societies provided many services for the black community, including schools for orphan children and help for the sick and disabled. Some societies were dedicated

Members of the Pennsylvania Society for the Abolition of Slavery, one of the groups that helped freedmen and strove to abolish the institution of slavery. The renowned abolitionist and journalist William Lloyd Garrison (1805-1879) is at the bottom right. *National Portrait Gallery.*

to gaining better wages and job security for black workers. Others were known more for their recreational activities and events that featured dancing, singing, and socializing. Baltimore's Society for Relief in Case of Seizure existed as a safeguard against free blacks being kidnaped into slavery.

By 1815 the Masons, a fraternal organization founded in Boston before the American Revolution, had four lodges (branches) in Philadelphia. They pooled their resources and built the country's first black Masonic Hall. Only one benevolent society existed in Baltimore in 1821. By 1835 there were thirty-five such groups with names such as the Friendship Benevolent Society for Social Relief, the Star in the East Association, and the Daughters of Jerusalem. Another major black fraternal organization, called the Grand United Order of Odd Fellows, was founded in 1843.

Black benevolent societies existed in the Deep South but were not welcomed by whites. Some communities even made it illegal to join one. Elsewhere in antebellum America, however, benevolent societies were very important social, cultural, and economic organizations for the free blacks who were members and for the black community at large.

Organized religion

Religion, especially Christianity, had a special meaning for blacks in antebellum America. Freed blacks often saw their manumissions as religious experiences, a rebirth made possible by the same God who had delivered the Jews from slavery in the Bible's Old Testament.

Free blacks had more control over their religious practices than slaves. They could choose to attend services with the whites or to practice their faith at black churches. Blacks who worshiped with whites in the Methodist, Baptist, Episcopal, and Presbyterian churches were often segregated from the white congregations, forced to sit in balconies or in pews at the back of the church. They had very little say in how the churches were governed.

Most free blacks belonged to Baptist churches. As early as the 1770s, a few black Baptist churches were established in Georgia and Virginia. But it was in the major cities

A service at an African
church in Cincinnati, Ohio.
*Archive Photos, Inc. Reproduced
by permission.*

of the North and West—Philadelphia, New York, Boston, Cincinnati, Detroit, and Chicago—that the Baptist church flourished. Where separate black Baptist churches existed, they were usually associated with a white Baptist church in the same area. Consequently, black Baptists did not have the same kind of network for communicating and organizing that black Methodists had established through the African Methodist Episcopal (AME) Church (see below).

The AME Church

A dispute over segregated church services led to the founding of the first independent church for blacks in America. In 1794, Richard Allen (1760–1831) founded the nation's first black Methodist church. Allen was born a slave but saved enough money to buy his own freedom from his

master in Delaware. In 1777, Allen moved to Philadelphia and became a preacher. When the officials of St. George Church, where he frequently preached, proposed separate seating for the large numbers of blacks who came to hear him, Allen left the church in protest. In 1787, Allen established the Free African Society, the first independent self-improvement organization for blacks in the nation. And in 1794, Allen and others founded the Bethel African Methodist Episcopal Church (Bethel AME, for short).

Bethel AME was the only black Methodist church in America until 1816. That year sixteen black Methodist congregations, from New York, New Jersey, Delaware, and Maryland, came together for a convention at Allen's church in Philadelphia. Together they withdrew from the white-dominated mother church and formed the nation's first independent black church, the African Methodist Episcopal (AME) Church. In this meeting, Allen was ordained a church elder and the AME Church's first bishop.

Richard Allen (1760-1831), the first bishop of the African Methodist Episcopal (AME) Church. AME was the first all-black religious denomination in the United States and is currently the largest African American Methodist denomination, with more than 2 million members. *Archive Photos, Inc. Reproduced by permission.*

Antislavery activism

AME Church membership grew as independent black churches opened throughout the North. As free blacks moved into the West, they founded more AME churches. By 1830, the AME Church had members in Canada, Haiti, and West Africa. The various churches all maintained connections with one another, and as an internationally organized network, they became very important in the antislavery struggle that took shape in the early 1800s.

Bethel AME, the mother church in Philadelphia, was very committed to ending slavery. Many of the leaders of the abolition movement—Frederick Douglass, Lucretia Mott,

and William Forten, to name a few—spoke from the church's pulpit. The basement of the church housed runaway slaves and was a "station" in the Underground Railroad, a secret network that helped slaves escape to free soil (see box titled "The Underground Railroad," Chapter 10). Bethel AME also raised large amounts of money to feed, clothe, and educate the black community, especially slaves seeking freedom.

Mother Bethel African Methodist Episcopal (AME) Church, Philadelphia, the first all-black church in the United States. *Archive Photos, Inc. Reproduced by permission.*

Names of Freedom

One of the first rights exercised by slaves who gained their freedom was to legally acquire a new name. As slaves, their masters had given them their names and often chose names that seemed to mock their slaves' degraded position in life—such as Caesar (a great Roman general) or Cato (a great Roman orator). Most masters recognized their slaves by their first name only, though many slaves took their master's surname (last name) as their own. When freed, many blacks saw advantages to being associated with their former white masters and kept their master's surname, but they often changed their first and second names.

Most free blacks chose English, not African, names. It was one way of trying to blend in and gain acceptance in the United States. Some blacks chose surnames based on the complexion of their skin, which explains why a great number of freed blacks had the last names Brown or Black. Other blacks chose names that reflected their occupations. A bricklayer might take Mason as a surname, gardeners perhaps chose Green, and blacksmiths and silversmiths found the name Smith appropriate. Some, inspired by their newly found liberty, chose surnames like

Sojourner Truth (c. 1797–1883), one-time slave, preacher, abolitionist, and feminist. Truth's slave name was Isabella Baumfree. She took the name Sojourner Truth in 1843 as she set out on foot as an itinerant preacher traveling from place to place. *Archive Photos, Inc. Reproduced by permission.*

Justice and Freeman. Others chose names from the Bible, such as Moses and Gabriel. A famous and highly skilled traveling preacher took the literal approach when she chose the name of Sojourner Truth (sojourner means "a temporary resident," or a traveler).

Proslavery activism

Between 1800 and 1830, there were at least three serious incidents of organized rebellion among slaves in the South (see "Major uprisings," Chapter 10). Many whites suspected that the revolts had been planned at religious gatherings, where they feared slaves had been incited by abolitionist literature. By 1835, most free blacks in the South had lost the right of free assembly. Any religious gathering of blacks, free or slave, had to be attended by a licensed white minister. Black ministers of the various denominations—Episcopal, Methodist, Baptist, and Presbyterian—were forced to leave their posts. Some ministers moved their congregations to the North.

In the last decades before the Civil War, the white-dominated churches of the South became the strongest allies of the slaveholders. Bishops and other high officials of the various churches were slaveholders themselves. One Episcopal bishop in Louisiana owned more than 400 slaves. In general, Presbyterians and Quakers did not own as many slaves as did the members of the Episcopal Church (in the Atlantic seaboard states) and the Baptist and Methodist Churches (in the cotton-belt states).

Education

In the Deep South, it was against the law to educate blacks, free or slave. White southerners were afraid that blacks who could read might be exposed to abolitionist literature or other rebellious ideas. Any organized attempts to establish public schools for blacks were strongly opposed by whites and ultimately failed. The small number of blacks who learned basic literacy skills were taught privately; some even taught themselves.

In the upper South and the North, free blacks had a better chance of receiving an education. Many communities provided public education for blacks. Although there were exceptions—in Boston after 1855, for example—blacks had to attend separate schools from whites. Separate schools for blacks were established in Massachusetts, Rhode Island, Connecticut, New York, New Jersey, and Pennsylvania. The existence of schools for blacks did not necessarily mean that they received a quality public education, as many states and localities never provided proper funding for their black school systems.

Public education opportunities for blacks in the West were very limited. Though free blacks were often forced to pay taxes to support public schools, they were not always allowed to send their children to those schools. In 1829, Ohio passed a law excluding blacks altogether from public schools.

Twenty years later, Ohio permitted black schools but provided very little financial support for them. Most free blacks in Indiana, Illinois, Michigan, and Wisconsin had to wait until after the Civil War before they were educated in any great numbers at the public's expense.

Self-help

In 1860, there were only 32,629 blacks in schools in the United States out of a total population of almost 500,000 free and 4 million enslaved blacks. In the absence of public education for blacks in antebellum America, black churches—at least where they were allowed to operate—filled the void as best they could. Many black churches ran Sunday Bible schools for children, and some churches offered regular classes during the weekdays for free or a small fee. By the 1850s, the AME Church was operating primary and secondary schools for blacks in many cities, including Philadelphia and Baltimore. Schools for blacks were established in other cities as well; some were made possible by large donations from individual wealthy free blacks, while others were funded by donations from black benevolent societies.

Black churches and benevolent societies also established institutions of higher learning for blacks. In 1856, the AME Church founded Wilberforce University in Ohio, and before the end of the century, the church set up four more colleges for blacks in Florida, South Carolina, Texas, and Georgia. Colleges for blacks established independently of black churches included the Institute for Colored Youth in Philadelphia (1842) and Avery College (1849) in Allegheny City, Pennsylvania. Before the Civil War, some blacks were also attending predominantly white colleges such as Oberlin, Franklin, Rutland, and Harvard University.

Fruit of the vine

The efforts of the black churches, schools, benevolent societies, and fraternal organizations of antebellum America produced a new class of educated and socially active blacks. Some of the greatest black leaders—the preachers, teachers, orators, and organizers who were to become so important in the struggle for the abolition of slavery—emerged from these black institutions.

Black poets, novelists, essayists, playwrights, historians, and newspaper editors were finally able to deliver black perspectives to the white population in their own voices. Black-owned and operated newspapers sprang up: *Freedom's Journal* started in 1827, and Frederick Douglass began publishing *North Star* in 1847.

The largest group of black writers were freed slaves, manumitted or fugitives, who wrote about their experiences in the first-person "narrative" form. Many of these autobiographies were published from 1840 to 1860, sometimes with help from the abolitionists who used them in their arguments against slavery. Perhaps the most famous and influential of them all was published in 1845, simply titled *Narrative of the Life of Frederick Douglass*. Other narratives published before the Civil War were written by William Wells Brown (1842), Lunsford Lane (1842), Moses Grady (1844), Lewis Clarke (1846), Julius Melbourne (1847), Henry Bibb (1849), J. W. C. Pennington (1850), Solomon Northrup (1853), Austin Steward (1857), and J. W. Longuen (1859).

CLOTEL;

OR,

THE PRESIDENT'S DAUGHTER:

A Narrative of Slave Life

IN

THE UNITED STATES.

BY

WILLIAM WELLS BROWN,

A FUGITIVE SLAVE, AUTHOR OF "THREE YEARS IN EUROPE."

With a Sketch of the Author's Life.

"We hold these truths to be self-evident : that all men are created equal ; that they are endowed by their Creator with certain inalienable rights, and that among these are LIFE, LIBERTY, and the PURSUIT OF HAPPINESS."—*Declaration of American Independence.*

The title page of William Wells Brown's novel *Clotel; or, The President's Daughter: A Narrative of Slave Life in the United States* (1853), the first published novel written by a black person in the United States.

Family

Family life for free blacks was much stabler than for enslaved blacks. Unlike slave marriages, unions between free blacks were legal and fairly secure, in that the married couple was not likely to be broken up by one of the partners being sold to another part of the country. Official marriages between free blacks, as between whites, required a marriage license and a formal civil or religious ceremony. If a free black wished to marry a slave, permission from the slave's owner was necessary. These unions were more informal and usually took place without a license from the state. Relations and marriages between free blacks and whites or Indians were also informal. Mixed-race couples were not allowed to marry.

In every state, free blacks were required by law to work and to support their children in a very visible way. Officials of the state had the power to declare parents "unfit" and could force the children into legal apprenticeships. Thousands of free black families in both the North and the South were broken up this way, as children were taken away from their parents and forced to work for white tradespeople for periods up to twenty-eight years.

The Abolition Movement

Early abolitionists

The Quakers (the Society of Friends, a religious body founded in England in 1647), played an important role in the early antislavery movement in England and its American colonies. Some Quakers based their opposition to slavery on their religion. One of the central beliefs of the Quakers was in the complete equality of humankind. Some used the Bible as a source for their arguments against slavery. Individual Quakers spoke out against it as early as 1657, but their ideas did not carry much weight in the organization, as Quaker leaders in London, Pennsylvania, and Rhode Island were deeply involved in the trans-Atlantic slave trade and owned slaves themselves.

In the United States, from the early 1700s, slavery became a controversial issue at most meetings of the Society. For example, in 1755, the Philadelphia yearly meeting ordered that members who traded in slaves should be officially admonished. In 1776, the Philadelphia meeting ruled that members would be dismissed from the Society if they did not free their slaves and provide them with compensation. The Quakers' opposition to slavery was largely responsible for

Pennsylvania declaring slavery illegal in 1780. (The Pennsylvania Colony, founded by William Penn, a British Quaker leader, had a large population of Quakers.)

Between 1780 and 1808, many state abolition and manumission (a formal release from bondage) societies were formed. Led by Quakers, evangelicals (Christian preachers of many denominations), and humanitarians, these early abolitionists aimed to end slavery gradually. They favored first ending the slave trade, then emancipating slaves over a period of time while providing compensation to the slaveholders. To that end, they petitioned and lobbied state legislatures from Massachusetts to Virginia. They secured legislation that prevented slavery in the Northwest Territory (1787), that shortened the apprenticeship periods for children of slaves in the North (see "Family," Chapter 9), and that prohibited U.S. participation in the trans-Atlantic slave trade (1807).

Abolition in the North

During the same time period (1780–1808), slavery became illegal in the North, either as the result of court rulings, as in Massachusetts in 1783, or as a result of acts passed by state legislatures, as in Connecticut and Rhode Island in 1784, New York in 1799, and New Jersey in 1804. It is hard to say how much credit for these changes belongs to the antislavery movement. Certainly the states in the North, where there were relatively few slaves, were more ready for change than the South.

The ideas of freedom and equality spawned by the American Revolution were still fresh in the North, and the influence of prominent whites who spoke out against slavery was also a significant factor in the postwar antislavery movement. No one as mighty as Thomas Jefferson or George Washington (who both owned slaves; see "Founding Fathers," Chapter 7) publicly spoke out against slavery, but some of society's leading white citizens took up the cause, such as Philadelphia's Benjamin Franklin (1706–1790; statesman, scientist, and philosopher) and Benjamin Rush (1745–1813; statesman, physician, and educator). Other leading whites who publicly opposed slavery included scholar Samuel Hopkins (1721–1803) of Rhode Island, clergyman Ezra Stiles (1727–1795) of Connecticut, clergyman and educator Jedidi-

Fact Focus

- The Society of Friends (Quakers) became a major force in the early antislavery movement in America and England.

- The African slave trade was illegal in England and the United States beginning in 1808.

- The American Colonization Society formed in 1816 and planned to ship blacks to a West African colony named Liberia, the "land of freedom."

- The Antislavery Society formed in England in 1823, and by 1826 it had seventy-one local chapters.

- During the 1830s, the British Royal Navy led patrols that captured an average of thirty slave ships off the African coasts each year, freeing 5,000 slaves.

- When the American Antislavery Society formed in 1833, only three blacks were among the sixty-two signers of the Society's Declaration of Sentiments.

- In the 200 years leading up to the Civil War, slaves engaged in about 250 serious revolts, conspiracies, and uprisings.

- In 1830, the first Free People of Color Congress met in Philadelphia and started what came to be known as the National Negro Convention Movement.

- In 1831, William Lloyd Garrison began publication of the abolitionist newspaper *The Liberator.*

- By 1840 there were more than 100 antislavery and abolition societies in the free states of the North, with at least 200,000 black and white members.

- From 1828 to 1845, the U.S. House of Representatives refused to even consider antislavery petitions from abolitionists.

- The autobiography of Frederick Douglass, *Narrative of the Life of Frederick Douglass,* became an international bestseller in 1845.

- In the fifty years before the Civil War, at least 3,200 "conductors" helped about 75,000 slaves escape to freedom on the Underground Railroad.

ah Morse (1761–1826) of Massachusetts, and author and dictionary creator Noah Webster (1758–1843) of Connecticut.

British abolitionists

The Society of Friends became a force in the antislavery movement in America and England. In 1761, the Quakers in England forbade their members to trade in slaves. The first abolitionist organization in England, The Meeting for Sufferers, was

founded in London by Quakers in 1783. That same year they petitioned Parliament (England's legislative body) to make slave trading illegal. In 1787, the various British abolitionist organizations came together to form the Society for Effecting the Abolition of the Slave Trade. In early 1807, after great pressure from the abolitionists and repeated legislative attempts in the House of Commons (one of the two sections of Parliament) led by William Wilberforce (1759–1833), Parliament outlawed the slave trade. The law took effect on January 1, 1808.

English Quakers and other abolitionists had an easier time than their American counterparts in their battle to end slavery. Slavery in England itself had been made illegal in 1772 in a historic decision by Lord Chief Justice Mansfield that freed some 15,000 slaves then living in the country. After the slave trade became illegal in 1808, the English abolitionists set their sights on ending slavery in all lands under British control. Wilberforce helped establish the Antislavery Society in 1823, and by 1826 it had seventy-one local chapters in England, with many Quakers as members and supporters. After years of intense political lobbying, on August 29, 1833, Parliament passed the Emancipation Act, freeing all slaves in the British Empire after a five-year period.

Abolition on the Atlantic

Beginning in 1808, the trans-Atlantic slave trade was no longer legal for American citizens or British subjects. The United States banned the trade according to an agreement reached at the Constitutional Convention twenty years earlier (see "A country divided," Chapter 11). The Danish, in 1804, were the first Europeans to ban the slave trade, but it was the British who took the leading role against the African slave trade among slaveholding nations.

Unlike the Americans, who outlawed the trans-Atlantic slave trade but made few provisions for catching and punishing violators, the British passed laws that contained harsh penalties for violators and rewards for those who caught them. Any British ship used in slave trading was confiscated by the government, and the owners were fined £100 for each slave bought, sold, or transported. British soldiers and sailors were paid a bounty for each captured ship and each freed slave. In 1808, after the slave trade was outlawed, two British ships were immediately sent to patrol the Atlantic coast of West Africa with the sole mission of intercepting slave traders.

After the end of the Napoleonic Wars with France in 1815, the British could dispatch more ships from the Royal Navy to the West African coasts for antislavery patrols. In the meantime, other countries had passed laws against the African slave trade: the Dutch in 1814 and the French and Portuguese in 1815. By 1820, most countries (except the United States) had granted the British the rights to search and seize slave ships sailing under their nations' flags. For many years, until the British and United States began "joint cruising" in the 1840s, slave ships could evade British and French searches simply by flying the American flag and claiming to be an American vessel.

A watercolor of the slave quarters of the Spanish ship *Albanoz,* painted by Lt. Francis Meinell of the British Royal Navy, whose ship captured the *Albanoz. The Granger Collection, New York. Reproduced by permission.*

The slave trade persists

In the 1830s, the United States and France stationed their own antislavery patrols off the West African coast. On the average, thirty slave ships were captured each year, and 5,000 slaves were freed and relocated to a colony in Sierra Leone, a small country on the West African coast. The number of freed slaves, however, was small when compared with the 80,000 to 90,000 slaves that were successfully transported to North and South America each year.

The United States protected slave ships by refusing to allow other countries to search American vessels, and many slave ships were still being outfitted (made ready to carry slaves) in U.S. ports. By the 1850s, two out of every three slave ships captured had been rigged by the Americans. And planters in the U.S. South kept the demand for African slaves high despite the ban (see "The African slave trade," Chapter 8). How many slaves were illegally brought into the United States after 1808 is impossible to know, but the effect of the Union's blockade of Southern ports in the U.S. Civil War (1861–1865) provides a clue. From 1860 to 1865, the number of slaves transported to the Western Hemisphere dropped from about 25,000 a year to around 7,000 a year.

Slave resistance

Slaves' resistance to slavery took on many forms, from passive to active, from individual to group, and from peaceful to violent. One passive strategy was for slaves to put on a show of obedience and meekness in front of their owners and overseers. Slaves sometimes faked being sick or wounded to avoid work. Behind their masters' backs, they worked as slowly as possible, or not at all—just enough to avoid the whip. In some cases, slaves cut off their own hands or toes or disabled themselves by other means as a way of taking revenge on their owners. Suicide was also common, and cases of infanticide (mothers killing their children) were not unheard of.

Slaves also directly resisted their owners in more violent ways. Slaves broke tools, destroyed crops, and worked farm animals to death. Slaves burned their masters' possessions with a vengeance. They torched crops, forests, barns, sheds, and homes. There were also many cases of slaves killing their masters or overseers—violently attacking them in the fields or silently poisoning them at mealtimes with arsenic or ground glass mixed in with gravy or other food.

One of the most effective ways to deprive a slave owner of his "property's" benefits was for the slave to run away. Men, women, and children fled from their owners by the thousands, alone, in pairs, and in groups. Their chances

The following labels appear on the map:

MAINE

MINNESOTA

WISCONSIN

VERMONT · NEW HAMPSHIRE

NEW YORK

MICHIGAN

MASSACHUSETTS

RHODE ISLAND

CONNECTICUT

UNORGANIZED TERRITORY

IOWA

ILLINOIS · INDIANA · OHIO

PENNSYLVANIA

NEW JERSEY

DELAWARE · MARYLAND

VIRGINIA

MISSOURI

KENTUCKY

TENNESSEE

NORTH CAROLINA

SOUTH CAROLINA

ARKANSAS

TEXAS

ALABAMA

GEORGIA

MISSISSIPPI · FLORIDA

LOUISIANA

Mississippi River

Hudson R.

☐ Free state
■ Slave state

Map showing some of the routes taken by slaves escaping on the Underground Railroad.

of being caught were high, and the punishments were harsh. How many tried, and succeeded or failed, is not known, but the number of fugitive slaves must have been significant, judging by the large number of newspaper advertisements offering rewards for their capture and return.

Some slaves fled to the northern states or Canada with the help of the Underground Railroad (see box on page

185). Other fugitive slaves tried to blend in with the free black populations in southern cities. Still others chose to band together in small camps in the swamps, forests, and mountains of the South, harassing the planters and stealing from them whenever possible.

Revolts and rebellions

From all appearances, it seems that southern slave owners led a double life. In public, they argued that blacks were very happy to be slaves, living and working under their masters' kindhearted supervision. In private, however, slaveholders often feared for their lives, especially in the Deep South, where slaves outnumbered their masters by quite a margin. The passage of the Black Codes (see Chapter 8), with their incredibly harsh restrictions on blacks, slave and free, were the products of a ruling class that felt unsafe and insecure in their position of power.

Despite the harsh consequences, however, a number of slaves led uprisings against their masters. If one of the definitions of heroism is acting out of one's sense of rightness without regard to the consequences, the thousands of slaves who revolted against slavery were surely heroes. They proved to their masters and their own people that blacks wanted freedom so badly that they would die fighting for it. If ending slavery was their goal, not one of the uprisings succeeded. Most rebel slaves ended up dead, not free. Their actions, however, forced the nation to confront the conditions of slavery that drove the slaves to organized rebellion and violence. Slave revolts, such as the one led by Nat Turner in 1831 (see below), also inspired the abolitionists to fight harder in their war to end slavery.

The record

The very first slave revolt in what is now the United States actually occurred in 1526 in the first known settlement on mainland North America (see "Slaves come to North America," Chapter 7). Of the 600 people who arrived in what historians believe was South Carolina, 500 were Spanish colonists and 100 were African slaves. Illness claimed the lives of many Spaniards, including their leader. The slaves revolted, and many fled to live with the local Indians. The remaining 150 settlers fled to Haiti, leaving the rebel slaves as the first permanent immigrants in America.

The first serious slave conspiracy in British North America occurred in Gloucester County, Virginia, in 1663. Very little is known about the event except that it involved slaves who planned to overthrow their masters and secure their freedom. The plot was betrayed by a white indentured servant, and the bloody heads of the unsuccessful rebels were displayed on local chimney tops.

One historian calculated that in the 200 years leading up to the Civil War, slaves engaged in about 250 serious revolts (conspiracies and uprisings). For a slave rebellion to be included in this count, it had to involve a minimum of ten slaves, and freedom had to be their goal. In the colonial period, slave uprisings occurred wherever there were slaves, from New York City to New Orleans. In antebellum (pronounced an-teh-BELL-um; meaning "before the war") America, slave revolts were confined to the slaveholding states of the South.

Major uprisings

Jemmy (1739)
One of the most significant early slave revolts occurred on September 9, 1739, at Stono, South Carolina (about twenty miles outside Charleston). Historians disagree on the name of the slave who led the uprising; some refer to him as Cato. The best information seems to point to a man named Jemmy as the man who led slaves in the killing of two warehouse guards and the seizure of weapons and ammunition. Jemmy, along with about 100 slaves who joined him on the way, began marching south to Spanish-held Florida, where they would be free.

Along the way they killed about twenty whites before the local militia formed a roadblock and fought the armed slaves in an intense battle. About fifty slaves were killed by the time the rebellion was over. Fourteen died in battle, and the rest of the captured slaves were either shot or hanged on

The Underground Railroad

The network of people, black and white, who guided runaway slaves to freedom and who sheltered them along the way came to be known as the Underground Railroad. The system began to take shape as early as the 1780s, when Quakers in a number of towns in Pennsylvania and New Jersey began assisting slaves in their escape. By 1819, towns in Ohio and North Carolina were acting as way stations and shelters for fugitive slaves. Long before the militant era of abolitionism began in 1831, the Underground Railroad was an established antislavery institution. Historians estimate that in the fifty years before the Civil War, at least 3,200 "conductors" helped about 75,000 slaves escape to freedom.

The term "Underground Railroad" was probably invented after 1831, about the time that steam railroads became popular. Some of the Underground Railroad's "lines" shared names with the nineteenth-century railroads that ran the same routes. In the early days, the "railroad" to freedom for fugitive slaves (mostly men) was a route traveled on foot, mostly at night, through swamps, up creek beds, across rivers, and over hills, using only the North Star as a guide.

As the traffic got heavier and more women and children slaves fled the South, escorts were provided and vehicles such as covered wagons and carriages were used to transport the human cargo from one "station" to the next. During the day, the fugitive slaves were hidden in barns and attics, where they would rest, eat, and prepare for the next leg of their journey.

The activities of the Underground Railroad were illegal, and people risked fines, jail, and sometimes death for participating. While the network's success depended on the coordination of hundreds of operators and conductors along the way, a few individuals stand out for their incredible accomplishments. Harriet Tubman, herself a runaway slave, made at least nineteen trips into the South and helped guide more than 300 slaves north to freedom. Levi Coffin, a Quaker and "president" of the Underground Railroad, helped more than 3,000 slaves escape. John Fairchild left his slaveholding family in Virginia and, posing as a slave trader and egg peddler, helped hundreds of slaves escape north from Louisiana, Alabama, Mississippi, Tennessee, and Kentucky.

the spot. Some of the heads of the defeated rebels were placed on milepost markers that lined the road back to Charleston. In response to the rebellion, South Carolina passed the Negro Act, making it illegal for blacks to assemble in groups, earn money, or learn to read. The Negro Act became the model for the Black Codes in the rest of the South.

A slave in New York City being burned at the stake after being found guilty of insurrection, 1741. *Archive Photos, Inc. Reproduced by permission.*

Gabriel Prosser (1800)

The so-called Gabriel Conspiracy, which took place in Henrico County, Virginia, was the first large-scale uprising planned, and as such, it struck sheer terror into the hearts of white slaveholders across the nation. A slave named Gabriel Prosser believed that God had chosen him to deliver his people from slavery. He persuaded his wife, family, and friends to join him in the effort. They made crude weapons—swords, bayonets, clubs, and even bullets for the few guns they had—and recruited more slaves. In a matter of a few months, they were ready to march on the city of Richmond, hoping to ignite a widespread rebellion among all slaves. On the night of August 30, 1800, about 1,000 armed slaves, some on horseback, met six miles outside the city, ready to attack.

Meanwhile, Governor James Monroe (1758–1831; later the fifth president of the United States) had learned of the plot. He declared martial law and called into service more than 650 troops to defend the city. As fate would have it, the slaves were unable to march on Richmond on the appointed night: an incredibly heavy rainstorm washed out a bridge that the rebels needed to cross to get to the city. They were forced to scatter, and in the days following the aborted attack most of the rebels were hunted down and captured. At least thirty-five rebels, including Gabriel Prosser, were hanged.

Denmark Vesey (1822)

The conspiracy led by Denmark Vesey (pronounced VEE-zee) in 1822 was one of the most significant and wide-reaching attempts to strike back at slavery. Vesey, who had purchased his freedom in 1800, made a respectable living as a hard-working carpenter. He was a literate man who hated slavery. In 1816, Vesey and other free blacks established a separate black Methodist church in Charleston, South Carolina. By 1820, the church had about 3,000 members, nearly one-third of the total membership of the country's African Methodist Episcopal Church (see "The AME Church," Chapter 9). The whites in Charleston shut down the African church in 1820, angering its members and inciting Vesey to action.

In December 1821, Vesey started to organize the area's slaves for an attack on Charleston. Vesey was the only non-slave involved in the plot. He was careful to select urban artisan slaves—mechanics, harness makers, blacksmiths, and carpenters—as leaders for the revolt. He appealed to his followers to recruit only slaves who could be trusted with the plans, but the secret was eventually leaked to the wrong person, who informed on the rebels to the authorities.

Vesey had set the date for the attack on Charleston for the second Sunday of July, 1822. When two of the leaders were arrested on May 30, Vesey moved the date ahead one month. Despite months of planning and the manufacture and stockpiling of bayonets and daggers, Vesey was unable to communicate the change of plans to the thousands of conspiring slaves, some of whom were eighty miles outside the city.

The planned attack, said by one of the witnesses to have involved as many as 9,000 slaves, never took place. In early June, authorities arrested 131 blacks in Charleston. Forty-nine rebels were condemned to die: twelve were eventually pardoned; thirty-seven were hanged, including Vesey. Four white men were fined and imprisoned for helping the blacks. In response to the conspiracy, the whites of Charleston tore down the city's African church.

Nat Turner (1831)

The uprising led by Nat Turner, known as the Southampton Insurrection ("insurrection" is another word for rebellion), was a slaveholder's worst nightmare. Turner was born a slave on October 2, 1800, and lived all his life in Southampton County, Virginia. Turner knew how to read and became very familiar with the stories in the Bible. He was also a preacher and sometimes conducted services of a Baptist nature.

After receiving what he considered a sign from God (a solar eclipse on February 12, 1831), Turner told four other slaves of his plans for a rebellion. They selected the Fourth of July as the date to strike. Turner was ill on that day, however, and the plot was postponed until another sign appeared, this time the "greenish blue color" of the Sun on August 13. On August 21, 1831, six rebels gathered at Turner's place and began their assault on the local white population.

Turner began the massacre by killing his master, Joseph Travis, and Travis's family. The rebels then took some arms and horses and began going from plantation to plantation killing whites. Within twenty-four hours, about seventy slaves had joined the revolt. By the morning of August 23, fifty-seven whites—men, women, and children—had been slaughtered. The rebels had covered about twenty miles and were marching toward the county seat, Jerusalem, where there was a warehouse of weapons. About three miles outside

town, the slaves were drawn into battle with bands of armed white men and forced to scatter.

A massacre of blacks immediately followed. Hundreds of white soldiers and militiamen hunted down and executed anyone they thought was connected to the revolt. At least 200 blacks were killed without trials. Those captured alive, about sixteen slaves and three free blacks, were condemned to hang. Turner himself avoided capture until October 30. After a short trial, Turner was hanged on November 11, 1831. A wave of terror rolled over the entire slaveholding South. Thousands of blacks were killed as whites took their revenge on any slaves suspected of plotting to revolt.

The Southampton Insurrection, like the uprisings led by Jemmy, Prosser, and Vesey, was a local event, yet it affected the entire nation, especially the slaveholding South. For slaveholders, the rebellions and conspiracies were reasons to

An engraving of the capture of Nat Turner. Turner remained hidden for two months after he incited an insurrection. During that time, troops killed an estimated 200 black people in Southampton County and beat his wife frequently, trying to learn Turner's whereabouts. *Courtesy of the Library of Congress.*

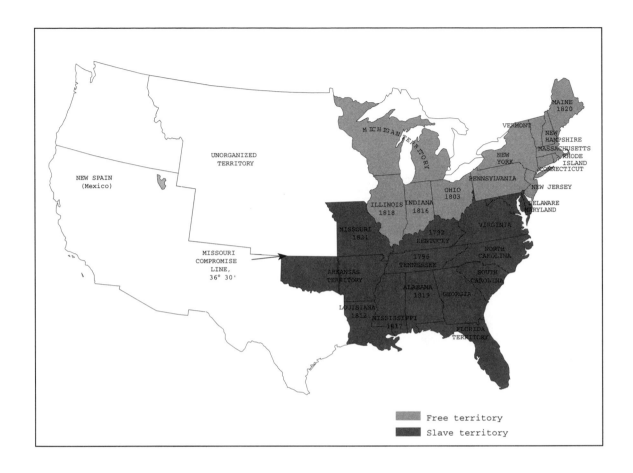

MAINE
1820

VERMONT

NEW
HAMPSHIRE

MASSACHUSETTS

RHODE
ISLAND

CONNECTICUT

NEW JERSEY

DELAWARE
MARYLAND

MICHIGAN TERRITORY

NEW
YORK

PENNSYLVANIA

UNORGANIZED
TERRITORY

OHIO
1803

NEW SPAIN
(Mexico)

ILLINOIS
1818

INDIANA
1816

VIRGINIA

MISSOURI
1821

1792
KENTUCKY

NORTH
CAROLINA

MISSOURI
COMPROMISE
LINE,
36° 30'

1795
TENNESSEE

ARKANSAS
TERRITORY

SOUTH
CAROLINA

ALABAMA
1819

GEORGIA

LOUISIANA
1812

MISSISSIPPI
1817

FLORIDA
TERRITORY

Free territory

Slave territory

Map of the United States in 1821, showing free territory and slave territory, and the Missouri Compromise line.

fear their slaves all the more and to pass even more restrictive laws to control them. With each uprising or conspiracy, blacks in the South lost more of their rights. For the antislavery movement, the slave rebellions focused the attention of the nation on the brutality of the slave system. And, as examples of the price slaves were willing to pay for freedom, the slave revolts and conspiracies inspired and helped to unify the abolitionists.

The rise of militant abolitionists

In 1821, Missouri became the twenty-fourth state in the Union. The question of Missouri's status as a slave or non-slave state sparked a national crisis. The U.S. Congress passed a series of measures in 1820 and 1821 known as the Missouri

Compromise. Congress admitted Missouri as a slave state and Maine as a free state. It also prohibited slavery in all other territory north of Missouri's southern boundary (the 36th parallel). Missouri was also allowed to keep a law in its state constitution that forbade free blacks from settling there.

The expansion of slavery into the new state of Missouri was a defeat for the abolitionists. It became clear to many in the antislavery movement that their efforts to change things gradually and peacefully were not working. In the decade following the Missouri Compromise, abolitionists started calling for an immediate end to slavery, and in some cases, for violent methods to achieve that goal.

In 1829, David Walker (1785–1830) published *Walker's Appeal ... to the Colored Citizens of the World But in Particular and Very Expressly to Those of the United States of America,* which shocked the nation in its call for blacks to violently rise up and defeat the forces of slavery. Walker's message to blacks, in shortened form, was: "Kill or be killed." The writings of Walker, a free black from North Carolina who had moved to Boston, were widely distributed in the North and secretly smuggled into the South, where the pamphlet was banned and slaveholders put a price on Walker's head. Walker died under mysterious circumstances in 1830.

In January 1831, William Lloyd Garrison began publishing the abolitionist newspaper *The Liberator.* For Garrison and his followers, the immediate and unconditional end of slavery was the only solution to the problem. Many southerners blamed the abolitionists, and Garrison (whose newspaper reprinted *Walker's Appeal* in serial form) in particular, for the violent revolt led by Nat Turner (see above). True or not, Garrison and his followers openly praised the violence of the uprising.

The question of colonization

Free blacks were at the forefront of the struggle from the beginning of the antislavery movement. One of their earliest successes was in opposing plans to deport blacks—those already free, and slaves manumitted for the purpose—to a colony in Africa set up with private donations and state and federal funds.

VOL. I.]   WILLIAM LLOYD GARRISON AND ISAAC KNAPP, PUBLISHERS.   [NO. 33

BOSTON, MASSACHUSETTS.]   OUR COUNTRY IS THE WORLD—OUR COUNTRYMEN ARE MANKIND.   [SATURDAY, AUGUST 13, 1831.

The masthead of William Lloyd Garrison's abolitionist newspaper, *The Liberator.*
Courtesy of the Library of Congress.

A plan to deport blacks to Africa, first proposed by Thomas Jefferson in 1777, picked up many supporters in 1815 after a private citizen, at his own expense, carried thirty-eight blacks to Africa. The American Colonization Society (ACS) formed in 1816 and planned to ship blacks to some land near the British colony of Sierra Leone, a small country on the west coast of Africa. The land, purchased in 1822 by the society, was named Liberia, the "land of freedom."

At first, the society had the support of several white abolitionist leaders, including Garrison, Arthur Tappan, Gerrit Smith, and James Birney. By 1832, there were 302 local and state branches of the ACS. And more than a dozen state legislatures, including those of some slaveholding states, had endorsed the society's plans.

Colonization was never all that popular among blacks in the South, but it wasn't entirely opposed, either. For blacks in the North, opposition to the ACS's plans was near unanimous. In 1817, 3,000 free blacks gathered in Philadelphia, under the leadership of Richard Allen (see "The AME Church," Chapter 9), and denounced the plans as an "outrage, having no other object in view than the slaveholding interests of the country." In the next ten years, anticolonization meetings were held by free blacks in many cities across the North.

By 1830, the ACS had persuaded only 1,420 blacks to move to Liberia. By the time of the Civil War, only 15,000 blacks had migrated to Africa, about 12,000 of them due

directly to the society's efforts. The idea of shipping blacks back to Africa never really took hold among blacks for many reasons, one of which was the strong and organized opposition to the plan by free blacks in the North. That opposition eventually led as well to white abolitionist leaders such as Garrison and Smith withdrawing their support from the ACS in 1831.

Black power

On September 15, 1830, Richard Allen organized the first Free People of Color Congress in Philadelphia. At that gathering, black delegates from six states began what came to be known as the National Negro Convention Movement. Every year until the Civil War, blacks convened in different cities "to devise ways and means of bettering our condition." The conventions organized boycotts of slave-produced goods, developed strategies for ending segregated travel on public coaches and steamboats, and tried to improve educational opportunities for blacks. By the 1850s, the conventions openly called for violent rebellion by blacks, advising "all oppressed to adopt the motto 'Liberty or Death.'"

Blacks also organized their own antislavery societies. By 1830 there were at least fifty such groups in cities such as New Haven, Boston, New York, and Philadelphia. In the North, black benevolent societies and fraternal organizations (see "Benevolent societies," Chapter 9), as well as black churches, were active in abolitionist causes (see "Antislavery activism," Chapter 9). Blacks gave their time, energy, and money to many of the local and regional antislavery societies and were especially active in organizing the American Antislavery Society in 1833 and the activities of the Underground Railroad right up to the outbreak of the Civil War.

Blacks created their own newspapers as well, with most of them dedicated to the antislavery crusade. Samuel Cornish and John Russworm started the country's first black newspaper, *Freedom's Journal,* in 1827. Other black newspapers published or edited by Cornish, most of them short-lived, included *Rights of All* (1829), the *Weekly Advocate* (1836), and the *Colored American.* Other black abolitionist newspapers included the *National Watchman,* the *Mirror of Liberty,* and the best-known of them all, the *North Star,* started in 1847 by Frederick Douglass.

The American Antislavery Society

In 1833, William Lloyd Garrison helped establish the American Antislavery Society (AAS) and served as its president from 1843 to 1865. At first, the AAS was dedicated to ending slavery through peaceful means by focusing on its moral evils. The AAS published antislavery newspapers and pamphlets, and by 1836 it had seventy lecturers traveling the country and delivering the abolitionist message. Many members of the AAS also participated in the Underground Railroad.

Impatient with the moderate methods of the AAS, in 1839 Garrison and his followers seized control of the organization and turned it in a more radical direction. Opposition to Garrison by the AAS's first president, Arthur Tappan

(1786–1865; prominent Massachusetts merchant), and others led to the formation of the American and Foreign Antislavery Society (AFAS). The AFAS continued to work with churches and believed that political action, not violence, was the best way to emancipation. In 1840, the members of AFAS became the core of the Liberty Party and nominated James Birney (1792–1857; publisher of the antislavery paper *Philanthropist*) as their candidate for president in 1840 and 1844. In 1844, Birney polled only 60,000 votes.

By 1840 there were more than 100 antislavery societies in the free states of the North, with at least 200,000 black and white members. Abolitionists in general, however, and Garrison's brand of antislavery activism in particular, were not always well received by the public or the government. Lecturers often found it hard to rent halls, and their meetings were sometimes broken up by angry mobs. And from 1828 to 1845, the U.S. House of Representatives refused to even consider antislavery petitions from abolitionists.

Harriet Tubman (1820–1913), the heroine of the Underground Railroad, standing (far left) with six slaves she helped guide to freedom. Tubman, an escaped slave, brought more than 300 slaves to safety. *Courtesy of the Library of Congress.*

Black abolitionists

Frederick Douglass (c. 1817–1875), abolitionist, writer, newspaper editor, and reformer. His book *Narrative of the Life of Frederick Douglass* (1845) revealed his fugitive slave status. *AP/Wide World Photos. Reproduced by permission.*

Many blacks served as agents and speakers for the various antislavery societies. Some were full-time employees of local or national chapters. Some of the more prominent agents, and the cause's more effective speakers, were Frederick Douglass, Theodore S. Wright, William Jones, Charles Lenox Remond, Sarah Parker Remond, Frances E. Harper, Henry Foster, Lunsford Lane, Henry Highland Garnet, and Isabella Baumfree, better known as Sojourner Truth (see box "Names of Freedom," Chapter 9).

Blacks wrote as well as spoke against slavery. A number of black abolitionist agents were also authors of autobiographies known as "narratives." From 1840 to 1860, a number of ex-slaves published their stories of enslavement and escape (see "Fruits of the vine," Chapter 9). The autobiography of Frederick Douglass, *Narrative of the Life of Frederick Douglass,* became an international bestseller in 1845. Abolitionists found these eyewitness testimonies of the brutality of the slave system very helpful in persuading people to join their cause.

Since many of the black abolitionists were ex-slaves themselves, their views of slavery and how to end it often differed from their white counterparts. Frederick Douglass knew the pain of being both a slave and a free black in America. In the first issue of his newspaper, *North Star,* Douglass made clear the unity between free blacks and slaves. "We are one," he wrote. "What you suffer, we suffer; what you endure; we endure. We are indissolubly united, and must fall or flourish together."

Common and uncommon goals

Alliances between black and white abolitionist leaders were sometimes strained. Many black leaders found it hard to trust white abolitionists such as Garrison and Birney, who had supported colonization up until 1831 (see "The question of colonization," earlier in this chapter). Further distrust was earned when the American Antislavery Society formed in 1833 and only three blacks were among the sixty-two signers of the society's Declaration of Sentiments.

Still, there was a great deal of cooperation between black and white abolitionists. White abolitionist leaders often attended, sometimes as featured speakers, the black conventions, churches, benevolent societies, and antislavery societies. Black abolitionist leaders also gave a great deal of time and energy to many of the mostly white antislavery societies. Frederick Douglass, for example, served as president of the mostly white New England Antislavery Society in 1847.

While black and white persons were genuinely united in their opposition to slavery, many black abolitionists had a larger vision. Free blacks also wanted the rights and privileges that went along with freedom. Yes, slavery must end, they argued, but blacks realized there was another obstacle to overcome in racism, the force that kept even "free" blacks from ever becoming equal with whites.

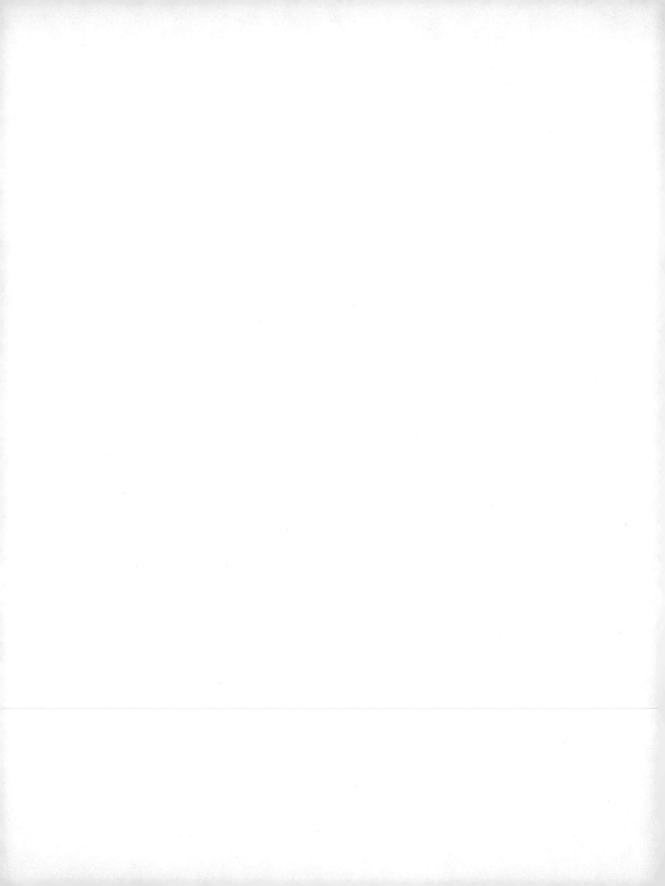

Civil War, Emancipation, and Reconstruction

A country divided

By the 1850s, the United States was unofficially divided into two opposing parts: the North and the South. The North's economy was more industrial, people lived mostly in cities, and there was no slave labor. The South depended on agriculture, people lived mostly in rural areas, and the economy was based on the labor of more than 3.5 million slaves. Though there were many other differences, the main problem for the two regions centered on slavery.

As the attack on slavery by the abolitionists of the North grew stronger (see Chapter 10), the South stiffened its defense of the institution. The South's most effective method of resistance was to threaten withdrawal from the Union. The tactic was first used by the slaveholding southern states at the Constitutional Convention in 1787. Most of the North had already abolished slavery, and some delegates were pushing for an official end to the African slave trade in the new nation (it had been outlawed briefly during the Revolutionary War). The South threatened to withhold its support from the proposed federal government. A

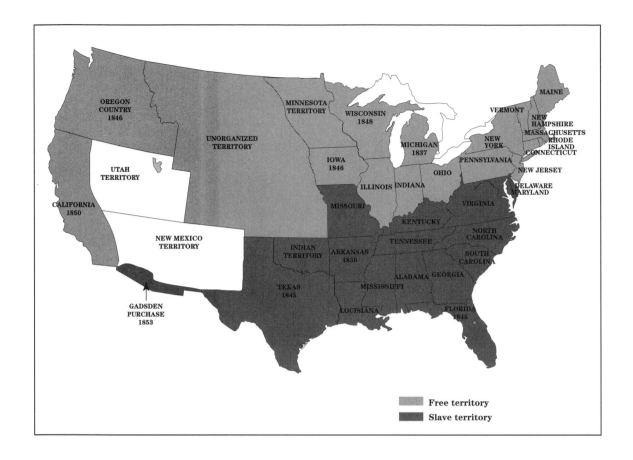

The following labels appear on the map:

OREGON COUNTRY 1846

UNORGANIZED TERRITORY

MINNESOTA TERRITORY

WISCONSIN 1848

MAINE

VERMONT

NEW HAMPSHIRE

MASSACHUSETTS

RHODE ISLAND

CONNECTICUT

NEW YORK

MICHIGAN 1837

PENNSYLVANIA

NEW JERSEY

UTAH TERRITORY

IOWA 1846

OHIO

DELAWARE MARYLAND

CALIFORNIA 1850

ILLINOIS

INDIANA

MISSOURI

VIRGINIA

KENTUCKY

NEW MEXICO TERRITORY

INDIAN TERRITORY

ARKANSAS 1836

TENNESSEE

NORTH CAROLINA

SOUTH CAROLINA

GADSDEN PURCHASE 1853

TEXAS 1845

MISSISSIPPI

ALABAMA

GEORGIA

LOUISIANA

FLORIDA 1845

Free territory
Slave territory

A map of the United States showing free territory and slave territory after the Compromise of 1850, in which California was admitted as a free state, the District of Columbia prohibited the slave trade, and the status of the territories of Utah and New Mexico was left to be determined. The fugitive slave laws were also greatly strengthened to appease the South.

compromise was eventually reached, permitting the African slave trade to continue for another twenty years and obligating all states to return fugitive slaves to their owners.

The Compromise of 1850

When gold was discovered in California in 1848 and many people started migrating west, the nation was once again forced to decide whether slavery would be allowed in new territories and states. Southern pro-slavers argued that slavery should be permitted. Northern abolitionists insisted that slavery should not be expanded. A third group, led by northern Democrats, thought that the question should be put to a vote by the people living in the new territories.

Fact Focus

- In 1852, *Uncle Tom's Cabin,* a novel about the horrors of slavery, sold 300,000 copies and persuaded thousands to join the antislavery crusade.

- On February 4, 1861, delegates from the seven rebel states of the South met in Montgomery, Alabama, and formed the Confederate States of America.

- On April 6, 1862, a total of 80,000 Union and Confederate soldiers met on a battlefield in Tennessee. By nightfall on April 7, 23,741 soldiers lay dead.

- From 1862 to 1864, more than 25 percent of slaves who sought refuge in Union camps died of starvation and disease.

- On January 1, 1863, Lincoln's Emancipation Proclamation freed 3 million slaves living in the Confederacy (about three-quarters of all slaves at that time).

- During the course of the war, more than 185,000 black men served in the Union

army and 29,000 black men served in the Union navy.

- Immediately after the war, in 1865 and 1866, Black Codes that were very similar to the prewar laws that dealt with blacks were established as the law of the land in the South.

- The Thirteenth, Fourteenth, and Fifteenth Amendments to the U.S. Constitution, ratified between 1865 and 1870, abolished slavery and established citizenship and voting rights for blacks.

- In 1867 in the South, the wages paid to freedpeople (ex-slaves) were lower than those paid to hired slaves before the war.

- As early as 1866, groups such as the Ku Klux Klan, the Knights of the White Camelia, and others used threats, force, bribery, arson, and even murder to keep blacks from voting in the South.

- By 1889, blacks had been elbowed out of their rights and were no longer a political force in the South.

After great debates, the U.S. Congress reached the Compromise of 1850. Among other things, Congress admitted California as a free state, left the status of territories to be decided later, outlawed the slave trade in the District of Columbia, and, most important, put real teeth into the fugitive slave laws of 1787 and 1793. The new law required federal marshals to arrest—on pain of a $1,000 fine—any black person who was accused of being a runaway slave. No warrant was needed if the claimant swore ownership. The accused had no right to a jury trial or to give testimony in their own defense. Anyone caught helping a fugitive slave was subject to six months in jail and a $1,000 fine.

The Compromise passed in part because of more threats from the South. Georgia, Mississippi, Alabama, and South Carolina were ready to pull out of the Union until they were promised that the fugitive slave act would be strictly enforced. The antislavery forces of the North were furious; they saw the Compromise of 1850 as a disaster. The fugitive slave laws directly threatened the freedom of approximately 50,000 runaway slaves in the North. Thousands of blacks immediately fled across the border to Canada. As slave catchers came north to find runaways, white and black abolitionists defended many fugitives from capture and even rescued a few already in the custody of federal marshals. Abolitionists also increased their efforts to help slaves escape by the Underground Railroad (see "The Underground Railroad," Chapter 10).

The Kansas-Nebraska Act of 1854

If anyone wondered what was in store for a nation so divided by the issue of slavery, they had only to look to Kansas in 1854. The Kansas-Nebraska Act of 1854, introduced in the Senate by Stephen Douglass (1813–1861; a Democrat from Illinois), organized Kansas and Nebraska as territories and left the question of slavery to be decided by the settlers when they applied for statehood. The act, in effect, erased the thirty-four-year-old prohibition of slavery above the Mason-Dixon line as established in the Missouri Compromise (see "The rise of militant abolitionists," Chapter 10), and once again the abolitionists were fighting mad.

The Kansas-Nebraska Act also made Kansas, in particular, a bloody battleground for proslavery and antislavery forces, as each side tried to establish their dominance before the vote. Thousands of settlers, from New England to the Deep South, poured into Kansas, established free-state towns or slave-state towns, and for the next few years fought one another for control.

In the early 1850s, the two major political parties of the country, the Democrats and the Whigs, split into northern

and southern wings. In 1854, after the passage of the Kansas-Nebraska Act (sponsored by the northern Democrats as a "compromise"), the northern Whigs united with antislavery Democrats and Free Soilers (an antislavery political party formed in 1848) and founded the Republican Party. The new party was firmly antislavery yet had a political program that was more broad-based than the failed Liberty Party of the abolitionists in the 1840s (see "The American Antislavery Society," Chapter 10). The southern Whigs joined the southern Democrats as a united party firmly on the proslavery side of the aisle. Emboldened by their political successes, the southerners began to press for the reopening of the African slave trade.

Dred Scott and Harriet Scott, engraved portraits. Dred Scott's lawsuit brought the issue of slavery all the way to the Supreme Court. *Archive Photos, Inc. Reproduced by permission.*

The Supreme setback

The *Dred Scott v. Sandford* decision handed down by the U.S. Supreme Court in 1857 was a huge victory for proslavery forces. Dred Scott was a slave who had filed suit in 1846, arguing that he and his wife should be free persons because they had lived with their owner for periods of time in territories where slavery was not allowed. At question was whether a slave was a citizen with the legal standing to sue in federal court, the status of slaves living on free soil, and whether Congress had the power to outlaw slavery in the territories.

The majority of the Supreme Court ruled that blacks, free or slave, were not citizens of the United States and therefore Dred Scott and his wife had no legal standing in court and were to remain slaves. The court also ruled that slavery was a property right established by the U.S. Constitution and therefore owners still retained title to their slaves, even when visiting or living on free soil. Further, the court ruled that territories were common lands of the United States where the property rights of all citizens—including slaveholders—applied. The court, in effect, declared the Missouri Compromise unconstitutional and opened all territories to slavery.

The abolitionists respond

The 1850s were a tough decade for the cause of abolition in the national political arena. Slaveholders won battle after battle in the U.S. Congress and the Supreme Court. Yet the abolitionists grew stronger and more determined as each year passed. Because of divisions within their ranks over what methods were best, abolitionists fought slavery with every weapon possible, from words to bullets.

In 1852, words were still the abolitionists' most powerful tool, and the publication of *Uncle Tom's Cabin,* a novel about the horrors of slavery, persuaded thousands to join the antislavery crusade. The book, written by Harriet Beecher Stowe (1811–1896), sold 300,000 copies in its first year and was dramatized in theaters all over the North. *Uncle Tom's Cabin* proved to be the abolitionists' single greatest literary assault on the South, forcing slaveholders to defend the cruelty and suffering of slavery and turning the tide of public opinion in the North against slavery.

In the 1850s, abolitionists led by William Lloyd Garrison (1805–1879; publisher of the abolitionist newspaper *The Liberator* and president of the American Antislavery Society) began actively calling for "disunion"—for the North to break away from the South. Garrison argued that disunion was the best way to stop the spread of slavery in the territories and that it would end the North's obligation to return fugitive slaves. Other abolitionists, such as Frederick Douglass (1817–1895; ex-slave and publisher of the abolitionist newspaper the *North Star*), opposed disunion and called for direct political action and the use of armed force to overthrow slavery.

The first shots

John Brown (1800–1859) was a white abolitionist who represented an even more radical viewpoint than Garrison or Douglass. Born in Connecticut in 1800, Brown was raised by parents who were very religious and very active in the antislavery movement. Brown made his mark in the movement in 1851 when he helped found the League of Gileadites, a small group of radical whites, free blacks, and runaway slaves committed to resisting the new fugitive slave laws (see "The Compromise of 1850," earlier in this chapter).

In response to the Kansas-Nebraska Act (see "The Kansas-Nebraska Act of 1854," earlier in this chapter), Brown and his sons moved to Kansas in 1855 to help establish the territory as free soil. Brown and his followers fought many armed and bloody battles in Kansas and Missouri for antislavery principles. For example, in May 1856, Brown and his group killed five southern settlers as revenge for the destruction of Lawrence, Kansas, a free-state town.

Brown's most famous act was his leadership in the October 16, 1859 raid on Harpers Ferry, Virginia. Brown and his twenty-one followers hoped to capture the federal arsenal and arm slaves for a massive uprising to end slavery. Brown's raiding party included two former slaves, three free blacks,

UNCLE TOM'S CABIN;

OR,

LIFE AMONG THE LOWLY.

BY

HARRIET BEECHER STOWE.

VOL. I.

ONE HUNDREDTH THOUSAND.

BOSTON:
JOHN P. JEWETT & COMPANY
CLEVELAND, OHIO:
JEWETT, PROCTOR & WORTHINGTON.
1852.

The title page of *Uncle Tom's Cabin* (1852), by Harriet Beecher Stowe. One of the most widely read books of the century, *Uncle Tom's Cabin* convinced many readers that slavery must end. *The Granger Collection, New York. Reproduced by permission.*

John Brown, kissing a baby as he walks to the gallows to be hanged.

and sixteen radical whites. After thirty-six hours and fifteen deaths, the well-planned but poorly executed revolt was crushed. Of Brown's group, ten were killed, five escaped, and the rest were hanged with their leader on December 2, 1859.

Brown's raid electrified the nation. Though black abolitionist leaders would not join Brown, and some, such as Frederick Douglass, actively tried to discourage him, no one questioned Brown's incredible commitment to the cause. To most abolitionists, Brown became a great martyr, an almost saintlike figure who gave his life in a holy crusade to end slavery. In the South, Brown was despised. His violent raid and plans for a large-scale revolt, and rumors of more to come, threatened the security of the South and inspired war preparations as far away as Georgia.

The disunited states

When the Republican Party candidate for president, Abraham Lincoln (1809–1865), was elected on an antislavery platform in November 1860, many southern slaveholding states finally did what they had threatened for seventy years— they withdrew from the Union and formed their own government. On December 20, 1860, South Carolina became the first state to secede. By February 1, 1861, six more states had followed: Mississippi, Florida, Alabama, Georgia, Louisiana, and Texas.

On February 4, 1861, delegates from the seven rebel states met in Montgomery, Alabama, and formed the Confederate States of America, or the Confederacy. The new nation's constitution outlawed the external slave trade but prohibited any laws that limited the rights of people to own slaves. On February 18, 1861, Jefferson Davis (1808–1889), a Mississippi plantation owner and former soldier, congressman, senator, and secretary of war, was inaugurated as president of the Confederacy.

When Lincoln was inaugurated in Washington, D.C., on March 4, 1861 as the sixteenth president of the United States, eight slave states still remained in the Union: Virginia, North Carolina, Tennessee, Arkansas, and the border states of Delaware, Maryland, Kentucky, and Missouri. Lincoln was determined to keep what was left of the Union together, even if that meant offending the antislavery wing of the Republican Party.

The war begins

The Civil War officially began on April 12, 1861, when President Davis ordered Confederate soldiers to open fire on Fort Sumter, a Union-held fort located in the harbor of Charleston, South Carolina. Union forces surrendered after a thirty-one-hour battle. The defeat cost the Union four more slave states, as Virginia, North Carolina, Tennessee, and Arkansas joined the Confederacy. Delaware and northwestern Virginia (which became the state of West Virginia in 1863) declared for the Union. Union troops occupied Maryland before it could vote, and a small Union army secured Missouri. Kentucky declared itself neutral (until the Confederates invaded in 1862; then it joined the Union).

War fever gripped both North and South, and thousands of men rushed to join the Union and Confederate armies. Many free blacks tried to enlist in the Union's army but were turned away. Some blacks volunteered to go into the South to organize slave revolts, but they were also turned down. The Union's refusal to enlist blacks was part of Lincoln's policy that billed the battle ahead as a fight to save the Union, not to end slavery. Enlisting blacks in the Union armies, Lincoln feared, would send the wrong message to the millions of Northern whites the Union would need to militarily defeat the Confederacy.

In the beginning of the war, Lincoln had every reason to expect the Union to prevail. The South had less than one-half the population of the North. Of the South's 9 million people, 4 million were slaves, leaving even less of the population available for military duty. The North was better equipped to wage war as well. It had twice as many rail lines to move troops and supplies on and five times as many factories to churn out arms, ammunition, and war-related materials. The Union also controlled the powerful U.S. Navy, which it used to effectively blockade the southern ports of the Confederacy throughout the war.

Ex-slave refugees

As Union troops invaded the South in the spring of 1861, thousands of slaves left their plantations and headed for safety behind the lines of the advancing army. At first there was no clear-cut federal policy for how to treat slaves seeking refuge with the Union armies. Some commanders in the field acted on their own, emancipating slaves (a policy

that Lincoln later reversed) and putting them to work (with pay) for the Union forces. Other commanders wanted to return the fugitives to their owners.

The Confiscation Act passed by the U.S. Congress on August 6, 1861 settled the matter. The law stated that any property used in aiding or abetting insurrection against the United States could be captured and kept as a prize of war. When the "property" consisted of slaves, the law declared them to be forever free. The Confiscation Act resulted in thousands of slaves seeking refuge and freedom on the lands occupied and controlled by the Union armies.

The ex-slave refugees were free, but they did not receive the best treatment by their Northern hosts. Again, the lack of a well-formed federal policy left most of the decision making to the field commanders. In Tennessee, for example, ex-slaves were sent to work for whites who leased abandoned plantations from the Union. And in Louisiana, ex-slaves were

Ex-slaves planting sweet potatoes on South Carolina plantation land during the Civil War, 1862. *Archive Photos, Inc. Reproduced by permission.*

hired out to loyal planters. The worst of it, however, was the suffering from starvation and diseases in the camps set up for the ex-slaves. Despite extensive relief efforts from private organizations in the North, from 1862 to 1864 more than 25 percent of the refugees in those camps died.

Some of the ex-slave refugee problems should have been solved in December 1862, when the head of the Union's Department of the South ordered that abandoned lands were to be used for the benefit of black refugees. Black families were to receive two acres for each working member and some farm tools. They were to plant corn and potatoes for themselves and cotton for the government. The actual amount of land available for such purposes, however, never met the demand. Instead the government sold off much of the abandoned lands to private buyers.

A turning point

Neither side imagined that the war would last so long or be so costly in terms of human life—at least not until the battle of Shiloh. On April 6, 1862, a total of 80,000 Union and Confederate soldiers met on a battlefield in Tennessee. By nightfall on April 7, 23,741 soldiers lay dead. The Confederate army retreated after Union reinforcements arrived, and the Union declared a victory. The battle, like so many more that followed, resulted in an incredible number of casualties on both sides no matter which side won.

By the spring of 1862, the Union had gained the upper hand in the war. Their armies and navy were successfully protecting their capital city in the east (Washington), blockading ports on the southern coasts, and capturing important land and cities to the west, such as New Orleans in April 1862. If the Union could capture the Confederacy's capital city of Richmond, Virginia, located just 100 miles southwest of Washington, the war would have an early end.

Instead the momentum of the war suddenly switched to the South as the Confederate armies, under the command of General Robert E. Lee (1807–1870), defeated Union armies in a series of battles in the summer of 1862. The Union losses were very high, and Northerners were beginning to demand

peace at any cost. The Confederacy was also very close to securing military intervention on their behalf from Europe, having argued that the South had every right to leave the Union and that the North was the aggressor in the war.

Abraham Lincoln (left, center) at the first reading of the Emancipation Proclamation. *Courtesy of the Library of Congress.*

Toward freedom

Faced with mounting losses on the battlefield and a lack of enthusiasm for the war from the public, Lincoln's policy toward emancipation (freedom from bondage) began to change in the summer of 1862. It was time, Lincoln decided, to rouse the North to a greater cause than just saving the Union. The war would be fought to end slavery, and blacks would be freed to help fight the war.

On June 19, the United States abolished slavery in the territories. On July 19, all slaves who made it into Union territory from "disloyal" masters (from Confederate states) were set free. Lincoln discussed issuing an emancipation proclamation with his cabinet as early as July 22, but he was advised to wait until the Union had a victory on the battlefield.

That victory came on September 17, 1862, at the battle at Antietam Creek, in Sharpsburg, Maryland. The one-day fight between the Union's 87,000 troops and the Confederacy's 41,000 troops was the Civil War's bloodiest day. The Union lost 12,000 men and the Confederacy nearly as many. The Confederate army retreated the next day and the Union declared a "victory."

Five days after the battle, on September 22, 1862, Lincoln solved many of the Union's political problems by issuing a preliminary draft of the Emancipation Proclamation, which he hoped would take effect on January 1, 1863. At the same time, he began to allow the enlistment of blacks into the Union's armed forces. Lincoln's change of policy pleased the abolitionists, who had urged emancipation all along. And since the war's goal was no longer just to save the Union, but to crush slavery, the sympathy of the antislavery Europeans turned to the North.

On January 1, 1863, Lincoln issued the final Emancipation Proclamation, setting free all slaves living in the Confederacy (roughly 3 million slaves; or about three-quarters of all slaves at that time). Almost 1 million blacks remained enslaved, most of them in the four border states loyal to the Union: Delaware, Maryland, Kentucky, and Missouri. And slaves were still not free in West Virginia, seven counties in eastern Virginia, and thirteen parishes in Louisiana, including the city of New Orleans.

Black sailors and soldiers

On September 25, 1861, the secretary of the U.S. Navy authorized the enlistment of slaves into the Union navy. By the end of the war more than 29,000 black men had enrolled for duty. The first call to arms for blacks from the Union army came in May 1862. Enough blacks enlisted to establish the "First South Carolina Volunteer Regiment." The group, however, was disbanded and sent home before it saw any action. Lincoln allowed a limited number of blacks to enlist in the Union army in the fall of 1862. Regiments of black soldiers were organized in Louisiana, South Carolina, and Tennessee.

In the spring of 1863, after the Emancipation Proclamation, many blacks rushed to join the Union army. Frederick Douglass and other black leaders acted as recruiting agents. By the end of the war more than 185,000 blacks had served in the Union army. About 93,000 came from the rebel states, 40,000 from the border slave states, and about 52,000 from the free states.

Black Union soldiers were called "United States Colored Troops" and were organized into segregated regiments of light and heavy artillery, cavalry, infantry, and engineers. With few exceptions, they were led by white officers. In the beginning, black soldiers were paid less than white soldiers. According to the Enlistment Act of July 17, 1862, the monthly pay of a white soldier with the rank of private was $16.50; blacks with the same rank received $10. After many protests from the black soldiers and their commanding officers, beginning in 1864, the War Department paid blacks the same rate as whites.

The 107th U.S. Colored Infantry poses for a Matthew Brady photograph. *Archive Photos, Inc. Reproduced by permission.*

The camp cook of the Army of the Potomac during the Civil War. *Archive Photos, Inc. Reproduced by permission.*

Blacks served the Union army in a variety of ways. Some blacks, such as Harriet Tubman (see "The Underground Railroad," Chapter 10), acted as spies. Some were organized into raiding parties. Many served as laborers for the Union cause, working on Union-controlled plantations and building fortifications for the army. One of the major complaints of black enlisted soldiers and their white officers was that they were used too much for manual labor and not enough for fighting. Finally, in 1864, the army limited the amount of "fatigue" duty assigned to black soldiers to the same as white soldiers.

According to one historian, black soldiers engaged in more than 250 battles with Confederate forces in the course of the war. More than 38,000 black soldiers died in the Civil War. The Confederacy held more than 3,000 black troops as prisoners in 1863, and in late 1864, more than 1,000 black prisoners of war worked on Confederate fortifications in Mobile, Alabama.

Black Union troops captured by the South before 1864 were not treated as prisoners of war. They were treated as fugitive slaves and returned to their states of origin. Throughout the war, Confederate troops were especially harsh on black Union soldiers, sometimes killing them in the field rather than taking them prisoner. Excessive manual labor, poor equipment, lousy medical care, the tendency to send blacks recklessly into battle, and the take-no-prisoners opposition from their enemies led to a 40 percent higher mortality rate for black soldiers than white soldiers.

Slaves in the Confederacy

Life during wartime for black slaves in the Confederacy was a time of great change. Between 1861 and 1865, thousands of slaves walked off their plantations and sought refuge behind the lines of advancing Union armies. For those slaves who stayed in the South, some out of loyalty, many refused to work or to submit to punishment. Slaves often assisted Union troops by providing information, destroying their masters' properties, and sometimes physically harming or even killing their masters.

Faced with an extreme shortage of labor due to the enlistment of many of its working men, the Confederacy found new ways to use its slaves. Slaves were put to work on farms that grew food crops of corn and wheat (instead of cotton) for the war effort. Slaves went to work by the thousands in the South's iron foundries, iron mines, coal mines, and salt factories. In 1863, the Confederate government even tried to force slave owners to hire out their slaves to work in the war effort. Both the slaves and their owners resisted.

Slaves were forced to perform many dirty and dangerous tasks for the Confederate armies. They repaired rail lines and bridges destroyed by the Union army. They worked in factories making gunpowder and arms. Slaves acted as teamsters, hospital attendants, ambulance drivers, and manual laborers on many construction and fortification projects. Most of the cooks for the Confederate army were slaves. They received $15 a month and clothing. If blacks ever served in battle as Confederate soldiers, it was at the end of the war, and their numbers were very small. Up until March 13, 1865, when President

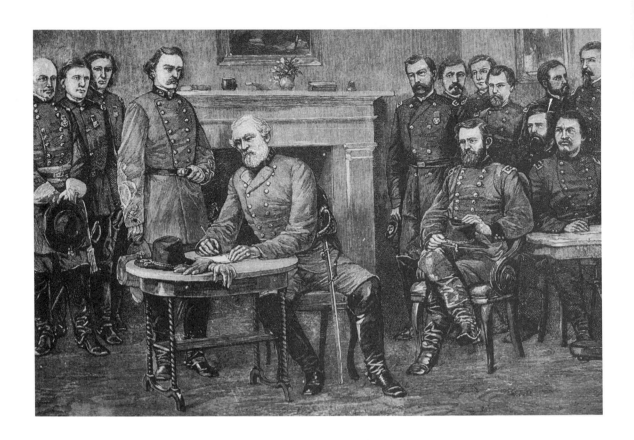

The surrender of
Confederate general Robert
E. Lee to Union general
Ulysses S. Grant at
Appomattox Courthouse,
Virginia, on April 9, 1865.
Archive Photos, Inc. Reproduced
by permission.

Davis put out a desperate call for troops of any color, the Confederacy refused to enlist black men in its armies.

The reunited states

The Civil War ended on April 9, 1865, when the Confederate army, led by General Robert E. Lee, surrendered at Appomattox Courthouse, Virginia. The casualties for both sides totaled 600,000, more than the number of combined casualties of all American wars since then. One of every four soldiers who served in the war died in battle or from disease. The South was in ruins. The Confederate capital of Richmond, Virginia, was just one of the many Southern cities destroyed by the Union army. The Union armies also laid to waste vast tracts of farmland as they advanced on, and occupied, much of the South.

Lincoln was elected to serve a second term as president in November 1864. He did not live long enough to serve

Former slaves greet black Union troops as the Civil War comes to a close.
Archive Photos, Inc. Reproduced by permission.

out his term, however, nor did he have much time to appreciate the Union's victory and the total abolition of slavery. On April 14, 1865, five days after the South surrendered, John Wilkes Booth, a Southern sympathizer, shot Lincoln. The president died the next morning.

Before he died, however, Lincoln had set a tone of healing, not revenge, for the war-torn nation. The Southern states had not actually seceded, Lincoln argued, they had only rebelled, and they should be welcomed back into the Union. Lincoln lived also to see the Thirteenth Amendment to the U.S. Constitution—which abolished slavery in America—passed by the U.S. House of Representatives on January 31, 1865, and well on its way to ratification (official approval by popular vote) by the states.

The ratification of the Thirteenth Amendment on December 18, 1865, was a great victory for blacks in America. It freed 4 million slaves and ended nearly 250 years of slavery for an entire race of Americans. The Thirteenth Amendment would not have been possible without the Union's victory in the Civil War. And the Civil War would probably never have happened if the abolitionist movement had not pushed the country into conflict on the slavery issue with such force for so many years. The end of slavery was a great victory for the thousands of free blacks and black slaves who, together with white abolitionists, fought the good fight on many fronts—social, political, economic, and military—for generations.

A step backward

The end of slavery was the beginning of another battle for black Americans and their allies—to secure citizenship and equal rights for blacks. The North forced the South to accept that blacks could no longer be their slaves, but the South quickly proved that it was not willing to move an inch toward equal rights and citizenship for its black population. Taking advantage of lenient amnesty (official pardon) policies established by Lincoln and his successor, President Andrew Johnson (1808–1875), Southern whites reestablished control over their state legislatures.

In 1865 and 1866, Black Codes, which were very similar to the prewar laws that dealt with blacks, were established as the law of the land in the South (see Chapters 8 and 9). Blacks were forced to work or they were declared vagrants. If blacks quit their jobs, they could be arrested for breach of contract. Blacks could not testify in court except in cases involving blacks. Blacks could be fined for violating curfews; possessing firearms; missing work; or speaking, gesturing, or acting in an "insulting" manner. Blacks, of course, could not vote.

Political Reconstruction

After almost two years of white home rule in the South, the Republican-controlled U.S. Congress intervened. First, on April 9, 1866, it passed a Civil Rights bill that repealed the Black Codes of the South. The bill granted citizenship to blacks, and equal rights with whites in every state and territory. Then in 1867, Congress passed a series of Reconstruction acts that drastically, but only temporarily, changed

the political landscape of the South. The acts divided the former Confederacy into five military districts under the command of army generals. They stripped the right to vote from most whites who had supported the Confederate government. Elections were ordered for state constitutional conventions, and black men were given the right to vote, in some states by military order.

A campaign to register voters in the South began in the summer of 1867. By November, more than 1.3 million citizens had registered, including 700,000 blacks. Black voters made up a majority in the states of Alabama, Florida, Louisiana, Mississippi, and South Carolina. Blacks were elected to constitutional conventions in every southern state but held a majority only in South Carolina. The state constitutions drawn up in 1867 and 1868 abolished slavery and gave all male residents the right to vote. Throughout the Reconstruction period, blacks were also elected to state legislatures and, in much smaller numbers, to the U.S. House and Senate.

At the federal level, the Reconstruction-minded Congress sent two important amendments of the U.S. Constitution

Freed slaves waiting for work opportunities. *U.S. Signal Corps, National Archives and Records Administration.*

Black men voting in
Washington, D.C., June 3,
1867. *Archive Photos, Inc.
Reproduced by permission.*

to the states for ratification. The Fourteenth Amendment, which granted citizenship to blacks, was made law on July 21, 1868. Ratification of the Fourteenth Amendment became one of the requirements for states to be readmitted into the Union. In an attempt to secure the right to vote for black men, Congress also passed the Fifteenth Amendment, guaranteeing the protection of U.S. citizens against federal or state racial discrimination, which was ratified by the states on March 30, 1870.

Relief and recovery

The Civil War and Reconstruction brought new freedoms to black Americans, but they also brought great suffer-

ing (see "Ex-slave refugees," earlier in this chapter). In March 1865, Congress established the Bureau of Refugees, Freedmen, and Abandoned Lands, or the Freedman's Bureau. Relief in the form of clothing, food, and schools for freedmen (ex-slaves, male and female) and refugees in the South had been provided by private associations and religious organizations based in the North since 1862. The Freedman's Bureau took the relief effort many steps further.

From 1865 to 1869, the bureau issued 21 million food rations; about 5 million rations went to whites, and the rest went to blacks. By 1867, forty-six bureau-run hospitals, staffed with surgeons, doctors, and nurses, had treated more than 450,000 cases of illness. The bureau also helped about 30,000 people resettle and distributed a small amount of abandoned lands to freedpeople.

The bureau's greatest achievement was the establishment of an extensive public school system in the South. To-

Government relief at the Freedman's Bureau. *Archive Photos, Inc. Reproduced by permission.*

gether with private agencies and religious organizations, the bureau set up and ran day schools, night schools, Sunday schools, industrial schools, and colleges. In 1869, there were 9,503 teachers in the bureau's schools, most of whom were from the North. In 1870, when the bureau ended its educational work, there were almost 247,333 students in 4,329 schools.

Black churches played an important role in providing spiritual and material relief (food, clothing, and schools) to blacks in postwar America. From around 1830 to the end of the Civil War, blacks were not free to worship as they wished in the South. With those restrictions gone, the number of independent black churches and their membership shot up dramatically. The oldest black church, the African Methodist Episcopal Church, had 20,000 members in 1856; in 1876 it had more than 200,000 members. Black Baptist churches in the South grew from a membership of 150,000 in 1850 to 500,000 in 1870.

Running in place

The greatest failure of Reconstruction was its inability to improve the economic conditions of blacks in either the North or the South. Blacks who moved to the North in search of better living conditions were often disappointed. They were able to find work only because the operators of the iron and cotton mills and the railroad builders often employed blacks at low wages in order to undermine white labor unions. Generally, white labor unions did not allow black members in the postwar years. Black laborers were forced to work for lower wages and gained a reputation as strikebreakers (people hired to replace striking workers). In December 1869, blacks formed the National Negro Labor Union. Denied connections to the white labor movement until 1880, the union focused on improving conditions for black workers.

Immediately following the war in the South, many freedpeople returned to the farms of their ex-masters and resumed work under conditions not much better than before slavery was abolished. Blacks now worked under a contract system with their employers. Plantation wages ranged from $9 to $15 a month for men, and from $5 to $10 a month for women (plus food, shelter, and fuel). In 1867, the wages paid

to freedpeople were lower than those paid to hired slaves before the war. Blacks who worked on a sharecropping system (a system in which one person farms land owned by another in exchange for a share of the crop) were no better off. Their expenses were sometimes higher than the value of their crops, and after paying the employer his share of the cotton and corn, many sharecroppers actually ended up in debt.

After the war, with few work opportunities, many ex-slaves returned to the plantations to work for their former masters, at very low wages or on a sharecropper basis. *Archive Photos, Inc. Reproduced by permission.*

Another civil war

The end of Reconstruction in the South was a gradual process. From 1870 to the end of the century, many of the political, social, and economic advances of blacks made in the postwar South were reversed. The growth of vigilante groups such as the Ku Klux Klan, the rise of the Democratic Party, and the eventual rewriting of state constitutions all contributed to the decline in the status of black Americans in the South.

This poster, created by Southern whites who opposed the Freedman's Bureau, demonstrates the kind of stereotyping and prejudice that faced black Americans after the Civil War. *Courtesy of the Library of Congress.*

The campaign to overthrow Reconstruction began in 1866 with terrorism (attacks on unarmed civilians). Secret societies of white southerners formed and, through the use of threats and violence, waged a crusade to deny political equality to blacks. Groups such as the Ku Klux Klan, the Knights of the White Camelia, the Pale Faces, and others used threats, force, bribery, arson, and murder to keep blacks from voting and to harass black and white Reconstruction officials and workers from the North. Enemies of these white vigilante groups were whipped, maimed, hanged, or run out of town; their houses and barns were burned, and their crops destroyed. Congress put an official end to the Klan and other terrorist groups with a series of laws in 1870 and 1871, but their actions continued with greater secrecy than before.

The rebirth of the Democrats as a political force in the South was in full swing by 1872, when, through a series of congressional amnesties, voting power was restored to all white southerners except a few ex-Confederate officials. Beginning in 1870 with the border states, the Democratic Party regained control of legislatures in one state after another in the South. By 1876, Democrats controlled every state in the South except South Carolina, Florida, and Louisiana. The withdrawal of all federal troops from the South in 1877 marked the formal end of the Reconstruction period and left the Democrats and their vigilante allies firmly in control of the fate of millions of black Americans.

The rebirth of white supremacy

The Fourteenth and Fifteenth Amendments to the Constitution provided protections for black Americans based on their race and status as ex-slaves. The Democrats, once in power, spent the next twenty-five years or so finding ways to legally deny blacks the right to vote or to participate in politics. Violence, intimidation, and deception played important roles. Vigilante groups simply told blacks to stay out of town on election day or face the consequences. Polling places were set up far from black communities or moved to a place known only to Democrats and their friends. Voting districts were constantly redrawn to divide up the black vote. By 1889, one historian concluded, blacks were no longer a political force in the South.

As the century came to a close, almost every state in the South began rewriting and amending their Reconstruction-era constitutions to include voting restrictions aimed at blacks. By these measures, most blacks, as well as some whites, were kept from the voting booths because they didn't have enough money to pay a poll tax, or they could not read and write, or they did not own enough property. On the surface, the laws never mentioned race or color, but their intention was never in doubt. For example, in Louisiana in 1896, more than 130,000 blacks were registered to vote. Two years after the adoption of a new state constitution in 1898, there were 5,320 registered black voters. In Alabama, only 3,000 blacks out of 180,000 blacks of voting age were registered in 1900.

The social forces that shaped the South's treatment of blacks in the post-Reconstruction era led to the adoption of the "Jim Crow" laws that would last until the civil rights movement of the 1960s. Beginning in Tennessee in 1870, and followed rapidly by the rest of the South, laws were passed that separated blacks and whites on trains, in depots, and on wharves. By 1885, most of the South required separate schools for blacks and whites, and by 1900, blacks were barred from white hotels, barber shops, restaurants, and theaters.

Slavery in the Twentieth Century

The end of Africa's western slave trade

Most of the slaves shipped to North and South America from 1518 to 1880 came from West Africa. In the nineteenth century, slaves were shipped to the Americas from East Africa as well. Beginning in the early part of the century, at least 25,000 slaves were being exported annually from the slave markets of Mozambique (pronounced moe-zam-BEEK) Island to Brazil. The Portuguese, Dutch, French, British, and Americans were all regular customers for slaves from Africa's east coast. Though the voyage around the southern tip of Africa to the Americas was much longer, slaves were cheaper than on Africa's west coast, and it was easier to evade the smaller British antislavery patrols (see "Abolition on the Atlantic," Chapter 10). It was not uncommon, however, for as many as one-half of the slaves to die on the voyage from East Africa to Cuba or Brazil.

By 1842, England, the United States, France, Denmark, Holland, and Spain had all passed laws against the trans-Atlantic slave trade. The slave trade from Africa to the Americas was only *legally dead,* however, and African slaves continued to be shipped across the Atlantic for another thirty-eight years (see "The slave trade persists," Chapter 10).

The abolition of slavery in the United States in 1865 dramatically decreased the number of slaves brought to the Western Hemisphere and contributed greatly to the end of the trade. Slavery gradually came to an end in Latin America, though the last two countries to abolish slavery were also Latin America's greatest slaveholders—Brazil and Cuba. In 1871, Brazil passed a gradual emancipation law, and in 1880 Cuba did the same. Though there were still slaves in Cuba until 1886, and in Brazil until 1888, the shipping of Africans across the Atlantic ended in 1880.

Africa's eastern slave trade

As the trade from West Africa to the Americas was winding down, slave traders turned their attention to East Africa and to the well-established slave markets of Arabia and the East. The Arab-dominated lands of northern Africa had been involved in the slave trade since 200 B.C.E., and by 900, there were many African slaves in Arab lands, as well as in India and China. For many years, slaves were just one of many exports from East Africa to these lands, including gold, iron, silver, mangroves (tropical trees), and coconut products.

In the 1800s, however, slaves became the chief export of East Africa, along with ivory. By 1840, Arab slave traders had moved deep into the forests of East Africa, as far south as Lake Victoria and the upper Congo, to capture and enslave Africans. Trading guns for slaves or taking them by force, the Arabs marched thousands of black Africans to the east coast for transport to the slave markets of Zanzibar, an island twenty-four miles off the coast of what is now Tanzania. At the time, Zanzibar was the capital of the Arab state of Oman and the main slave export market for the whole East African coast. Though Oman outlawed the export of slaves in 1845, at least two-thirds of the 20,000 to 40,000 slaves brought to Zanzibar annually were shipped to Arabia (the Arabian Peninsula of southwest Asia), Iraq, Persia, and Turkey. The other one-third of the African slaves were put to work on the island's Arab-owned clove, cacao (beans used to make chocolate), and coconut palm plantations.

Fact Focus

- Though there were still slaves in Cuba until 1886, and in Brazil until 1888, the shipping of Africans across the Atlantic Ocean to the Americas ended in 1880.

- As a result of mass enslavement by King Leopold of Belgium, between the late 1870s and 1919 the population of the Congo Basin in Africa was reduced from 20 million to 10 million.

- Under Joseph Stalin's rule (1927–1953), as many as 5 million to 8 million people were in "corrective labor camps" in the USSR at any one time.

- By late 1944, there were 7.5 million civilians and 2 million prisoners of war (captured soldiers) working as slaves in Nazi Germany.

- Modern forms of slavery include chattel slavery, serfdom, debt bondage, child labor, child prostitution, child pornography, the use of children in armed conflict, servile forms of marriage, forced labor, and the "white slave" traffic, or sexual slavery.

- In 1992, it was estimated that there were hundreds of thousands of political prisoners in China's vast network of labor reform camps.

- In 1996, there were between 10 million and 15 million bonded child workers in India. In Pakistan, there were at least 4 million bonded child workers.

- Human-rights groups estimated that in the 1990s, between 30,000 and 90,000 Sudanese were enslaved in an ongoing civil war in that African nation.

- In 1996, there were 26,047 reported cases of slavery in Brazil, mainly involving Indians who worked in charcoal production.

- In 1999, one human-rights group claimed that the African nation of Mauritania contained the world's largest concentration of chattel slaves—an estimated 390,000 people.

- According to Anti-Slavery International, there were more than 200 million slaves in the world in 1999.

The Egyptians were also heavily involved in trading black African slaves throughout the nineteenth century. The main source of slaves from 1821 to 1860 was the Upper Nile region, just south of Khartoum (pronounced car-TOOM), in the territory of Sudan (the region of North Africa from the Atlantic Ocean to the Upper Nile, south of the Sahara Desert). As many as 50,000 African slaves a year were floated down the Nile to the slave markets of Egypt until British, French,

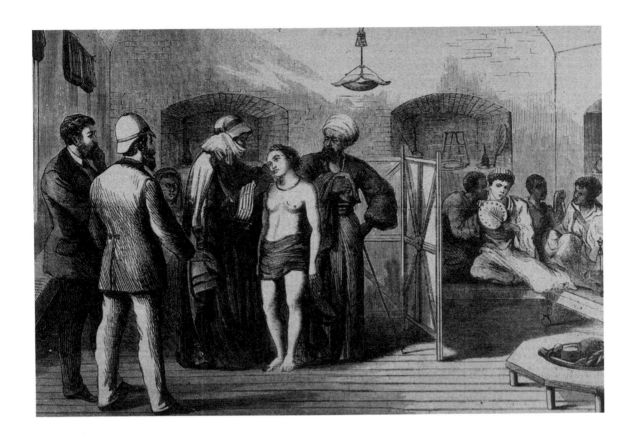

An Arab slaver in Basra, a port in what is now Iraq, in the nineteenth century.
Archive Photos, Inc. Reproduced by permission.

and German missionaries intervened. Driven off the Nile, the slave traders moved to the desert, where from 1860 to 1876, more than 400,000 black Africans were taken from the Sudan for sale as slaves in Egypt and Turkey.

Europeans in Africa

As the twentieth century began, most of Africa was under direct European control. In 1884, at the Conference of Berlin, the countries of Germany, France, England, Portugal, and Belgium each staked out territories in Africa that they wished to occupy and control. The map of Africa changed almost overnight as the Europeans divided the lands of the vast continent among themselves. Germany lost most of her African possessions in World War I (1914–1918), but most of the European powers maintained control of their colonies until after World War II (1939–1945).

In 1885, King Leopold (1835–1909) of Belgium was granted by the Berlin Conference the right to rule over the Congo Basin (now the Democratic Republic of Congo, formerly Zaire, and before that, the Belgian Congo), an area of central Africa seventy-five times the size of Belgium. King Leopold named his personal kingdom the Congo Free State and told the world he wanted to rescue the African people from Arab slave traders and bring them education and "civilization."

Holocaust in Africa

The reality was that King Leopold replaced the Arab slave trade with a far more brutal system of slavery. Leopold's strategy was to plunder the area of its natural resources using the forced labor of the enslaved African population. Without ever setting foot in the Congo, Leopold directed Belgian troops to round up whole communities of Africans and put them to work harvesting ivory and wild rubber and building facilities needed for trade, such as railroads and ports. Leopold, and the private companies he worked with, imposed an almost-impossible-to-meet quota system on the natives and, when they failed to meet it, amputated the hands of the workers and kidnaped the women and children as punishment. As Leopold's private African kingdom eventually fell apart, his troops resorted to wholesale slaughter as punishment.

When the world finally learned the truth of Leopold's deadly system of slavery (see box titled "A Twentieth-century Abolitionist"), they forced the king to give up control of the Congo to the Belgian government in 1908. A Belgian government commission investigated Leopold's reign of terror and found that from the late 1870s to 1919 (the year of the report), the population of the Congo Basin had been reduced from 20 million to 10 million, making it, as Adam Hochschild in *King Leopold's Ghost* called it, "a death toll of Holocaust proportions." Most of the people died from starvation and disease, a direct result of being driven from their homes and food sources. Other African natives died from the horrible conditions of their enslavement. Many of the dead had been murdered by Leopold's forces.

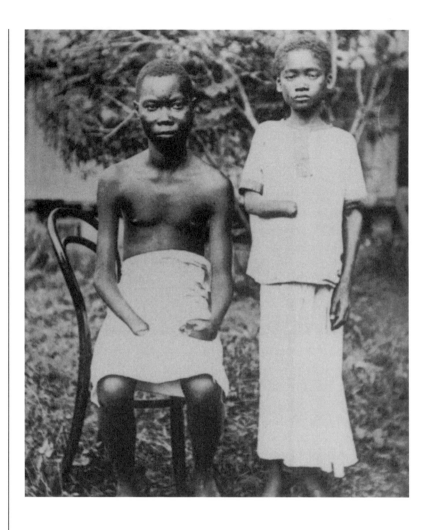

Two young boys in the Belgian Congo during King Leopold's reign there. Mola, seated, lost his hands to gangrene after being tied too tightly by soldiers. Soldiers cut off the right hand of Yoka, standing, in order to claim bounty for having killed him. *Anti-Slavery International. Reproduced by permission.*

Forced labor in the USSR

From 1927 to 1953, the Union of Soviet Socialist Republics (USSR) was ruled by the dictator Joseph Stalin (1879–1953). During Stalin's rule, the government of the USSR enslaved millions of Soviet citizens in labor camps in Siberia, Central Asia, and above the Arctic Circle. In 1918, one year after the Russian Revolution and the overthrow of Russia's czarist system (a country ruled by a czar, or king), the Soviets wrote their Labor Code and in Article 1 declared that "all citizens be subject to compulsory labor."

The concept of forced labor and exile for criminal and political prisoners was not new to Russian society. In czarist Russia, as late as 1914, at least 30,000 convicts were assigned to hard labor in the mines and on construction projects. Russian czars did not hesitate to send personal and political enemies into forced labor or exile, and Russia's colonization of Siberia and the Far East were helped along by the thousands of Russians sent into exile as punishment by the czar. From 1904 to 1917, Stalin himself was exiled to Siberia by the czar for his political activity.

Russia's rulers in the Soviet era (1917–1991) took the concept of forced labor for convicts—especially political prisoners—a giant step beyond the old system. The Soviet system widened the definition of crimes punishable by forced labor or exile to include so-called "crimes against the state." At times, that might have meant no more than being *suspected* of disagreeing with the government's tightly controlled social and economic policies. People were arrested, removed from their offices and jobs by the secret police, and sentenced without trials.

Slavery Soviet-style

Under Stalin's rule, as many as 5 million to 8 million people were in "corrective labor camps" in the USSR at any one time. Stalin used his huge prison workforce in a variety of ways to bolster the Soviet economy without having to pay for labor. Prisoners built and maintained roads and rail lines and constructed housing and hydroelectric plants (which harness running water to produce electricity). They labored in the coal, gold, chrome, and ore mines and in the oil fields. Prisoners also worked in

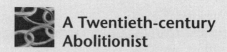

A Twentieth-century Abolitionist

King Leopold's slaughter of the people of the Congo might have gone on even longer if not for the efforts of Edmund Dene Morel (1873–1924). Around 1897, Morel was an employee for a Liverpool-based shipping line in the port of Antwerp, Belgium. Morel noticed that ships from the Congo came in loaded with ivory and rubber but ships going back to the Congo were full of army officers, arms, and ammunition but no goods. The flow of goods to Belgium without an equal flow of goods in trade back to the Congo could only be explained one way, Morel figured: the rubber and ivory of the Congo were being obtained with slave labor.

Over the next few years, Morel spent his time as an investigator, journalist, public speaker, and government lobbyist in a crusade to end Leopold's rule in the Congo. Morel's efforts resulted in the founding in 1904 of the twentieth century's first human-rights movement, the Congo Reform Association. With thousands of members and branches in Europe and the United States, the association and its government supporters forced Leopold to surrender control of the Congo Free State to the government of Belgium in 1908.

Building the Turkmen-Siberian Railway in 1929. Sentenced by the Soviets to forced labor camps, Russian prisoners in Siberia labored in building railroads, plants, and housing, as well as in mining. *Photograph by M. Alpert. Corbis/Novosti. Reproduced by permission.*

agriculture, fishing, lumbering, and manufacturing. The prisoners were paid in food, not wages. Their living conditions were so poor that the death rate at many labor camps was 30 percent a year.

The use of prison labor does not always constitute a form of slavery. The conditions of Soviet-style forced labor, however, were nothing short of slavery. People were arrested without reasonable cause, shipped on trains like animals to faraway places, forced to do unbearable work, and frozen and starved to death. In 1956, three years after Stalin's death, Soviet leaders granted an amnesty to a large number of labor-camp prisoners, though many were forced to remain in exile in remote regions of the USSR. "Corrective labor" as a governmental policy designed to control political dissent continued under the new leadership, and it is reported (though figures are unavailable) that the practice is still alive after the formal breakup of the USSR in 1991.

Slavery in Nazi Germany

Slavery as practiced by the Nazis (the National Socialist German Workers' Party) in Europe during World War II was one of the most brutal systems that the world has ever known. As the German armies conquered their European neighbors—Russians, Poles, Slavs, Italians, and others—they herded civilians and soldiers by the millions into boxcars and shipped them to Germany to work as slaves, where many of them died of overwork, starvation, and lack of shelter and clothing.

In 1939, the German leader, Adolf Hitler (1889-1945), drafted 7 million Germans for the war effort. Faced with a shortage of workers, the German strategy was to invade and conquer all non-German countries, plunder their resources, and enslave their populations. At first, hundreds of thousands of Russians died in German hands of cold and starvation. By 1942, when the war had dragged on longer than Hitler expected, German policy changed. Greater care was taken to keep Russians, and other captives, alive so that they could work on Germany's farms and in its mines, factories, and households. By late 1944, there were 7.5 million civilians and 2 million prisoners of war (captured soldiers) working as slaves in Germany.

Most of the 3 million Russian civilians sent into slave labor were women. Some were forced to work as domestic servants in German households; others worked on farms and in factories. Beginning in June 1944, Germans rounded up Russian youths from the ages of ten to fourteen and shipped them to Germany to serve as apprentices to tradesmen.

Throughout the war, millions of Slavic and Italian slaves worked on Germany's farms. They were housed like animals in barns and stables.

Extermination through work

Most of Hitler's weapons—the tanks, guns, and ammunition—were made by slaves. Germany's chief weapons manufacturer, the Krupp firm, controlled factories, mines, and shipyards in twelve nations of German-occupied Europe. The Krupp works used male, female, and child slaves by the thousands. When Nazi Germany was defeated in 1945, Krupp had about 100,000 slaves in 100 different factories. Through the course of the war, Krupp used the inmates of 138 concentration camps (camps where the Nazis imprisoned and killed Jews and other prisoners) as well. Krupp set up a plant in the Auschwitz concentration camp, for example, where skilled Jewish inmates were forced to make weapons parts.

One of the main goals of Nazi Germany was to rid society of people it perceived as "undesirable." As noted by Milton Meltzer in *Slavery: A World History*, by 1942 Hitler developed a strategy to liquidate (kill) "Jews, foreign saboteurs, anti-Nazi Germans, gypsies, criminals, and antisocial elements" through a policy of "extermination through work." Hitler's agents seized whole factories of workers, transporting the uncooperative in chains to various Krupp-owned factories. At first the minimum age for slave laborers was seventeen. By 1944, however, the Germans were forcing children as young as six years old to work in the factories.

Holocaust in Europe

The foreigners (non-Germans) in the labor camps died in great numbers. Overwork, overcrowding, unsanitary conditions, poor-quality food, a lack of housing and clothes—all led to great suffering and death through diseases, starvation, and cold. Many prisoners worked and died in the same clothes they had on when they arrived. Some had no shoes even in the winter and had to use blankets as coats. The rate of tuberculosis (pronounced too-burr-cue-LOW-sis; a highly contagious and deadly disease) in the camps was four times the nor-

mal rate. The horrors of Nazi Germany's slave-labor camps were surpassed only by the horrors of its concentration camps, where 6 million Jews were systematically murdered.

Hitler's war machine was defeated in 1945. In 1948, at the Nuremberg trials of Nazi war criminals, Alfried Krupp, the head of the company, was sentenced to twelve years in prison and ordered to give up all his personal property and wealth for the crime of "exploitation of forced foreign labor." In 1951, the U.S. High Commissioner in West Germany pardoned Krupp and restored his fortune, estimated at $500 million.

Jewish women at the Plaszow concentration camp in Krakow, Poland, are forced to pull carts of quarried stone, 1944. *Photograph by Raimund Tisch. USHMM Photo Archives.*

"Comfort women" in World War II

One of the horrifying and sometimes unreported aspects of war is the abuse of women that occurs, with enemy

A group of Filipino women who say the Japanese forced them to be "comfort women" in the 1930s and 1940s react with dismay when they hear that the Tokyo District Court has ruled against their claims for compensation and an apology, 1998. *Photograph by Bullit Marquez. AP/Wide World Photos. Reproduced by permission.*

soldiers raping, kidnaping, and otherwise preying upon civilian women in conquered territories. Before World War II, Japan occupied vast territories in Asia, including China, Korea, and the Philippines. According to a large group of survivors, women in some of these areas were kidnaped or forced to go to Japan's battlegrounds to serve as sex slaves for the Japanese soldiers. They were classified as military supplies when they were transported. On the battle fields they were known as "comfort women."

As many as 200,000 women from the ages of eleven to thirty-two were inducted into sexual slavery against their will by the Japanese. A majority of the women came from Korea. They were kept in small rooms, where they were forced to serve large numbers of soldiers daily. Shame and physical and emotional damage prevented many from going back to their homes when World War II was over. At the end of the twentieth century, women who had survived organized and presented a claim to the Japanese government, asking for compensation (money to repay them for their suffering) and an apology. The Japanese government rejected their claims.

The end of the twentieth century

Modern forms of slavery

Slavery as practiced in the second half of the twentieth century came to include a wide variety of human-rights violations. In 1956, the United Nations defined slavery as the condition of someone over whom any or all of the powers connected to the right of ownership are exercised. Over the years since then, the UN has dedicated itself to ending all forms of slavery, including chattel slavery, serfdom, debt bondage, child labor, child prostitution, child pornography, the use of children in armed conflict, servile forms of marriage, forced labor, and the "white slave" traffic, or sexual slavery.

Counting the number of slaves in the world at the end of the twentieth century was not easy. Estimates vary from source to source and according to what form of slavery was considered. According to Anti-Slavery International (ASI), a London-based organization founded in 1839, there were more than 200 million slaves in the world in 1999. Most of the slaves, according to ASI, lived in Asia, Africa, and Latin America.

The International Labor Organization (ILO) in 1998 estimated the number of children exploited in labor markets around the world at between 200 million and 250 million, with nearly 95 percent living in developing (poor) countries. Child labor, the ILO contended, was widespread and growing in 1998.

A 1996 United Nations report noted that children were being sold for prostitution, pornography, and adoption at increasing rates worldwide. In Asia alone, more than 1 million children were exploited sexually and lived in conditions virtually identical to slavery. According to a U.S. Department of Health and Human Services report, cited by the UN, up to 300,000 child prostitutes were walking the streets of the United States, many no older than eleven or twelve and some as young as nine.

Child labor abuse was common in the United States in the nineteenth century. *National Archives and Records Administration.*

As the twentieth century came to a close, modern slavery, in some or all of its various forms, existed in dozens of countries around the world. The examples of slavery listed below represent only a handful of the places in the world where slavery continued through 1999. For more information

This woman (left) is one of dozens of deaf Mexicans who were rescued in 1997 after having been kept in slave-like conditions in New York City, forced to sell trinkets in the subway for the smugglers who had brought them into the country. Modern slavery often victimizes people who are vulnerable, such as immigrants, children, and in this case, people with disabilities. *Photograph by Gino Domenico. AP/Wide World Photos. Reproduced by permission.*

on slavery in the places listed below and the many other countries where slavery was practiced in the twentieth century, contact the organizations listed in the "Directory of Human Rights Groups" at the end of this chapter.

Asia

China

Many forms of slavery existed in China at the end of the twentieth century. Some were as ancient as the Han

Dynasty of the third century B.C.E.; others were as new as the latest political leadership in the People's Republic of China. In China, as in the rest of Asia (including Japan), the selling of children into slavery has been a common practice for many centuries. The practice is known as *mui tsai,* a Chinese term for child adoption. Traditionally, extreme poverty has forced parents to sell their children. Young girls, at the age of four or five, were sold into domestic slavery. Other children were forced to work in mines, small factories, and shops. Though slavery had been abolished in China in 1908, there were about 4 million children trapped in *mui tsai* in 1930.

The sale of children into slavery continued in China into the 1990s, along with another ancient Chinese form of slavery: the sale of girls and women into marriages and prostitution. From 1991 to 1996, according to official figures from the Chinese, police caught and prosecuted 143,000 slave dealers and rescued 88,000 women and children who had been sold into slavery, marriage, or prostitution. The real number of women and children was much higher, according to human-rights groups, which argued that the Chinese government downplayed the number of victims out of embarrassment.

The Communists outlawed wife selling after they took over China in 1949, but it and child slavery persisted fifty years later because the conditions that were responsible for these activities—extreme poverty and high unemployment—were still present. Also, the demand for abducted women has been high in China because of a severe shortage of females in a population that has traditionally favored male births. In 1998 there were 130 males for every 100 females in China. In terms of sheer economics, it was cheaper to buy a wife illegally ($240 to $480) than to pay a traditional bride's dowry (at least $1,200).

China's forced laborers Like the Soviets, the Chinese used forced labor as a punishment and "corrective" for all kinds of crimes. In 1951, two years after the establishment of the People's Republic of China, the Chinese leader Mao Zedong (1893–1976) began a policy of "reform through labor." As in the USSR, the Chinese government forced political opponents and dissidents into labor camps, where they worked on various state construction projects such as roads, railways, and water conservation.

A 1954 law identified persons who were targeted for arrest and detention at labor camps as "counter-revolutionary elements, feudal landlords, and bureaucrat-capitalists." By 1959, according to the International Labor Organization, the list had grown to include "vagrants, persons who refused to work, persons guilty of minor offenses, and those who, for various reasons, had no means of existence."

Slave products for export In 1992, it was estimated that there were hundreds of thousands of political prisoners in China's vast network of labor reform camps, some of which were nothing more than secured factories staffed with inmates. For years the official policy of China has been to use prison labor to produce cheap products for export, including clothes, shoes, bicycles, circuit boards, hand tools, steel pipe, leather, tea, wine, and many other products. Despite a 1930 law against importing prison-made goods, many of these products still made their way to U.S. store shelves. Germany and Japan also provided large markets for Chinese prison products.

In China most of the prisoners in the labor camps were treated no better than slaves. According to the human-rights group Asia Watch, prison workers labored long hours on dangerous jobs, received no pay, got little or no medical services, and lived on meager food rations that were withheld if production quotas were not met or as punishment for other infractions. Other punishments included beatings, torture, and solitary confinement. Political prisoners were treated especially poorly, reported Asia Watch, as most of them were forced to work in the confinement of their prison cells.

India, Pakistan, Nepal, and Bangladesh

In 1999, there were millions of people, mostly children, in slavery in India, Pakistan, Nepal, and Bangladesh. Part of the labor system in these countries is known as bonded labor, which is a modern term for the age-old practice of debt slavery. The victims were mainly children between the ages of four and fourteen who were sold into bondage by their parents to pay debts or to provide income for their families.

A group of Thai girls, mostly about twelve years old, pose in 1980 after being rescued from slavery in a textile factory. They are a few of thousands of youngsters in Thailand sold by their parents every year at a market in Bangkok's railroad station. *AP/Wide World Photos. Reproduced by permission.*

India passed laws against this form of child slavery in 1978 and again in 1986, yet the New York-based Human Rights Watch estimated that in 1996 there were between 10 million and 15 million bonded child workers in India. In Pakistan, the estimated number of bonded child workers varied depending on the source. In 1993, the Pakistan Human Rights Commission, a nongovernment organization, put their number at 20 million. A child labor survey conducted in 1996 by the Pakistani government, however, declared that there was a maximum of 4 million bonded child workers in the country.

Carpet slaves The children of South Asia were forced to work under slavelike conditions in a variety of industries. In India, Pakistan, and Nepal, which account for two-thirds of the world's trade in carpets, 70 percent of the carpet makers were under the age of fourteen in 1992. Children were forced to work at their looms for seventeen to eighteen hours a day, seven days a week. They lived and worked without proper light, ventilation, or sanitary facilities. Respiratory illnesses from wool dust were common, as were cases of anemia, tuberculosis, skin diseases, cuts, spinal deformation, and blindness. Punishments for these "carpet slaves" included beatings, mutilations, and the withholding of food. For girls it was worse than for boys, as some were raped and sold into prostitution. In some regions of Pakistan, overwork and diseases killed up to 50 percent of the carpet slaves before they reached the age of twelve.

In addition to making carpets, children in these countries manufactured many other products for the world market, including the United States. In 1996, for example, Pakistan's top five exports to the United States included three products made mostly by bonded child workers—carpets, sporting goods, and surgical instruments. Soccer balls, clothing, and footwear were also products made by child labor in Pakistan that found their way to store shelves in the United States and around the world.

Bonded child laborers in India, Pakistan, Nepal, and Bangladesh also worked in a variety of other jobs in the cities and the countryside. Some children worked as agricultural laborers—looking after livestock; digging canals; and cutting grass, wood, and hay. Children were also brick kiln workers, rag and paper pickers, and quarry miners. The bonded children of South Asia lived as orphans—without their most basic needs as children ever being met.

Africa

Sudan

From 1983 to 1998, an ongoing civil war in Sudan, Africa's largest country, resulted in the deaths of 1.5 million people, the displacement of another 4 million, and the enslavement of tens of thousands, mostly women and children. Except for a ten-year period (1972 to 1982), Arab Muslims in northern Sudan have been battling black Christians in the

John Eibner of Christian Solidarity International pays an Arab trader the equivalent of $13,200 in Sudanese money to buy 132 slaves and rescue them from slavery, 1997. *Photograph by Jean-Marc Bouju. AP/Wide World Photos. Reproduced by permission.*

south since the country gained its independence from the joint rule of Egypt and Britain in 1956.

Beginning in 1989, the government of Sudan, from its capital city of Khartoum in the north, has pushed to impose the religion of Islam and the Arabic language on the entire country, including the south, where they faced armed opposition from the Sudan People's Liberation Army (SPLA). Caught in the middle were the women and children of the million-member Dinka tribe, the largest ethnic group in southern Sudan and the main supporters of the SPLA.

The slave trade in Sudan was conducted mainly by the Popular Defense Force (PDF), a government-sponsored Arab militia. The PDF regularly raided civilian villages and cattle camps in the south and hauled away hundreds of black Africans at a time to be marched north and sold into slavery. Human-rights groups estimated that in the 1990s, 30,000 to 90,000 Sudanese were enslaved in such a manner. The captives were sold to wealthy Arabs in the north for as little as $15.

Young men were forced into the military or killed. Children were forced to work as domestic servants and agricultural laborers and women as servants and concubines (sex slaves).

Mauritania

In 1999, one human-rights group claimed that the African nation of Mauritania, a former French colony in the southwest Sahara Desert, contained the world's largest concentration of chattel slaves—an estimated 390,000 people. That number was much higher than other estimates of slavery in Mauritania in the 1990s. The U.S. State Department's human-rights report for 1994 documented 90,000 slaves, and in 1997, one expert on Mauritania estimated that there were about 100,000 slaves in the country.

It should be noted that in 1992, Mauritania had just over 2 million people, with blacks making up only 20 percent of the population, or about 400,000 people. Therefore, even

Moctar Teyeb, an escaped slave from Mauritania, addresses a news conference in Boston in 1999 as part of the American Anti-Slavery Group's awareness campaign to end modern-day slavery around the world. *Photograph by Stephan Savoia. AP/Wide World Photos. Reproduced by permission.*

the lower estimates of the number of black Mauritanian slaves would represent a significant part of the nation's minority population.

In 1996, human-rights activists told U.S. congressional subcommittees that Arab slave traders "capture [African] children and in some circumstances women to breed slaves." Slaves, according to David Hect in a 1997 *New Republic* article, "may be exchanged for camels, trucks, or money." Slaves were also subject to beatings, mutilations, and torture, including the "camel treatment," the "insect treatment," and the "burning-coals treatment." Testimony from individuals to the committee was backed up by the human-rights group Africa Watch.

Mauritania obtained its full independence from France in 1960. The nation did not officially abolish slavery until 1980. Despite the ban on slavery, tens of thousands of blacks remained the property of their Arab masters through the 1990s. The slaves were subject entirely to their masters' will. They worked long hours without pay, had no access to education, and were not free to marry or associate freely with other blacks.

Latin America

Brazil

In the Amazon region of Brazil in the 1990s, many poor people were trapped in a system of forced labor and debt slavery. People came from all over Brazil to the Amazon forest looking for work and ended up as slaves, forced to labor in forest clearance, charcoal production, mining, and prostitution.

Workers were recruited with promises of decent wages and living conditions, but when they arrived at the mines and charcoal camps, they found inadequate shelter and lousy food. They also found themselves in debt. Not only did they owe money for their transport to the mining camps, charcoal farms, and construction projects, but also all of their food, work supplies, and medicine could only be bought from the "company store" at prices several times their market value. The result was that most workers ended up enslaved for life, never able to work off their debts.

The Pastoral Land Commission, a Catholic Church organization, reported 26,047 cases of slavery in Brazil in 1996, mainly involving Indians who worked in charcoal production. Whole families, including children as young as nine, gathered, stacked, and burned wood for twelve hours a day to meet production quotas. Charcoal workers and miners were kept under control by a variety of methods, according to the UN Commission on Human Rights, including "beatings, inhuman, cruel, and degrading treatment, and killings of workers trying to flee such conditions."

The practice of forced prostitution was closely linked to the isolated labor camps of the Amazon. Women were promised jobs in supply stores and restaurants but ended up being forced to work as prostitutes to pay off transportation and other debts. The women were often victims of beatings and imprisonment and were tortured or killed if they tried to escape.

Directory of Human Rights Groups

Slavery existed in many countries around the world throughout the twentieth century with no end in sight for the twenty-first. To find out more information about worldwide slavery in the past and the present, contact one or more of the following human-rights organizations.

Amnesty International USA
322 Eighth Avenue
New York, NY 10001
Phone: 212-807-8400
Fax: 212-463-9193
E-mail: admin-us@aiusa.org
Web site: http://www.amnesty.org/

Anti-Slavery International
The Stableyard
Broomgrove Road
London SW9 9TL, England
E-mail: antislavery@gn.apc.org
Web site: http://www.charitynet.org/~ASI
Founded: 1839

Christian Solidarity International
c/o Rev. Hansjurg Stuckelberger
Zelglistr. 64
Postfach 70
CH-8122 Binz, Switzerland
Phone: 41-1-980-4700
Fax: 41-1-980-4715
Founded: 1977

International Labor Organization
4, route des Morillons
CH-1211 Geneva 22, Switzerland
E-mail: webinfo@ilo.org
Web site: http://www.ilo.org
Founded: 1919

Human Rights Watch
350 Fifth Avenue, 34th Floor
New York, NY 10118-3299
Phone: 212-290-4700
Fax: 212-736-1300
E-Mail: hrwnyc@hrw.org
Web site: http://www.hrw.org/contact.html
Founded: 1985

Bibliography

The following list focuses on works written for readers of middle school or high school age. Books aimed at adult readers have been included when they are especially important in providing information or analysis that would otherwise be unavailable, or because they have become classics.

Books

Adams, Brian. *Atlas of the World in the Middle Ages*. New York: Warwick Press, 1981.

Aptheker, Herbert. *American Negro Slave Revolts*. New Edition. New York: International Publishers, 1974.

Baldson, J. P. V. D., ed. *The Romans*. New York: Basic Books, 1965.

Bennett, Lerone, Jr. *Before the Mayflower: A History of Black America*. 6th ed. New York: Penguin Books, 1993.

Bevan, E. R. *Ancient Mesopotamia: The Land of the Two Rivers*. Chicago: Argonaut, 1918.

Biel, Timothy Levi. *The Age of Feudalism*. San Diego, CA: Lucent Books, 1994.

Blassingame, John W., ed. *Slave Testimony: Two Centuries of Letters, Speeches, Interviews, and Autobiographies*. Baton Rouge: Louisiana State University Press, 1977.

Bradley, Keith. *Slavery and Rebellion in the Roman World*. Bloomington: Indiana University Press, 1989.

Bradley, Keith. *Slavery and Society at Rome.* Cambridge, England: Cambridge University Press, 1989.

Bright, John. *A History of Israel.* 3rd ed. Philadelphia: Westminster Press, 1981.

Bush, M. L., ed. *Serfdom and Slavery.* New York: Addison Wesley Longman, 1996.

Carter, Alden R. *The Civil War.* New York: Franklin Watts, 1992.

Chirichigno, Gregory C. *DebtSlavery in Israel and the Ancient Near East.* Sheffield, England: JSOT Press, 1993.

Cottrell, Leonard. *Land of the Two Rivers.* New York: The World Publishing Company, 1962.

Donadoni, Sergio, ed. *The Egyptians.* Chicago: The University of Chicago Press, 1997.

Finley, M. I. *Ancient Slavery and Modern Ideology.* New York: The Viking Press, 1980.

Fladeland, Betty. *AngloAmerican Antislavery Cooperation.* Urbana: University of Illinois Press, 1972.

Frankel, Noralee. *Break Those Chains at Last: African Americans, 1860–1880.* New York: Oxford University Press, 1996.

Frankfort, Henri. *The Birth of Civilization in the Near East.* Bloomington: Indiana University Press, 1951.

Franklin, John Hope. *From Slavery to Freedom: A History of Negro Americans,* 3rd ed. New York: Alfred A. Knopf, 1967.

Garland, Yvon. *Slavery in Ancient Greece.* Revised and expanded edition. Ithaca: Cornell University Press, 1988.

Gregor, Arthur S. *How the World's First Cities Began.* New York: E. P. Dutton and Co., 1967.

Hillyer, V. M. *The Medieval World.* New York: Meredith Press, 1966.

Hochschild, Adam. *King Leopold's Ghost.* New York: Houghton Mifflin, 1998.

Hollister, Warren C. *Medieval Europe: A Short History.* 7th ed. New York: McGrawHill, 1994.

Ketchum, Richard M., ed. *The American Heritage Picture History of the Civil War.* New York: American Heritage, 1960.

Marsh, Henry. *Slavery and Race.* West Vancouver, BC: David & Charles Ltd. 1974.

Meltzer, Milton. *All Times, All Peoples: A World History of Slavery.* New York: Harper & Row, 1980.

Meltzer, Milton. *Slavery: A World History.* Updated edition. New York: De Capo Press, 1993.

Mendelsohn, Isaac. *Legal Aspects of Slavery in Babylonia, Assyria, and Palestine.* Williamsport, PA: The Bayard Press, 1932.

Northrup, David, ed. *The Atlantic Slave Trade.* Lexington, MA: D.C. Heath and Company, 1994.

Rodriguez, Junius P., ed. *The Historical Encyclopedia of World Slavery.* Santa Barbara, CA: ABC-CLIO, 1993.

Saggs, H. W. F. *Peoples of the Past: Babylonians.* London: British Museum Press, 1995.

Sawyer, Roger. *Slavery in the Twentieth Century.* London: Routledge & Kegan Paul, 1986.

Smith, Brenda. *Egypt of the Pharaohs*. San Diego, CA: Lucent Books, 1996.

Snell, Daniel C. *Life in the Ancient Near East, 3100–332 B.C.E.* New Haven: Yale University Press, 1997.

White, Deborah Gray. *Let My People Go: African Americans, 1804–1860*. New York: Oxford University Press, 1996.

Articles

Aikman, David. "Slavery in Our Time: Black America Slowly Rediscovers Slavery—in Africa." *American Spectator,* February 1997: 52–53.

Ascherson, Neal. "Touch of Evil." *Los Angeles Times,* January 10, 1999: BR7.

Aziz, Majyd. "The Magnitude and Multitude of Child Labor in Pakistan." *Economic Review,* July 1998: 27.

Fang, Bay. "China's Stolen Wives." *U.S. News & World Report,* October 12, 1998: 35–36.

"For Sale: People." *Commonweal,* January 17, 1997: 5–6.

Harding, Jeremy. "Into Africa." *New York Times,* September 20, 1998: G8.

Hecht, David. "Virtual Slavery." *New Republic,* May 12, 1997: 9–10.

Mackenzie, Hillary. "Slavery in Sudan." *Scholastic Update,* December 14, 1998: 18.

"ModernDay Slavery." *Current Events,* March 26, 1999: 1–3.

Raghaven, Sudarsan. "A Global Outcry Against Slavery ... Just Adds to Bhutto's Problems." *Business Week,* November 11, 1996: 4.

"Sale of Children Must Be Eliminated." *UN Chronicle,* June 22, 1996: 61.

"The New Abolitionists." *Christian Century,* Janury 15, 1997: 39–40.

Index

Illustrations are marked by (ill.)

255

Archaic Greece 37
Argentina 101
Arguin 80
Armor 65 (ill.)
Ashanti 75–76, 78
Ashur 21
Asia Minor 48
Assyrians 16, 21–25, 31–32
Athenian slave girls 40 (ill.)
Athens 38, 40–41, 43
Athens' slave society 39
Atlantic Slave Trade 73–88, 90,
    120, 175, 178–79
Attucks, Crispus 124, 125 (ill.)
Augustus Caesar 45–46, 50, 53, 55
Avery College 172

B

Babylon 19, 23, 24 (ill.)
Babylonia 18, 20–21, 24, 32
Babylonians 16, 23, 29
Bangladesh 12, 243–44
Baptist church 222
Baptists 166–67
Bavarians 64
Belgian youth 232 (ill.)
Benevolent societies 165–66, 172,
    194
Benin 75, 77
Bethel African Methodist Episco-
    pal (AME) Church 168–69,
    169 (ill.)
Bible 30
Biblical slave laws 33
Biology 123–24
Black Codes 139–43, 146, 148,
    183, 185, 218
Black Death 5, (ill.), 6, 71
Black Sea 38
Black soldiers 212–15, 217 (ill.)
Boston Massacre 124–25
Branding 50, 53, 114
Brazil 9, 12, 101–02, 105–08, 228,
    248
British 84–86, 90, 109–10, 112,
    123–24, 177–79
Brown, John 205–07, 206 (ill.)
Brown, William Wells 173
Bruegel, Pieter 71

Bureau of Refugees, Freedmen,
    and Abandoned Lands
    221–22
Burgundians 64

C

Canaan (Palestine) 30
Caribbean 91 (ill.)
Carthage 46, 47 (ill.), 48
Catholic Church 9
Celtic 66
Central America 91 (ill.)
Certificate of indenture 111 (ill.)
Charlemagne 62–64, 64 (ill.)
Charles the Bald 65
Charles II 85
Charleston, South Carolina 146,
    187–88
Chattel slavery 1, 3–7, 12, 139–40
Child labor 12, 243–44, 240 (ill.),
    247
Child pornography 2, 12
Child prostitution 12
Children, selling into slavery 12,
    18, 33, 242
Chile 101
China 12, 241–43
Christianity 61, 64, 68, 84, 122,
    166
Christians 62–63
Christian Solidarity International
    250
Citizenship 44
Citizenship rights 53
City slaves 8, 146
City-states 17–18, 37, 39
City-states, Greek 38, 41–42
City-states, Sumer 17
Civil War (See American Civil
    War)
Civil War camp cook 214 (ill.)
Classical Greece 39
Claudius 53
Claver, Peter 105 (ill.)
*Clotel; or, The President's Daughter:
    A Narrative* 173 (ill.)
Code of Hammurabi 19–21
Coffin, Levi 185
Coffle 133, (ill.)
Coinage 38
Colombia 100

Industrial slaves 8
Institute for Colored Youth 172
International Labor Organization
     (ILO) 239, 250
International slave market 47
Iraq 19
Irrigation farming 15–16, 25
Islam 68
Israel 29–31, 34
Israelites 29, 31 (ill.)
Italy 38, 44, 57, 72

J

Jamaica 96
Jamestown, Virginia 110–11, 122
Japan 238, 242
Jefferson, Thomas 124, 128
Jemmy 184–85
Jerusalem 23, 31–32, 32 (ill.), 46,
     68–70
Jews 29, 236
"Jim Crow" laws 226
Johnson, Andrew 218
Joseph 30
Joshua 30
Judah 31–32
Judaism 68
Julius Caesar 46

K

Kansas 202
Kansas-Nebraska Act of 1854
     202–03, 205
Kidnaping 4, 36
King Ferdinand 81
King John of England 70
Knights 58, 65, 65 (ill.)
Knights of the White Camelia
     224
Krupp, Alfried 236–37
Ku Klux Klan 223–24

L

Labor camps 11, 233, 242–43
Lagash 17

Las Casas, Bartolomé de 82
Latin America 7, 9, 12
Latin America, colonial 89–108
Laws, governing slavery 20
Lee, Robert E. 216, 216 (ill.)
Leeward Islands 81
Legal status 53
Leopold of Belgium 11, 231–33
The Liberator 191, 192 (ill.)
Liberia 192
Liberty Party 195, 203
Libyans 25
Lincoln, Abraham 207, 211–12,
     211 (ill.), 216–17
Lisbon, Portugal 80
Liverpool 85–86
Lombards 64
Lord Dunmore 125
Louis the German 64
Lucullus 55

M

Magna Carta 70
Manumission 9–10, 21, 29, 34,
     43–44, 53–55, 92, 105,
     116–17, 175–76
Mao Zedong 242
Marcus Crassus 55
Maroons 96
Marriage 9, 29, 122–23, 148–49,
     173–74
Marriage between slaves 9
Maryland 115
Mason-Dixon line 202
Masons 166
Massachusetts 119-121
Mauritania 12, 247–48
Medical treatment 146–47
Mediterranean region 37–38
Mediterranean Sea 48, 68
The Meeting for Sufferers 177
Menes 25
Mesopotamia 2–3, 15–24
Methodist 166
Mexico 83
Middle Ages 5, 57–72, 74–75
Middle Kingdom (Egypt) 25
Middle Passage 8, 86–87, 110
Mines 43, 50
Missionaries 104, 230

Missouri Compromise 190–91, 202–04
Monasteries 62
Money 43
Monroe, James 187
Morel, Edmund Dene 233
Moses 30
Mother Bethel African Methodist Episcopal (AME) Church 169 (ill.)
Mount Vesuvius, Italy 54
Mulattoes 150
Muslims 6, 65, 68, 70
Muslim slave traders 74 (ill.)

N

Narrative of the Life of Frederick Douglass 173, 196
National Negro Convention 193
National Negro Labor Union 222
Native Indian enslavement 8
Natural reproduction 49
Nazi Germany 235–37
Near East 6
Nebraska 202
Nebuchadnezzar II 23, 32, 32 (ill.)
Negro Act 185
Nepal 12, 243–44
New Babylonian Empire 23
New England Antislavery Society 197
New Hampshire 119–21
New Jersey 118
New Kingdom (Egypt) 25, 27–29
Newspapers 173
New Testament 62
New World 7
New York 116–17
New York City 116
Nigeria 75, 77
Nile River 25, 30
Nineveh 21
Nobles 58
Normandy 67
North Africa 50
Northrup, Solomon 137–38, 161–62
North Star 173, 194, 196

O

Odyssey 35
Old Kingdom (Egypt) 25
Old Testament 16, 30, 33, 122
Old Testament laws 34
Oman 228
107th U.S. Colored Infantry 213 (ill.)
Overseer 127 (ill.), 142–44

P

Pakistan 12, 243–44
Pale Faces 224
Palestine 29–30, 68
Palmares 106
Panama 100
Peasants 5–6, 27, 36–37, 49, 58 (ill.), 59, 67, 71
Peasants' Crusade 68 (ill.)
Peasants, Egyptian 26
Peasant wedding 71 (ill.)
Peculium 54
Peloponnesian Wars 41, 42 (ill.)
Pennsylvania 118
Pennsylvania Society for the Abolition of Slavery 165 (ill.)
People's Republic of China 11
Persian Gulf 17
Persians 23, 25, 33, 41
Peru 101
Pharaohs 16, 24–26
Piracy 4, 36, 48
Plague 5 (ill.), 71
Plantations 8, 83 (ill.), 92, 136–39, 142–45, 147, 209, 223
Plebs 44
Pompey 49, 55
Pope Gregory I 62
Pope Urban II 68–69
Portugal 79, 104
Portuguese 73, 80, 84, 89, 101, 105, 107–08
Presbyterian Church 166
Prisoners of war 4, 16, 18, 20, 22, 27, 29, 33, 36, 39, 41, 46–47, 63, 74–75, 235
Promised Land (Palestine) 30
Proslavery activism 170–71
Proslavery poster 224 (ill.)

W

Walker, David 191
Walker's Appeal ... to the Colored Citizens of the World 191
Washington, George 125, 127 (ill.), 128
West Africa 7, 73–75, 77–78, 80, 82, 84, 86
Western Roman Empire 45
West India Company 116
West Indies 8, 81–84, 90, 92–93, 97, 120
Whigs 202–03
Whitney, Eli 130
Wife selling 242
Wilberforce University 172

Wilberforce, William 178, 178 (ill.)
William of Normandy 67
Williams, Nancy 152
William the Conqueror 67 (ill.)
World War II 235–38

Y

Yahweh 33

Z

Zanzibar, Oman 228